BREXIT MEANS BREXIT:

How the British Ponzi Class Survived the EU Referendum

Michael William

Copyright © 2017 Michael William

All rights reserved.

ISBN:

ISBN-13: 978-1976206832
ISBN-10: 1976206839

PREFACE

This book is a post-Brexit referendum update. It is intended to draw upon my two previous books (*The Ponzi Class: Ponzi Economics, Globalization and Class Oppression in the 21st Century*; and *The Genesis of Political Correctness: The Basis of a False Morality*) and apply the arguments to the current political dimension. It is not necessary to have read those two books to understand this one, but direct references to issues in them are bracketed for information purposes. This is a much lighter read, the detailed research already being done in the two previous books.

Following the British EU referendum vote and the election of President Trump in the USA – with his bald rejection of political correctness, commitment to securing the USA's borders and his stated aim of entering into better bilateral trade deals – someone on social media commented that 'The West fights back'. That comment was perhaps accurate at the moment it was made. Since then, other voter rebellions in France and Holland have failed; candidates and governments advocating the status quo have prevailed. Meanwhile, Brexit has been postponed, and at the time of writing, President Trump is floundering.

My two previous books provided an exposure of historical facts and ideological conflict and were calls to action. This book is ultimately more pessimistic and more of a wake-up call. The patriotic cause, certainly across the Anglo-Saxon West, and the West in general, needs to take stock, regroup and counterattack – or else the West's fight back is in danger of becoming a spectacular belly flop in slow motion.

Michael William
August 2017

Also by Michael William

The Ponzi Class: Ponzi Economics, Globalization and Class Oppression in the 21st Century
The Genesis of Political Correctness: The Basis of a False Morality
Multiculturalist Ideology (Part One): A Rationale For Race War Politics
Multiculturalist Ideology (Part Two): The Rising Tide of Race War Politics

Contents

PREFACE..3
INTRODUCTION...7
PART ONE..11
THE EU REFERENDUM AND ITS AFTERMATH....................11
    THE ECONOMIC CASE FOR REMAIN..........................22
    REFERENDUM RESULT AND THE AFTERMATH..........47
    THE POLITICAL FALLOUT..62
    SUMMARY...67
PART TWO..71
BUSINESS AS USUAL...71
    FOREIGN AID..71
    QUALITY OF LIFE..81
    TRADE POLICY...88
    THE PONZI CLASS AND PONZI ECONOMICS.............95
    POLITICAL CORRECTNESS.......................................111
    RACE WAR POLITICS...125
    IMMIGRATION...139
    SUMMARY...176
PART THREE..181
MAYISM..181
    SUMMARY...220
PART FOUR..225
THE JUNE 2017 GENERAL ELECTION................................225
    SUMMARY...248
CONCLUSION..259
APPENDIX A...265
WHITE PAPER..265

The United Kingdom's exit from and new partnership with the European Union..265

APPENDIX B..273

TORY PARTY JUNE 2017 GENERAL ELECTION MANIFESTO 273

INTRODUCTION

In my book *The Ponzi Class: Ponzi Economics, Globalization and Class Oppression in the 21st Century*, I wrote:

> 'The policy is one of Ponzi economics for the benefit of the Ponzi class. The British economy is being run as a Ponzi scheme and faces the ultimate outcome of any Ponzi scheme: financial ruin amidst a pile of debt and unpaid bills. The policy of Ponzi economics is part and parcel of the current manifestation of free trade – globalization; and the rise of the Ponzi class – a class, despite some internal differences, who are politically correct with a belief that they are entitled to spend public monies on themselves and encompass most of the three main political parties, the banks, multinationals, the corporate sector, the unions, most charities, the media, senior civil servants and an array of quangos. They are the ruling class.'

And:

> 'Free trade was once again embraced and evolved into globalization as Keynesianism evolved into Ponzi economics, with assets consumed as income, escalating debts and a much lower standard of living for ordinary people. Class oppression is not by the bourgeoisie, it is by an unrepentant Ponzi class. Via the tax system, the Ponzi class help themselves to ordinary people's monies, spend it as if it were their own and then run up debts and leave unpaid bills in addition. Ordinary people are losing a large part of their incomes, their pensions and even their homes if they need residential care in old age, assuming that they can even afford to own their own home. Business owners can be swindled by the banks and lose

everything. Children lose their inheritance. Thatcher's property-owning democracy has given way to a beds in sheds lawyers' dictatorship.'

That book was published in December 2015, and its sister book, *The Genesis of Political Correctness: The Basis of a False Morality*, was published in January 2016. Since then, the world of politics has changed – across the West, at least – as a result of the Leave vote in the British EU referendum. The term Brexit is familiar across the world. The Brexit vote has even been a factor in the successful campaign of the new President Trump in the USA. Restless peoples across Europe turn increasingly towards those parties in their own countries that oppose the status quo. The EU is nervous. 'Populism' is condemned.

Meanwhile, in Britain, we have been told that 'Brexit means Brexit,' although quite how Brexit is interpreted is disputed. We have concepts of soft Brexit, hard Brexit, and even dirty Brexit. The idea that Brexit means exit is apparently too simple.

The purpose of this book is to examine the extent to which the Brexit vote changed British politics and the hegemony of the Ponzi class. This book will rely upon the arguments and facts, figures and statistics contained in *The Ponzi Class* rather than laboriously rehashing them, although some more-up-to-date information will be set out. That information and the accompanying analysis will show that little of substance has changed. Nor is it likely to. While the media is excited at the issues surrounding Brexit, and while there has been the creation of a new government department for Brexit, the fact is it is business as usual apart from some awkward parliamentary votes and some legal action. Nothing substantial has changed. Britain continues on its downward path. The Ponzi class continues in power with the same economic outlook and steeped in political correctness.

This book is divided into four parts. First, it will give a summary of the EU referendum and its aftermath, not least to put what followed into context. Second, it will compare important aspects of the issues set out in *The Ponzi Class* and *The Genesis of Political Correctness* with the problems Britain still has. It will be seen how little has been disturbed by the Leave vote. Third, it will examine the emergence of Mayism – the ideology of the May Government. Despite what May might wish, her government will be defined by Brexit, and her government's approach to that task is central to the economic and political future of Britain. Fourth, it will explore key aspects of the June 2017 general election and the consequences of the outcome.

In particular, very importantly and perversely, with an aggressive commitment to globalization, Britain's longstanding unilateral free-trade mantra has emerged stronger than ever, as has the commitment to the false morality of political correctness. The potential consequences of this combination should not be underestimated.

PART ONE

THE EU REFERENDUM AND ITS AFTERMATH

The EU referendum vote was on June 23, 2016. That vote came after a particularly combative campaign in which an avalanche of threats and abuse was hurled at the Vote Leave campaign. Of importance, the official campaign was Vote Leave – not UKIP nor its offshoot Leave.eu. The strategy of Vote Leave was to downplay UKIP and entice as many Tories as possible to lead the Leave campaign. This upset the UKIP leadership and caused some anger in that they felt they were not given the prominence they felt they deserved. Also, the Vote Leave campaign did not promote an anti-immigration case to the extent that the UKIP leadership wanted. Some senior figures in UKIP joined Vote Leave, and some Tories and others joined the Leave.eu campaign, which fought its own battle despite its lack of official status.

The Remain campaign seemed more united, although there was some disquiet about the Labour leader's lack of enthusiasm. Jeremy Corbyn, despite his previous longstanding hostility to the EU, did make a few speeches in favour of staying in. The campaign to remain was dominated by what was called Project Fear, which both Osborne and Cameron vigorously rammed at the electorate. Unusually, Project Fear involved a multitude of civil society and international entities attempting to frighten and threaten the British voters into doing as they were told and vote Remain. Even then US President Obama joined in.

Project Fear included: Cameron's claim that the Calais camp of illegal immigrants might be transferred to Britain; Osborne's claim that pensioners would lose £32,000 from their pensions; the Treasury's claim that house prices would fall by 10% to 18% within two years; Cameron's claim that there would be an increase in mortgage interest payments of around £1,000 per annum; Osborne's claim that households would be £4,300 poorer by 2030; Osborne's claim that there would be an immediate year-long recession with up to 820,000 jobs being lost; Obama's claim that Britain would be at the 'back of the queue' for a trade deal; Donald Tusk's claim that Brexit would threaten 'Western political civilization in its entirety'; Cameron's claim that there might be war and genocide in Europe: 'Can we be so sure that peace and stability on our continent are assured beyond any shadow of doubt'; and Cameron's claim that the ISIS leader Abu Bakir al-Baghdadi and Putin would be 'happy' if there were a Brexit vote.

Osborne even produced a number of reports from the Treasury, at taxpayers' expense, which claimed that a vote to leave would produce an economic Armageddon. Osborne was much criticized for producing a 'punishment budget' proposal, and just before the referendum polling day, Osborne said that 'On Friday morning you will see the first reaction in the financial markets because they've placed all these bets that they will move money out of Britain if Britain votes to Leave' and that 'I have a responsibility to the people listening to this programme to do all I can to protect them. But I have to tell you that you cannot in the end protect people from the economic shock that leaving the EU would bring about.' At the time, the polls suggested that the Remain campaign held a lead of 53% to 47%.

A major controversy was Turkey. Just before the referendum voting day, Cameron told the television programme Question Time: 'I can't find a single expert anywhere in the country or in Europe who thinks that Turkey's going to join the EU in the next three decades,' and he refused to commit to using a veto on Turkish membership, as 'It's not going to come up.' On the same day, President Erdogan's top aid, Ilnur Chevik, said on Newsnight:

> 'We are really flabbergasted! We thought Mr Cameron was our chief supporter for our quest in European Union membership. We felt that when we needed

him, he was going to be there. Turks felt that the British were the driving force behind our EU membership and that they were supporting us right to the hilt. But the way Mr Cameron put it — he didn't believe anything, apparently, in our full membership. He was only deceiving us and he was just buying time.'

On the June 23, EU diplomats said that they would recommence talks on Turkey's accession to the EU the following week.

There were two main televised debates, the first of which was between Boris Johnson (Tory MP), Andrea Leadsom (Tory MP) and Gisela Stuart (Labour MP and the chairman of Vote Leave) for Leave, and Nicola Sturgeon (SNP leader), Angela Eagle (Labour MP) and Amber Rudd (Tory MP) for Remain. This first debate came the Tuesday after the beginning of the purdah (disallowing state resources being used for Remain) and at a time when Remain was comfortably ahead in the polls following a large output of economic threats from Osborne. This debate was the first time that the voters could judge the two sides on an equal footing. Given the pounding that the Leave side had had to endure, this was also their first opportunity to fight back. On the day of the debate, the Remain campaign exuded supreme confidence.

In their opening statements, Boris Johnson, who spoke first, said that Britain should 'take back control' (an idea that the Leave side would push) and dismissed the 'prophets of doom' who rubbished the option to leave. Amber Rudd said that the Leave side were vague as to the outcome of a Leave vote and that 'Just don't know is just not good enough.' Regarding the EU, Gisela Stuart asked of people, 'Would you join today?' and said that the project had become a nightmare. Nicola Sturgeon lauded the EU as being a collection of independent countries working together. Andrea Leadsom asked, 'What is the best thing for our children and grandchildren?' and described the EU as yesterday's game. Angela Eagle warned that 'there would be no turning back' from whatever choice the voters made.

The first topic for discussion was immigration. Amber Rudd began and described the issue as 'a complex problem' before making a jibe at Boris Johnson: 'I fear that the only number that Boris is interested in is the one that says No 10.' (This was the first of many personal attacks on Boris Johnson, whom the Remain team had obviously decided to target. This 'get Boris' tactic had limited effect, as Boris Johnson tended to ignore it, allowing the attacks to bounce off him, and also because of the effective contributions played by both Andrea Leadsom and Gisela Stuart.)

Nicola Sturgeon demanded higher levels of government spending for the public services and housing, not a reduction in immigration. Gisela Stuart pointed out that she was an immigrant herself and contrasted the circumstances in place when she had come to Britain with the total lack of control today. Boris Johnson said that the levels of mass immigration needed democratic consent and further pointed out that 'a city the size of Newcastle is arriving every year.' Andrea Leadsom said that 'If we stay in the EU, there is no chance of controlling immigration.' Angela Eagle, like Nicola Sturgeon, demanded more government spending and that a Migration Impact Fund should be brought back.

The immigration issue precipitated an argument about money. Boris Johnson said that if Britain ended the EU contributions, then Britain could spend that money 'on all sorts of priorities', including the NHS. Amber Rudd contested this on the grounds that the claim that Britain would save £10billion was untrue, as Britain would not save money by leaving. Nicola Sturgeon claimed that a £350million-per-week figure given (on the side of a Vote Leave campaign bus) as the cost of the EU contribution was 'an absolute whopper'. Angela Eagle told Boris Johnson to 'get that lie off your bus.' Andrea Leadsom said that the £350million was an ONS figure, a gross figure, and that out of the net payments, there could be enough saved by leaving the EU to allow more for the NHS. Amber Rudd totally rejected this and said that 'being in the EU makes us money – there is no saving from leaving the EU.'

The next issue debated was the economy. Andrea Leadsom pointed out that only 6% of firms exported to the EU, and Gisela Stuart said that 'the EU's economy is broken' and that 'it is nonsense that you have to choose between trade and democracy.' Amber Rudd claimed that nine out of ten economists were agreed in favour of the Remain case, that 'there is a consensus', and that it would be 'right to listen to the experts'. Gisela Stuart countered that 'there is really just one expert, I think, that matters, that is you the voter' and said that her late husband had been an economist and had sometimes got it wrong.

Nicola Sturgeon alleged that worker's rights and protection were 'real gains' of EU membership. Angela Eagle brought up the Economists for Brexit who had said that Britain should 'eliminate manufacturing', and she complained that this would mean many would lose their jobs. This anti-manufacturing point was ignored by the Leave team. Gisela Stuart brought up the size of Britain's trade deficit and expected a free trade deal, as it was in the EU's interest. Trade would go on.

Boris Johnson quoted a remark that Nicola Sturgeon had previously made about the Remain campaign being 'miserable, negative and fear-based'. He wondered how she would classify the Remain campaign's arguments in the debate. (This was a point he continued to have fun with throughout the debate).

Amber Rudd said that 'we should be leading not leaving,' that she had spoken to firms such as Siemens and Airbus who favoured Remain and that no international organization supported Leave. Angela Eagle claimed that 3million jobs depended on trade with the EU and that Boris Johnson was only interested in one job. (Boris Johnson: 'I missed the insult.') Gisela Stuart was unimpressed, saying, 'I've heard a lot of this before,' regarding matters such as joining the ERM and the euro. Andrea Leadsom reiterated that small businesses 'are the experts'.

The next issue was the NHS. Gisela Stuart said that in order to plan for public services, there was a need to take back control and that because NHS entitlement was based on residency, then there had to be control and planning. She further pointed out that this was a once-in-a-generation choice that went well beyond fear-based arguments.

Nicola Sturgeon claimed that there were 200,000 foreign workers in the NHS, that its problems were due to 'austerity cuts', and that the Leave side should not 'blame immigrants'. Angela Eagle said the 'NHS is facing a crisis' and that the Leave campaign was 'obsessed' with immigration. She further dismissed as 'a fallacy' that leaving would mean extra money for the NHS. Andrea Leadsom countered that Britain should save the £10.6billion annual net payment to the EU and spend that money on priorities, describing this as the 'independence dividend'.

Amber Rudd claimed that the EU makes Britain 'stronger and richer' and that 'there is no Brexit bonus'. Andrea Leadsom said that 'it is absolute nonsense' and 'scaremongering' and that people would see through it. Amber Rudd was adamant that the economy needed Britain to be in the EU and accused the Leave campaign of 'sneering at experts'. Gisela Stuart pointed out that 'the economy thrives because we have decent products, not because there is the Single Market.'

The next issue was rights. Andrea Leadsom said that the major rights people enjoyed had been introduced prior to joining the EU. Gisela Stuart said that 'employment rights require jobs' and not the EU. Boris Johnson asserted that 'we do not need the EU to guarantee our humanity.' Nicola Sturgeon said that Boris Johnson was keen to deregulate on leaving the EU, and Amber Rudd invited people to consider the company included in the Leave campaign and wondered how moved Nigel Farage, the UKIP leader, was with women's rights and mentioned a fridge (a former UKIP MEP had once joked that women did not clean behind the fridge enough).

Andrea Leadsom condemned these attacks, particularly from Nicola Sturgeon, as being the 'lowest of the low' and said that what Nicola Sturgeon was saying was: 'We should stay in the EU because as this country elected a Conservative government, we need to stay in the EU so that it can overrule a democratically elected government and do what she wants it to do. That is absolutely outrageous.'

The next issue was sovereignty. Gisela Stuart said that on June 23, the question was if the voters would defend their democracy, and she further described the EU as 'a sclerotic creature'. Boris Johnson believed that sovereignty belongs to the people and described the EU as an anti-democratic superstate. Nicola Sturgeon said that it would send a dreadful message to the world to cut ourselves off. Boris Johnson accused Nicola Sturgeon on being keener to be ruled from Brussels than from Westminster.

Andrea Leadsom said:

> 'This isn't a pooling of sovereignty. This is a takeover by an unelected European superstate. It's absolute nonsense to say it's a pooling of sovereignty. We cannot control our borders, we cannot control our taxes, we cannot control our rules and regulations ... It's a disaster and it's getting worse. We have to take back control.'

Amber Rudd said: 'We are not a passenger in this,' and that people should not allow Leave to mislead them.

The final issue was trust. Boris Johnson said that he was relying on hard, cold facts. Gisela Stuart highlighted that 'The Status quo is not actually on the ballot paper' and that Britain therefore needed to take back control and vote Leave.

There were then closing statements. Andrea Leadsom said: 'For me as a mother, for my children ... this is a vote for once in a generation and it's quite clear to me that the EU is yesterday's game ... With all my heart as well as with all my head, I desperately urge you to take back control.' Amber

Rudd said: 'What we've heard is complete fantasy from the Vote Leave team. It reminds me of the Wizard of Oz ... when you pull back the curtain, there is nothing there ... From Boris, well, he's the life and soul of the party but he's not the man you want driving you home at the end of the evening.' Gisela Stuart said that this was 'our last chance' and that 'A vote to stay is dangerous, it means handing over more and more money to unelected elites and bureaucrats every year.'

Nicola Sturgeon summed up her views that the EU had brought peace, the Single Market, protection in the form of various rights, and the freedom to travel and that 'The UK, France, Germany are all independent countries but independent countries that choose to work together for the greater good. Let's keep hold of all of these gains.' Boris Johnson took a different view: 'I think the last couple of hours and the whole campaign is the contrast between this side offering hope and that side offering nothing but fear about life outside. They say we can't do it on our own. We say we are a great country. We say we can.' He continued: 'They say that we have absolutely no choice but to stay locked in the back of the EU car, driven in the wrong direction going in a direction we do not want to go; we say we can take back control.' For Angela Eagle: 'I have fought the Tories all my life, but this is not a referendum on the government; it's about the future of our country and the Labour party believes passionately that our future lies in Europe.'

The outcome of the debate was that the Leave campaign surged to being only just behind the Remain campaign in the polls. Though devoid of government financial support and state resources, the Leave campaign had done well in the debate, and the Remain campaign was struggling. Steadily the polls narrowed, and then Leave edged ahead. The campaign became increasingly heated.

The murder of Jo Cox, a Labour MP, stopped the campaigning. This murder, which took place a week before the vote, was a dramatic shock. It was seized upon by the

Remain campaign to vilify the Leave campaign. Unfortunately, the murder coincided with a controversial poster unveiled by the Leave.eu/UKIP campaign. This 'Breaking Point' poster highlighted the EU's failure to manage the immigration crisis. It was denounced as racist.

At the forefront of the charge to link the Brexit campaign with the evil act of a mental defective was none other than Hillary Clinton, who wrote on Twitter on the Friday after the murder (italics my own emphasis): 'It is cruel and terrible that her life was cut short by a violent act of *political intolerance*.' David Cameron, that same Friday, said: 'Where we see hatred, where we find division, where we see intolerance we must drive it out of our politics and out of our public life and out of our communities.' Also on Friday, the ardent leftie Polly Toynbee wrote in *The Guardian*:

> 'There are many decent people involved in the campaign to secure Britain's withdrawal from the EU, many who respect the referendum as the exercise in democracy that it is. But there are others whose recklessness has been open and shocking. I believe they bear responsibility, not for the attack itself, but for the current mood: for the inflammatory language, for the finger-jabbing, the dog-whistling and the overt racism.'

The following Sunday, in a telephone conference, Will Straw, the Stronger In's campaign director, said:

> 'We need to recognise that people have been pulled up short by Jo Cox's death and it is now time to make a very positive case for why we want to be in the European Union ... to call out the other side for what they have done to stir division and resentment in the UK.
>
> That is something we must all do ... This is what we think is the closing argument of the campaign, reflecting all the arguments that we have been

setting out for many months but also the new context that we're in.

What we want to say is people should vote Remain on Thursday for more jobs, lower prices, workers' rights, stronger public services and a decent tolerant United Kingdom.'

Stephen Kinnock, a Labour MP and son of the former Labour leader Neil Kinnock, wrote in *The Guardian*:

> 'We must unite and act to defeat the forces of division, intolerance, populism, nationalism and cynicism that have been bubbling under for years, and that have come to the fore in recent weeks. This will be a long and difficult journey, but we owe it to Jo to make it. And it's a journey that starts on Thursday.'

The supposed Tory Baroness Warsi claimed to have left the Brexit campaign to join the Remain side, complaining: 'Are we prepared to tell lies, to spread hate and xenophobia just to win a campaign?' Few in the Brexit campaign were even aware that she had purported to be on their side in the first place.

There were a number of others, in particular George Osborne, who made similar comments. In response to the attacks on the 'Breaking Point' poster, Nigel Farage, the UKIP leader, said:

> 'What we are seeing here is the Prime Minister and Remain campaign trying to conflate the actions of one crazed individual with the motives of half of Britain who think we should get back control of our borders and do it sensibly.'

The killer was someone who had a long history of mental health issues and apparently was in a state of crisis the night before he committed his atrocity. In addition, he had obsessive compulsive disorder and aggressively cleaned himself with Brillo pads. He had acquired a shotgun (of some description) sometime previously; in 1999, the killer had bought a manual from a US far-right website that had instructions on how to build a 'pipe pistol'. Those who knew him said that he never discussed politics and did not know what his political views were. The police treated the murder as an act of terrorism.

The Remain campaign moved ahead in the polls and stayed ahead for the remainder of the campaign. The second major debate took place on the Tuesday before the vote. The Leave side was unchanged, whereas the Remain side put up Ruth Davidson (the Tory leader in Scotland), Sadiq Khan (the Labour London mayor) and Frances O' Grady (general secretary of the TUC). The same arguments were in contention. Those on the Remain side were bold in their assertion that they had won the economic argument. Khan alleged that Vote Leave had lost the debate on the economy and was just telling lies. O' Grady insisted that in the event of leaving the EU, 'we will pay with our jobs and our wages.' Interestingly, Gisela Stuart reminded that reform of the EU was not possible and that Cameron had got nothing in his purported renegotiation.

One change was that the Leave team backed away from any idea of reducing immigration and restricted themselves only to taking back control of the borders. This gave the Remain team some merriment. The loss of nerve, although understandable given the allegations made following the murder of Jo Cox, was a threat to the Leave case.

The debate was evenly matched until the closing statements. The last to speak was Boris Johnson, who, to a standing ovation from a large part of the audience, said:

> 'There is a very clear choice between those on their [Remain] side who speak of nothing but fear of the consequences of leaving the EU, and we on our side who offer hope. Between those who have been

endlessly rubbishing our country and running it down and those of us who believe in Britain.

They say we can't do it. We say we can. They say we have no choice but to bow down to Brussels. We say they are woefully underestimating this country and what it can do.

If we vote to leave we can take back control of our borders, of huge sums of money, £10billion a year net, of our tax raising powers, of our trade policy, and of our whole law making system – the democracy that is the foundation of our prosperity. *And,* if we stand up for democracy we will be speaking up for hundreds of millions of people around Europe who agree with us but who currently have no voice.

And if we vote leave and take back control, I believe that this Thursday could be our country's independence day.'

On June 22, 2016, the eve of the vote, not only did the gloves come off, but Liz Hurley came out for Brexit and posted a photo of herself covering her naked body with a Union Jack cushion.

THE ECONOMIC CASE FOR REMAIN

During the referendum campaign, particularly before the purdah period of the campaign proper, the Treasury issued several reports into the alleged consequences of a Leave vote. Other Remain organizations did likewise. The voters were deluged with scare stories as to the supposed adverse economic effects of leaving the EU. The Treasury reports were the product of taxpayers' money, utilized government resources, used official economic data and were presented by Osborne as being authoritative.

The first of these reports was entitled 'Alternatives to membership: possible models for the United Kingdom outside the European Union'. In assessing this report, three factors need to be borne in mind. Firstly, irrespective of membership of the EU, there will be trade between the EU and Britain. Pure free trade is a theory, and the EU does not have free trade in agricultural produce, for example, nor does it have free trade with the wider world. The issue is therefore the extent to which Britain needs to vary existing arrangements.

Secondly, the report repeatedly lauded Britain's service sector, which was described as accounting for 80% of the economy. The report argued that Britain was a service sector success story and needed to be in the Single Market to export services. This mantra was defective, as the British manufacturing sector has performed very badly and spent 2015 in recession in large part due to its inability to compete with foreign producers. The service sector, due to its very nature, does not face the same level of foreign competition. Many services simply cannot be traded internationally. Furthermore, as the Polish Eurocrat Elżbieta Bieńkowska conceded in January 2017, in reference to services, the common economic area 'does not function properly'.

It was not the case that Britain is good at services; it was the case that the service sector has not been decimated by foreign competition. Such evidence that there is shows that the service sector is more liable to fail than to successfully compete. For example, the financial sector shows that Britain's banks and building societies were mostly taken over by foreign competitors. To open up the service sector to foreign competition creates the danger that it will suffer the same fate as British manufacturing.

Thirdly, membership in the Single Market requires acceptance of certain conditions. The report defined the Single Market thus:

> 'A single market is a common trade area that extends beyond the deepest and most comprehensive Free Trade Agreements. It works to remove all regulatory obstacles to the free movement of capital, people,

goods and services. It stimulates competition and trade, improves economic efficiency and helps to lower prices. The EU's Single Market is the largest in the world.'

By definition, therefore, membership in the Single Market involves 'free movement' of people ('the obligation to treat the citizens of other EU states the same as nationals and remove unjustified obstacles to their movement within the EU') – ie uncontrolled and unlimited mass immigration. Membership in the Single Market is akin to membership in the EU and is not the same as free trade; it involves an attempt to pretend that there is a single market in the EU – there is not; for example, the labour markets across the EU are different, with different wage rates reflecting different national histories (see *The Ponzi Class*, page 314). To end mass immigration requires leaving the Single Market. Free movement of people is not an add-on to the Single Market but an integral, non-negotiable part of it. Those who want Britain to remain in the Single Market *want* to see uncontrolled and unlimited mass immigration.

The report listed a number of bullet points of Single Market 'trade-offs' in the event of a Leave vote:

> '• in return for full access to the EU's free-trade Single Market in key UK industries, we would have to accept the free movement of people;
> • access to the Single Market would require us to implement its rules. But from outside, the UK would no longer have a vote on these rules. And there is no guarantee that we could fully replicate our existing cooperation in other areas, such as cross-border action against criminals;
> • full access to the Single Market would require us to continue to contribute to the EU's programmes and budget;
> • an approach based on a Free Trade Agreement would not come with the same level of obligations,

but would mean UK companies had reduced access to the Single Market in key sectors such as services (almost 80 per cent of the UK economy), and would face higher costs;
- we would lose our preferential access to 53 markets outside the EU with which the EU has Free Trade Agreements. This would take years to renegotiate, with no guarantee that the UK would obtain terms as good as those we enjoy today; and
- in order to maintain the rights of UK citizens living, working and travelling in other EU countries, we would almost certainly have to accept reciprocal arrangements for their citizens in the UK.'

As the first four of the above bullet points relate to the Single Market, which Britain is now committed to leaving, although the Remainers dispute this, then the arguments raised have been superseded by the Leave vote. Rolling over existing arrangements is far easier than starting from scratch, and so a new trade agreement should be straightforward – if both the EU and Britain wish to maintain a free trade arrangement. Given the scale of Britain's trade deficit with the EU, then it is in the EU's interests to keep free access to the British market. Although, given Britain's devotion to unilateral free trade and globalization, it may not be necessary for the EU to enter into a free-trade agreement in order to get free access to the British market, and it would be in their best interests to close their markets to Britain, overtly or covertly, while enjoying continued free access to the British market.

Regarding the final bullet point, Britain has citizens living in many countries around the world and has managed to make agreements with those countries without difficulty.

The report then defined and criticised a number of alternative models that Britain would have to choose from on leaving the EU: the Norway model (and also the Swiss model, the Turkey model and the Canada model), bilateral agreements, and WTO only, which it described as 'the most complete break with the EU' and said would 'not entail accepting free movement, budgetary contributions or implementing EU rules' but would 'cause a major economic shock to the UK'.

It should be noted that membership of the European Economic Area (EEA), of which Norway is a member, is intended to be a stepping stone to full EU membership. That is why members are expected to adhere to EU regulations. Since Britain is leaving the EU and has no intention of rejoining there is no reason to join the EEA and hence be saddled with EU rules or having to make payments to the EU. Likewise, both Switzerland and Turkey had aspirations to join the EU, although Switzerland has subsequently changed its mind.

Bilateral agreements were quickly negotiated by Britain in 1932 following exit from the Gold Standard and the country's abandonment of its then policy of unilateral free trade (*The Ponzi Class*, pages 131 to 141). There is no reason to believe that Britain will be unable to conclude such agreements. The EU-Canada deal took a long time to negotiate because they did not have the same level of standards that exist between Britain and the EU. If all else fails, then the WTO could be the basis of trade, although, in practice, the WTO rules will vary according to implementation – there will be bilateral trade arrangements even if they are not willingly agreed on.

The report stated that Britain would have to make 'difficult choices' and consider 'the obligations required for [continuing] access which would almost certainly include the need to adopt EU rules, make financial contributions, and accept the free movement of people'. This would only apply, however, if Britain is to remain in the Single Market or joins the EEA.

Regarding the WTO, the report pointed out that the EU 'imposes a common external tariff on countries outside, except those that have negotiated preferential trade agreements with it' before giving a list of tariffs for different categories of goods. Of the categories and tariff rates, many of the categories are items of goods which Britain imports rather than exports (eg textiles, tea, tobacco, and most of the clothing is now imported). The majority of the categories of items are subject to low tariffs of 12% or less, with many being subject to less than a 5% tariff. Confectionery might be attracting a high tariff, but Britain has gradually sold off much of its confectionery firms (eg Cadbury), with production being transferred abroad. Only animal products, beverages and tobacco, and sugars and confectionery have tariffs higher than 20%. Apart from 'cereals & preparations', all other categories have tariffs lower than 12%.

The report highlighted the importance of the car industry and that currently Britain is able to export to the EU without tariff or regulatory barriers, in contrast to the 10% tariff placed on those countries that did not have a preferential trade agreement. Of course, Britain could conclude a preferential trade agreement with the EU, and, in the absence of such, the EU would likewise be liable to tariffs on its exports to Britain.

The report did not address the scale of the selloff of British industry, the deindustrialization that Britain has experienced or the reasons for that. It did not delve into the very significant balance of trade deficit that Britain has with the EU or the damage that that deficit is doing to the British economy and the adverse effects on ordinary people. All of this was ignored.

The document floundered about at length trying to debunk the WTO model. At times, it was perverse, at times untruthful, and at times barmy. It had the brass neck to allege:

> 'The EU, for example, has used its collective weight to impose tariffs against the dumping of Chinese steel imports. If the UK attempted to take similar measures on its own, they would carry less weight (the UK economy is about a sixth of the total EU economy in size, so such measures would have correspondingly less impact).'

In fact, the EU failed the British steel industry, which had one plant permanently closed and jobs across the remaining sites put under threat due to Chinese dumping of steel, selling it at below their own cost of production. The other EU countries were less affected by this, as they quietly favour their own industries for local contracts, whereas Britain enforces the rules as simplistically and as stupidly as possible. Britain is fully committed to *unilateral* free trade.

The report alleged that 'If reciprocal tariffs were introduced on imports from the EU, these goods would become more expensive.' This might be true, but there is no obligation to buy those EU imports. For example, Britain could import sugar far more cheaply from the Caribbean. Britain is unable to feed itself and would greatly benefit from being able to import cheaper foodstuffs from non-EU countries, and this would help push down the cost of living.

Crucially, the report referred to Britain's fish exports, ignored Britain's fish imports, and made no mention at all of Britain being able to recover control of its fishing grounds (in 2015, EU fishing vessels caught more than four times as much fish in British waters than British vessels caught in EU waters). This was a major omission. Re-establishing Britain's own territorial waters, in the same way as all other sovereign countries, would create jobs in Britain's fishing and fishing-related industries. This is a major benefit of leaving.

Most important of all, the report did not consider British interests and confined itself to a passive, reactive indecisiveness regarding the use of tariffs:

> 'Lowering tariffs would make imports cheaper, but there is no guarantee that this would be reciprocated. If we chose to go down this route, the UK would need to lower tariffs on all imports, for the EU and the rest of the world alike. If we had already lowered tariffs, giving duty-free access to the UK market, other countries would have no incentive to give

preferential access to their own markets for UK companies. We would have lost a significant lever in trade negotiations. The UK would face a stark choice: lower tariffs for all countries in the world, or raise tariffs with respect to the EU. The first option would undermine our position in future trade negotiations. The second option would raise costs for businesses and consumers.'

It is this wishy-washy 'analysis' that lies at the heart of Britain's long-term economic decline. Nowhere in the document did it compare the advantages of regaining the freedom to establish a national trade policy with the consequences of continued membership. Britain has a substantial trade deficit with the EU, and Britain has continuously had a payments deficit since 1983. This is a serious problem. Britain has been funding this deficit by selling assets and by borrowing. The document did not explain what will happen when the assets run out and when further borrowing is not possible.

By comparison, the USA imposed large tariffs on Chinese steel imports, while British ministers sat doing nothing other than to claim that the plight of the British steel industry was in the hands of the EU. The EU did nothing. The US steel plants have been saved; one British steel plant was closed. By comparison, the then US presidential candidate and now president Donald Trump openly stated that he would use tariffs to protect US industries from hostile competition from countries that are not abiding by free-trade rules.

Britain faces the problem of massive trade deficits with China and the EU, both of which have artificially manipulated their currency values. China manipulates its currency for trade advantage, whereas the one-size-fits-all euro is too high in value for the southern EU states and too low in value for the northern EU states. This means that the markets for British goods in Southern Europe are in recession, while the northern EU states enjoy artificially low export prices and also benefit from British goods being artificially highly priced due to the euro.

The Treasury's second report was entitled 'HM Treasury analysis: the long-term economic impact of EU membership and the alternatives'. In the forward, Osborne asked: 'Does Britain want to continue to be a country that faces out to the world? Do we want to be promoting our case at the top table of the world's institutions? Is our national security best served by retreating from the world?' Osborne stated that 'Using detailed analysis and rigorous economic modelling, this document sets out the Treasury's assessment of the long-term economic impact of staying in the EU compared to the alternatives.' The report rehashed arguments from the previous one, confined itself to the alternatives it defined and was therefore, by definition, biased (Osborne was aggressive about this: 'No country has been able to negotiate any other sort of deal, and it would not be in the EU's interest to agree one'), and insisted that 'to put it simply, families would be substantially worse off if Britain leaves the EU'. Even a casual glance at this 200-page document reveals it to lack any semblance of objectivity.

The report started with an executive summary, which was telling. It quickly asserted that 'Much of the UK's economic success is built on its long history as an open trading nation. Openness to trade and investment will be a key driver of the UK's future economic security.' Consequently:

> 'The key economic criteria for judging the UK's membership of the EU against the alternatives are therefore what it would mean for the UK's economic openness and interconnectedness. This needs to be considered alongside the obligations that come with securing that access and the influence the UK has over those obligations.'

From the outset, the report defined the issue in a way that facilitated the conclusions it wanted to give. We were told that in order to achieve 'openness' (eg allow foreign firms to buy up the best of Britain's assets), we must be prepared to accept the 'obligations' (such as mass immigration) that the EU was forcing upon us.

The executive summary repeated the simplification of the alternative models set out in the previous report and stated:

> 'The analysis in this document shows that under all 3 models, the UK's economic openness and interconnectedness would be reduced. Trade and investment flows would be lower. The UK would be permanently poorer if it left the EU and adopted any of these models. Productivity and GDP per person would be lower in all these alternative scenarios, as the costs substantially outweigh any potential benefit of leaving the EU.'

We were told that there would be 'substantially weaker tax receipts' and 'higher government borrowing and debt, large tax rises or major cuts in public spending'.

The executive summary continued:

> 'The total cost of leaving is likely to be higher. The new settlement for the UK negotiated by the Prime Minister in February 2016 included an ambitious agenda of economic reform in the EU. This will include the next stage of development of the Single Market, with a focus on bringing down the remaining barriers to trade in services, energy and digital, alongside completing major ongoing trade deals. If the economic benefits of reform are realized this could increase UK GDP by up to a further 4%.'

It further alleged that if Britain were to leave, then these reforms would be 'less likely to happen'.

There were repeated assertions that the EU had increased the 'openness' of the British economy as a result of the Single Market and the EU's trade deals with other countries. It alleged that the benefits were greater than the costs of EU membership. It alleged that: 'Trade as a share of national income has risen to over 60% in the past decade, compared to under 30% in the years before the UK joined the EU' (this specious allegation is dealt with below), and that Britain should accept that 'EU membership means accepting the regulatory framework associated with it.'

The executive summary was adamant that Britain must remain in the Single Market and had to comply with the terms of that membership including the need 'to accept the free movement of people and continue to make financial contributions to the EU'.

At one point, the executive summary came close to admitting that Britain would be better off out of the EU when it stated: 'To allow the UK to access the Single Market without agreeing to the rules of the Single Market would put their own businesses and consumers at a disadvantage!' In other words, were Britain to leave and yet be allowed to trade freely with the Single Market, then British businesses would be better off. The Osborne pitch was completely dependent upon his assertion that the EU would refuse to make a free trade deal and that such a deal was absolutely necessary.

Of the main body of the report, there were four main issues. Once again the service sector was prioritized – in particular, banking: 'The financial services industry is crucial to the success of the UK economy. EU financial integration have helped UK financial firms grow both in size and in the breadth of services they offer. Financial services exports have increased from 1.6% of GDP in 1991 to 3.5% of GDP in 2015.' As with the ruinous return to the Gold Standard after World War One (WWI), the interests of the City were considered more important than the interests of manufacturing. It cannot be stressed too much that the reason why the service sector is supposedly so successful compared to manufacturing is because manufacturing has been decimated by foreign competition, including by unfair trade practices of other countries (eg Chinese counterfeiting – see *The Ponzi Class*, pages 248 and 266 to 270).

Secondly, the report lauded trade with other countries as being the only thing that matters. For example, it stated: 'The key economic criterion for judging the UK's membership of the EU against the alternatives is, therefore, what it would mean for the UK's economic openness, access to global markets and its ability to trade with the EU and the rest of the world.' To be clear, by trade, the report added both imports and exports: 'openness to trade, defined as total trade (exports and imports) as a share of UK GDP, has increased significantly over the past 5 decades – rising from 23% of GDP in 1965 to 64% in 2015'. This is a nonsense argument. By this 'logic', the more Britain imports and the bigger the trade deficit, the better. The report set out a table showing that Britain has a trade surplus with the rest of the world (despite the huge trade deficit with China), whereas there was a massive trade deficit with the EU.

Thirdly, the report argued that funding the deficit was a reason to vote to remain in the EU: 'The UK ran a trade deficit of £67.8billion with the EU (3.6% of GDP) in 2015. This was comprised of a deficit in goods of £88.7billion (4.8% of GDP), but a surplus in services of £20.9billion (1.1% of GDP).' It also said:

> 'The UK's current account deficit means it is also a net borrower from the rest of the world. In turn, this implies the UK is exposed to changes in the perceived riskiness of lending to the UK. This exposure has been noted by the Governor of the Bank of England, who has said "the possibility of a risk premium being attached to UK assets because of certain developments exists, and that plays into the riskiness of the situation". In other words, if concerns about lending to the UK increase, investors will require a return – or premium – for bearing that risk, making it more expensive for the UK to fund its current account deficit.'

And it argued: 'there might be a sudden stop in the UK's ability to finance its large current account deficit outside the EU'.

Thus, rather than pay for imported goods by successfully exporting goods, under the Tories, Britain should be content to run a massive trade deficit and to sell off assets and borrow to fund that deficit. China, for example, should be allowed to manipulate its currency, hack into computers, produce counterfeit goods, exploit other protectionist measures, and then not spend the money it gets for its exports to Britain on British goods but lend that money back so that we pay them interest on it. This is not an economic model but a national bankruptcy model. The EU is little better, exploiting the one-size-fits-all euro to push down the prices of the manufactures from Northern Europe and, hence, leave Britain with a substantial trade deficit with them. Meanwhile, mass immigration continues uninterrupted, with the government pocketing any extra tax revenues paid but doing little if anything to meet the costs of that immigration, such as the strains on hospitals, schools, roads, housing, etc, under the assumption that yet more immigrants will come to meet future costs. This is Ponzi economics (*The Ponzi Class*, the chapter 'Ponzi Economics').

It should be noted that Osborne's forecasts were based upon continuing very high levels of immigration (contrary to stated government immigration policy) and that the ONS had recently estimated that the population of Britain might even reach 80 million by 2039 (being around 65 million in 2016).

Fourthly, the report perversely tried to turn the trade deficit into a pro-EU factor:

> 'The UK's current account deficit is identified by many of the studies as a risk. The decline in investor confidence could be amplified should overseas investors reassess the sustainability of the UK current account, leading to a sharp fall in sterling. A sterling

depreciation is a common feature of the external analysis, with a trade-weighted fall of 15% to 20% anticipated by Citi, Goldman Sachs and HSBC. Most analyses recognise the potential for higher inflation caused by the exchange rate depreciation to reduce household real incomes and further depress consumer spending. Citi estimate Consumer Price Index (CPI) inflation at 3% to 4% year-on-year for several years, and HSBC see inflation increasing by up to 5 percentage points in the near term depending on how far import price rises are passed on to consumers.'

The report set out no programme to bring Britain's trade back into balance. The sensible solution to the risks posed by the trade deficit is to eliminate that trade deficit and for Britain to stand on its own two feet as a self-sustaining independent country.

The third Treasury report, written by Osborne, was entitled 'HM Treasury analysis: the immediate economic impact of leaving the EU', and it coincided with the dispatch of the postal vote forms. By this stage of the referendum, even some Tory MPs were infuriated with the bunkum emanating from Osborne, and there was talk of a leadership challenge once the referendum was over.

Once again, Osborne had written the forward. He started as he meant to go on, with dire allegations that a vote to leave the EU would be apocalyptic not only for relations with the EU but also 'our relationship with the rest of the world', which would be affected by 'instability and uncertainty that would [be] trigger[ed]', as 'a vote to leave would represent an immediate and profound shock to our economy'. According to Osborne, the economy would go into recession, with between 500,000 and 800,000 losing their jobs, with higher inflation and higher government borrowing. Sterling would fall. Even house prices 'would be hit', and there was the danger in his 'more acute scenario' that 'The rise in uncertainty could be amplified, the volatility in financial markets more tumultuous.'

Osborne claimed that there would be three causes of a shock to the economy: a transition effect, an uncertainty effect, and a financial effect. The transition effect supposedly meant that the long-term effects (alleged in the Treasury's previous report) would take place immediately. The uncertainty effect alleged that 'Businesses and households would respond to this [uncertainty] by putting off spending decisions until the nature of new arrangements with the EU became clearer' and that 'immediately' following the vote:

> 'Businesses would reduce investment spending, such as the purchase of new machinery and moving to new premises. They would also cut jobs, consistent with lower expectations of external demand and financial investment, including from overseas, in the future. Individuals would adjust their purchases of major items, particularly where they involved extra borrowing, on the basis of lower future incomes.'

Regarding the financial effect, the report claimed that 'In the immediate aftermath of a vote to leave, financial markets would start to reassess the UK's economic prospects. The UK would be viewed as a bigger risk to overseas investors, which would immediately lead to an increase in the premium for lending to UK businesses and households.' It claimed that personal investments 'would also decline' and that inflation would increase due to a fall in sterling. These bald assertions were an attempt to predict stock exchange speculation, and then the report proceeded to give exact figures by using specially written computer models: 'For this document's analysis, a comprehensive UK uncertainty indicator was constructed. The Bank of England has also used a similar indicator to evaluate movements in uncertainty' – about which the less said the better. In a speech during the referendum, David Davis MP (who is now Brexit Secretary) said:

'The assumptions that the Treasury and the IMF have plugged into their models are essentially that we will lose trade in Europe and not gain any in global markets. Neither, in my view, are remotely plausible. All their calculations are doing is putting an implausibly precise number on an entirely improbable scenario. Just look at the Chancellor's latest claim that Brexit will plunge us into recession later in the year. By predicting what is the absolute bare minimum for a technical recession, this forecast is a victory for precision over accuracy, and for politics over economics. A forecast designed to deliver the maximum scary headlines with minimum justification. As with the last Treasury forecast, dubious assumptions have led to the required outcome. The Chancellor has been given a result which allows him to link a potential recession, the main cause of which is actually that "dangerous cocktail" of global risk that he so recently warned us of, to Brexit.'

Having contrived its doom-laden prediction, the report proceeded to try and convince that things could even be worse. It held out the prospect of 'tipping points', higher inflation, higher unemployment, increased government borrowing, and even a 'sudden stop' of 'financial inflows, reflecting concerns about the size of the current account deficit'. Nor did the report include any allowance for 'a sharp tightening of fiscal and monetary policy to restore credibility'.

By contrast, the report saw no problem with the balance of trade deficit, which it admitted was high: 'The UK current account deficit of 7.0% of GDP in 2015 Q4 is high by historical and international standards.' That was a gross understatement. The report continued: 'the UK's current account deficit remains reliant on inflows of capital from abroad. Some of these inflows are linked to business related to the UK's access to the Single Market, including financial services.' Inadvertently, the report did aver that the deficit was a risk:

> 'The extent to which a large current account deficit can be sustained, and the pace at which it adjusts to a more sustainable level, depends on the willingness of foreign investors to hold assets in that country. This in turn would depend on a broad range of factors, including the structural features of the economy (such as how open an economy is), the size and composition of its external liabilities and other external variables.'

This waffle abdicated responsibility for the deficit to foreigners rather than government economic policy or the competitiveness of industry, and shifted cause of the deficit away from the Single Market.

A variety of think tanks and economic organizations intervened in the referendum to support the Remain campaign. The output was consistently wild and dishonest. One such intervention, shortly before polling day, was from the IMF. In its June report on Britain, the IMF focused on Britain's referendum. Despite being more concise, more readable, and easier to understand than one of Osborne's efforts, even so, the report had a number of clangers and clearly had Osborne's fingerprints all over it.

The executive summary was usefully one page long. It described the alternatives to EU membership as being either becoming members of the EEA, or 'bespoke arrangements', or 'defaulting' to WTO rules. The report asserted:

> 'Studies that find net gains, or only very small losses, tend to assume the potential for rapid expansion of trade from new trade agreements with other economies or a substantial boost to productivity from reducing EU-sourced regulation. While theoretically possible, in practice the effects on output are unlikely

to be sufficiently large to make the net economic impact of exiting the EU positive.'

The executive summary openly acknowledged:

'The economic consequences for other countries would mainly be negative, albeit smaller than for the UK, and concentrated in the EU. Within the EU, losses would vary widely, reflecting variation in trade and financial exposures to the UK. Ireland, Malta, Cyprus, Luxembourg, the Netherlands, and Belgium would likely be most affected.'

Therefore, from the outset, the report's flaws were clear. It simply assumed that there would be a reduction in trade with the EU without explaining from whom consumers alternatively source their demand for goods, and that the reduction in trade would be harmful to both Britain and the EU. This was because, we were to believe, the EU would refuse to roll over existing trade arrangements, albeit with some modifications (for the Common Agricultural Policy or the Common Fisheries Policy, for example), even though there would be adverse consequences for the EU countries for not doing so – as the IMF acknowledged. Meanwhile, Britain would be allegedly unable to increase trade with other countries via new free-trade deals and so would suffer a fall in output. It should be noted that the home market and its importance was totally ignored.

The main text of the report upped the ante by alleging that 'the balance of evidence points to notable downward economic risks to the UK economy' stemming from 'reduced trade access' which 'would be magnified if exit from the EU were also accompanied by restrictions on migration'. The IMF even alleged that 'there is little evidence that EU immigrants have caused job losses and lower wages for UK citizens ... the evidence seems consistent with the notion that EU migrant labour has allowed UK firms to better match workers to jobs, allowing them to work more efficiently and boosting demand for labour overall.' The strain on public services was totally ignored. The IMF's convoluted, threadbare reasoning strayed well beyond its economic remit. They were peddling a Ponzi argument.

The IMF stated that there would be an increase in unemployment if Britain voted Leave, as the 'untested exit process could be damaging for investment, consumption, and employment; the exchange rate could act as a buffer, but not by enough to offset the negative effects on demand and output.'

The IMF repeated the Osborne/Treasury line that 'The single market is more than a free trade agreement (FTA) or customs union – the intent is a zone in which there are no barriers to the movement of goods, services, capital, and people', and it emphasized the EU's trade deals with other countries, and also 'prospective agreements under negotiation with a further 67 economies, including Brazil, Canada, India, Japan, and the US, with the aim of not only removing tariffs, but – more importantly – opening up markets in services, investment, and public procurement. These markets are 10½ times the size of UK GDP.' Britain's ability to compete was an issue ignored.

The IMF also played up the fact that 'The process for negotiating withdrawal and a new agreement under Article 50 would set off a complicated process that would run through the European Council, European Commission, European Parliament, and Council of the European Union' and that it is unclear whether a new agreement would need unanimity as it 'would depend on the nature of the agreement.'

Regarding trade arrangements with other non-EU countries, the IMF revealingly admitted that the British government 'views that it is not possible to apply the principle of "presumption of continuity",' and, hence, Britain 'would not be able to ensure continuity by right, and agreements in which it participates via EU membership would be subject to renegotiation'. It was the *British* Tory government that asserted this, not the other countries.

The IMF managed a spectacular belly flop regarding the issue of the balance of trade deficit. The IMF stated:

> 'The UK runs a trade deficit with the EU, whereas it maintains a small surplus with the US and Japan. This deficit is mostly in goods; the UK runs a surplus in services. However, whereas the value of the UK's exports to the EU is 13 percent of UK GDP, the value of exports from the rest of the EU to the UK is 3 percent of rest-of-EU GDP. Expressed in nominal terms, a quarter of UK imports come from Germany; Germany, France, and the Netherlands account for nearly one-half of imports originating from the EU. Spain, Belgium, Italy and Ireland are also significant trading partners. However, when exports to the UK are expressed as a share of the GDP of the source country, the UK market is most important for Ireland, Malta, Cyprus, Belgium, and the Netherlands.'

This was, of course, all a play on statistics. The scale of the imports from Germany should be noted. The IMF proceeded to claim that 'the financial sector is highly exposed to a loss of access to the single market'. The IMF did not stress that using the Treasury's own figures, financial services exports in total were only 3.5% of GDP in 2015, with the exports to the EU being only a part of this total figure.

The IMF referred to Patrick Minford (one of the Economists for Brexit) and compared his computer models and simulations with those of others. It quietly attacked the Minford suggestion that Britain reduce all tariffs to zero upon leaving the EU and that all production be shifted 'entirely to services, at the expense of agriculture and manufacturing'. It speculated on the consequences of tariffs being imposed on British exports and the prospects of zero tariffs being applied to imports, but it did not delve into the consequences of tariffs being imposed on imports, despite the size of Britain's trade deficit. Crucially, it continued (italics my own emphasis):

'A permanent reduction in export demand would be associated with a permanent depreciation in the real exchange rate, *to eventually restore the current account balance to equilibrium*. This would cause imported goods to become more expensive. Exports would be more competitively priced, but not by enough to fully offset reduced export demand from higher trade barriers. Losses would likely be accentuated to the extent that reduced trade brought reductions in productivity and foreign investment. *Restrictions on inward migration* would also damage not just labour supply but, potentially, skill levels and efficiency.'

What the IMF said was biased, economically and logically illiterate, and was the key item of the report.

The exchange rate has failed to redress Britain's trade deficit over the last 30-odd years. Even when sterling fell after the 2008 crash, the fall was insufficient to redress the deficit or return Britain to growth. After the exit from the Gold Standard in September 1931, sterling fell 30% within months, yet still Britain suffered from a trade deficit, and it was only tariff reform that restored growth. First, the Abnormal Importations Act, passed in November 1931, allowed import duties of up to 100% on certain goods (in practice, the maximum imposed was a duty of 50%); then, decisively, the Import Duties Act was passed, which placed a 10% tariff on all imported goods apart from those specifically exempted (mainly raw materials, food and Empire primary produce). In April 1932, the nominal rate was doubled to 20% on all items apart from some specifically omitted. By the end of April 1932, only 30% of imports were free of any duty. By the end of 1932, most manufactured and semi-manufactured goods were subject to a 20% tariff, with some at a 33⅓% tariff. In 1935, the tariff on iron and steel was increased to 50% to force the European cartel to agree to a quota to be imported into

Britain, and the measure was reversed back to the original level of 33⅓% within a few months when agreement was reached. The effect of the tariffs was dramatic. In 1931, during the 1929–32 slump, output fell in Britain by 5.6%. In 1932, Britain's per capita incomes increased by 0.2%, by 2.5% in 1933, and by 6.3% in 1934. As producers concentrated on supplying the home market, Britain boomed (*The Ponzi Class*, page 140).

The IMF report assumed that a depreciation in sterling would be sufficient to eliminate the trade deficit, although it did aver that there might be a reversion to WTO rules. It openly assumed that this rebalancing of the economy would be achieved alongside 'restrictions on migration', in which case, the increase in output, due to extra exports and/or import substitution, could only be achieved by increased productivity in that the same national population would produce more and firms would be required to use their existing workforce more efficiently and/or invest in more productive machinery. Despite what the report averred, this is all to the good.

What is impossible is for British industry to eliminate the trade deficit with the existing workforce without both a major increase in output (GDP growth) and an increase in productivity and efficiency. If Britain's deficit with the EU is taken to be a ballpark figure of £80billion, then, by definition, British production would need to increase by £80billion to bridge that deficit. Either we export £80billion more or import £80billion less (because we are now buying British goods rather than foreign ones) or, more likely, a combination of both. Those who would now benefit from these extra sales would, in turn, having more to spend, buy more from others, who, in turn, would do likewise. Thus output would increase further (Keynes stressed the importance of the multiplier effect).

Despite what the IMF said, if the trade deficit is eliminated, then Britain will boom. That is an arithmetical certainty. The government deficit would melt away as increased tax revenues poured in and the Osborne austerity policy would become redundant (it should be noted that Labour preferred to remain in the EU and have Osborne's austerity policy). Britain does not need 'rapid expansion of trade from new trade agreements with other economies'. It is the home market which matters, and that market is totally within the domain of the British government. The policy to be pursued on regaining control is a policy of eliminating Britain's trade deficit. Increased demand from the home market will increase Britain's GDP growth rate.

The Economists for Brexit, referred to by the IMF, produced their own report entitled 'The Economy after Brexit – Economists for Brexit'. They predicted that Britain would enjoy economic success after leaving the EU. Importantly, the Brexit economists based their case on a policy of *unilateral* free trade. In practice, this would be a policy only of tariff-free imports, with other countries imposing whatever tariffs they like on British exports. Patrick Minford, one of the eight economists, told the BBC:

> 'Whereas what we are assuming is that we take advantage of leaving the EU to have free trade with the rest of the world unilaterally – we simply say to the rest of the world sell to us at your prices. That brings down the costs to the consumer and transforms the economy in our modelling because consumers have lower prices, wages fall for employers because they are still better off with lower wages because the prices are falling. So there's this dynamic unleashed into the economy, that's completely absent from these other analyses because they just assume we stay with the EU tariffs.'

Importantly, the economists for Brexit argued for both lower prices of imports, a good thing, and lower wages, which is not necessarily a good thing for ordinary people if overall prices do not fall as much. Pushing wage rates down is difficult and is likely to lead to a fall in living standards. A policy of unilateral free trade is dangerous, as it ignores the historical failure of that policy for Britain and would be a positive reason for the EU to exploit the open British market while they restrict British exports to the EU.

The Economists for Brexit made an important point about the need to confront vested interests: 'In any industry there may be firms that think they will benefit from Remain. But their interests, as with other vested interests, are theirs, not the UK's. Therefore, the views of business are likely to vary by size of firm, by the sector they are in, and by their business model.' Those multinational firms arguing for continued EU membership and mass immigration are acting in their own vested interests and not the national interests. The interests of the Ponzi class and the national interests are not one and the same.

The Economists for Brexit were dismissive of the fixation with the Single Market:

> 'People talk about Britain "having access" to the Single Market, as though it were some sort of a room, with a door through which you may or may not be admitted, depending upon your EU membership. But this is nonsense. All countries in the world have access to the EU Single Market. It is simply that, in order to sell goods into it, they have to agree to meet its standards. But that is true wherever you try to sell goods. As it happens, plenty of countries around the world have had great success selling into the Single Market without themselves being members of it. The United States is the largest exporter to the EU (exporting more to the EU than does the UK), followed by China. As for the importance of being able to influence EU rules, neither of these other countries has any influence on them. Nor do they have a single Member of the European Parliament (MEP) or a representative at any European meeting.
>
> By contrast, the downside of belonging to the Single Market is you must apply all its rules and regulations throughout the whole economy. In the UK's case,

only 12% of our GDP is directly accounted for by exports to the EU. But this means that 88% is not. Yet that 88% also must obey all the EU's rules.'

Patrick Minford himself wrote about trade in the report. He estimated that tariff and non-tariff barriers had increased prices by about 20%. He advocated that Britain should simply leave the EU and not bother with a trade agreement and rely on WTO rules: 'Thus, the best outcome for us as a nation is trading on the basis of WTO free market prices without so-called free trade agreements negotiated with any country'; he also said that 'One thing we do not have to do, and should not do, is enter into any other trade agreements. The WTO rules are there to police the world market in which the UK can best thrive.'

The report concluded:

> 'It is interesting to see, after Brexit, the UK becomes a more 'normal' economy, with growth reviving, monetary policy 'normalising' and inflation getting back on track. The fall in the exchange rate and the direct improvement in the current account largely correct the recently persistent current account deficit. The PSBR, as a share of GDP, continues to fall towards balance at the end of the decade, with faster growth of nominal GDP.'

In fact, the PSBR, according to the Economists for Brexit figures, continues virtually unchanged from the Treasury forecast, and the trade deficit continues at a very high level indefinitely into the future. On this basis, the path mapped by the Economists for Brexit was one leading to economic failure. The damage caused by immigration was briefly touched upon and not properly dealt with, although the downward pressure on wages was highlighted. The policy option of unilateral free trade was not an attractive one, but the option of simply leaving rather than chasing a new free-trade agreement was rightly preferred.

The harm caused by the trade deficit cannot be overstated. For example, there is a diminution of tax revenues. Between 2000 and 2012, tax paid by small businesses rose almost three-fold – despite the lending squeeze caused by the credit crunch. Meanwhile, large businesses were paying 20% *less* tax despite a 65% increase in profits. Had the tax paid by large businesses increased in line with that of small businesses, then the government would be receiving £50billion a year more in tax. Part of the reason is down to corporate tax dodging, and partly it is down to the scale of the foreign takeovers of British industry (*The Ponzi Class*, pages 271 to 278).

In 1991, British pension funds and insurance companies held 50% of British shares long term. That figure had fallen to 15% by 2015, with foreign ownership increasing to 41%. The Treasury itself reported that between 1997 and 2007, foreign ownership of quoted British companies rose from 30% to 50%. Between 2005 and 2015, £440billion worth of British companies was sold to foreigners. Those sectors most affected by foreign takeovers were paying lower or virtually the same levels of tax, and thus a falling share of the total. This trend cannot continue indefinitely. The various Osborne/Treasury reports, the IMF report, a variety of other Remain reports, and even the Economists for Brexit report (advocating unilateral free trade) all failed to address the need to eliminate Britain's trade deficit with the EU.

REFERENDUM RESULT AND THE AFTERMATH

On polling day, *The Financial Times* claimed that a Brexit vote would damage 'not only the UK but Europe and the West'. Polls suggested that the Remain side led by 48% to 42% with 11% undecided. At one North London polling station, flags and bunting were taken down at a cricket club which was being used as a polling station after Remain campaigners complained that the St George's Cross (English) flag was Brexit propaganda. In another incident, one voter was turned away because she wore a Union Flag dress. Sixty-eight-year-old Teresa Hicks was threatened with the police when she objected to being refused the right to vote and asked if the same objections would be raised if someone turned up in a burka.

Many Leave campaigners urged voters to use a pen to vote rather than a pencil in order to prevent ballot fraud. In Chichester, police were called after a complaint about Leave campaigners handing out pens outside a polling station. Even though the Electoral Commission said that it was legal for voters to use pens, some councils objected and threatened to disallow such votes.

On polling day evening, Nigel Farage, the UKIP leader, told Sky News: '[It] looks like Remain will edge it.' An Ipsos Mori poll put Remain at 54% and Leave at 46%. However, the outcome was a Leave victory. In England, the vote was 47% Remain, 53% Leave; for Scotland, 62% Remain, 38% Leave; Northern Ireland, 56% Remain, 44% Leave; Wales, 47% Remain, 53% Leave. In London, it was 60% Remain, 40% Leave. The English are now a minority in London. In essence, the result was an English rebellion with Welsh support.

Within days of Britain's EU referendum, France, the Netherlands, Italy and Denmark all experienced strong demands for their own referendums. In France, Marine Le Pen described the vote as a 'victory for freedom' and called for all countries to have their own referendum. In the Netherlands, Geert Wilders tweeted: 'Hurrah for the Brits! Now it's our turn. Time for a Dutch referendum.' The German Die Welt newspaper reported that the German government was worried that France, the Netherlands, Austria, Finland and Hungary might all opt to likewise leave the EU.

Events moved very quickly. On the June 24, 2016, it was disclosed that both Boris Johnson and Gove, amongst 84 MPs, had signed a letter of support for Cameron whatever the referendum outcome as backbench moves gathered momentum to oust him. Even so, on that same day, Cameron resigned as prime minister. He said:

> 'I was absolutely clear about my belief that Britain is stronger, safer and better off inside the European Union and I made clear the referendum was about this and this alone. But the British people have made a very clear decision to take a different path and as such I think the country requires a fresh leadership to take it in this direction.'

Osborne went to ground.

Also on June 24, 2016, Jean-Claude Juncker, the EU communications president, stated that the 'union of the remaining 27 members will continue' before meeting with European Parliament President Martin Schulz, President of the European Council Donald Tusk and Dutch Prime Minister Mark Rutte. A statement was issued after the meeting which said that they respected the British vote and urged the British government 'to give effect to this decision of the British people as soon as possible, however painful that process may be. Any delay would unnecessarily prolong uncertainty.' Jean-Claude Juncker said that the EU would adopt a 'reasonable approach' and that 'It's not an amicable divorce, but it was not exactly a tight love affair anyway.'

A plan had been drawn up (by the Tory MPs Bill Cash and John Redwood) for a 'Brexit Act' or 'Restoration of Sovereignty Act' to repeal the 1972 European Communities Act and incorporate existing EU regulations into British law to be reviewed in the future. However, Cameron's resignation froze the process of government as the Tories entered a leadership struggle. There was a widespread view that the new leader needed to be a Leave campaigner.

On June 27, 2016, it was reported that there were talks about Osborne joining a Boris Johnson/Gove dream ticket for Tory Party leadership. Boris Johnson praised the way in which Osborne and Cameron had led Britain to an 'outstandingly strong' economy. If true, this came to nought.

The campaign for Tory leadership took an unexpected turn. Boris Johnson was the favourite Leave candidate. Gove was supporting Boris Johnson, but on June 30, 2016, it was reported that a leaked email showed the friction within the Boris Johnson leadership campaign. Gove's wife wrote: 'Crucially, the membership will not have the necessary reassurance to back Boris, neither will Dacre/Murdoch [of the *Daily Mail* and News Corp] who instinctively dislike Boris but trust your ability enough to support a Boris-Gove ticket. Do not concede any ground. Be your stubborn best.'

Without warning Boris Johnson, with whom he had been socializing the night before at an event, Gove, who had been taking advice from Osborne, announced his own candidacy on the final day for the submission of nomination papers. Gove's candidacy was supported by a number of key Boris Johnson campaign members. The suddenness and lateness of Gove's defection plunged the Boris Johnson campaign into crisis due to the nomination deadline. Furthermore, Gove told the BBC:

> 'After the referendum result last week I felt we needed someone to lead this country who believed heart and soul in leaving the European Union. I also believed we needed someone who would be able to build a team, lead and unite. I hoped that person would be Boris Johnson. I came in the last few days reluctantly and firmly to the conclusion that while Boris has great attributes, he was not capable of uniting that team and leading the party and the country in the way that I would have hoped.'

For many years, Gove had insisted that he had had no leadership ambitions of his own.

At a packed event expected to launch his campaign, after taking advice from his campaign team, Boris Johnson made a speech setting out his beliefs and a summary of his career. Then he turned to the issue of being prime minister and said: 'But I must tell you, my friends, you who have waited faithfully for the punch line for this speech, that having consulted colleagues and in view of the circumstances in Parliament, I have concluded that person cannot be me.'

Theresa May attracted quick and widespread support from the Tory MPs, including seven Cabinet ministers. She was the establishment candidate. A poll of ordinary party members also gave May a lead. Andrea Leadsom, the prominent Leave campaigner who had announced her candidacy after failing to get assurances from Boris Johnson, once Boris Johnson had withdrawn, became the Leave candidate, attracting the bulk of the Leave supporters. Iain Duncan Smith said: 'Having known Andrea for some considerable time, I have huge confidence in her strength her experience, her wide range of capabilities, her calm manner and her ability to achieve objectives even against considerable odds.' Of her candidacy, Leadsom said: 'I was thinking about what is in the interests of the country, because to me the clear priority is to deliver on the referendum. We have been given an instruction, we now have to get a grip and get on with it.'

Gove, who had been described as a 'cuckoo in the nest' by fellow Tory MPs, was damaged by his betrayal of Boris Johnson and was unable to reach beyond his core supporters, despite a spirited effort. Gove said:

> 'What this country needs in a prime minister is not just a cool head but a heart burning with the desire for change. What this country needs is not just a plan to make do and mend but a vision to transform our country for the better. I have that vision. The one thing I want to make clear is I believe the person who is PM of the country is someone who argued for and believes in the mandate of the British people. And Theresa May did not argue for and did not make the case for Britain leaving the EU, and that is a fundamental division of principle between us.'

The day after he announced his own candidacy, Gove presented a full manifesto of policies. In launching his campaign, Gove said: 'All my political career, I've been driven by conviction, not ambition, by a belief I was doing what's right not what's expedient. I stand here – and I am standing for the leadership – not as a result of calculation I am standing with a burning desire to transform our country.' Ominously, he also said that he would wait until 2017 before invoking Article 50. Ken Clarke condemned Gove for 'student union' politics, and Nadine Dorries, a Boris Johnson supporter, tweeted: 'I am utterly astounded to discover that some MPs are actually backing Gove. Clearly, honesty and honour not a consideration for some.'

Arron Banks, a UKIP donor who vocally backed Leadsom, told the BBC:

> 'If Theresa May wins, UKIP will be back with a vengeance. I think if Andrea Leadsom wins, it will be a slightly different scenario. I think we potentially could be talking about a new party, and I think there are very good sound reasons for that as well. Perhaps more direct democracy. The elites have hated the referendum, because it took the power away from them.'

Banks also told the Sunday Express: 'We [himself and other donors] might be prepared to put £10million into a new UKIP to fight Theresa May. If May wins, then UKIP is back in full force on absolute steroids.'

In July 2016, a note, allegedly carried by a Leadsom organizer, was photographed on the Tube Central Line. The note included references to the Human Rights Act, making positive discrimination illegal, and to waging 'war on political correctness'. The division between Leadsom and the very, very politically correct May was not confined to leaving the EU.

May presented herself as the unity candidate and said:

'There is a big job before us: to unite our party and the country, to negotiate the best possible deal as we leave the EU, and to make Britain work for everyone. I am the only candidate capable of delivering these three things as prime minister, and ... I am also the only one capable of drawing support from the whole of the Conservative Party.'

May had around 88 MPs supporting her, Leadsom had around 19 with another 30 former Boris Johnson-supporting MPs joining (including Boris Johnson himself), while Gove mustered around 18, Stephen Crabb had 21 and Liam Fox had 9. After the first round of voting of the Tory MPs, only May, Leadsom and Gove remained. In the second round of voting, May secured 199 votes, Leadsom got 84, and Gove 46. The contest came down to a battle between Leadsom and May in the final runoff. Leadsom could see that May had overwhelming support, and with the Tory grandees, establishment and the press against her, she withdrew. Leadsom had been under relentless press attack, especially about the importance she attached to being a mother, which was spun as being a criticism of May (who was childless) despite the fact that Leadsom had been stressing the matter throughout the campaign (for example, see the opening and closing statements in the first debate above). The outcome was that the Brexiteers failed to win control of the Tory Party.

Osborne, who was pushing to be foreign secretary if he could not stay on as chancellor, was sacked in a face-to-face meeting with May and left Downing Street by the back door. May told Osborne to spend some time getting to know the Tory Party and to 'Go away, and learn some emotional intelligence.'

The Remain campaign's Project Fear was quickly shown to be a sham. Retail sales rose by 1.4% in July compared to the 0.2% predicted by economists and the apocalyptic forecasts by the Remain campaign. In July 2016, the Council of Mortgage Lenders disclosed that home loans were at an eight-year high – despite the referendum vote. In August 2016, it was revealed that Britain's car industry had enjoyed the largest production for 16 years, with more than 1million vehicles being produced for the first seven months of the year. Goldman Sachs, JP Morgan and Morgan Stanley, which had forcefully backed Remain and even donated £1.25million to the Remain campaign, in September admitted that their doom-laden forecasts for the economy were wrong. Despite the odd outbreak of gloom from the Remoaners, the economy continued to do far better than forecast. Project Fear was proven to be a pack of lies.

Despite the vote to leave, the May Government embarked on an exercise of foot dragging. Instead of repealing the 1972 European Communities Act and leaving (it is the 1972 Act which makes EU law supreme, and repeal of the Act is the only way to leave), the government decided to adhere to the Lisbon Treaty, go down the Article 50 route, and do nothing to leave until negotiations with the EU were complete. Furthermore, the government put off the triggering of Article 50 until 2017. Article 50 is a negotiation process and nothing more. By itself, adhering to the untried Article 50 does not get Britain out of the EU.

That there would be a delay in Brexit was clear from the immediate response to the referendum result. In July 2016, Philip Hammond told MPs:

> 'If a treaty between the United Kingdom and the European Union 27 is deemed to be a mixed competence, it will have to be ratified by 27 national parliaments. I believe I am right in saying that the shortest time in which that has been done in respect of any EU treaty is just under four years – that is after taking into account the time it takes to negotiate.'

John Redwood, MP, said: 'People will not accept a process that takes six years or anything like that. They have voted to leave and they want to leave now.' Redwood believed it was achievable for Britain to be out by Christmas. Redwood also said: 'The UK did not recently vote for a slightly beefed up version of Mr Cameron's attempted renegotiation with the EU. We voted to leave, to take back control of our laws, our money and our borders. Those phrases were repeated throughout the Leave campaign, heard and understood by many, and approved by the majority of voters.' Redwood was ignored. In November 2016, May told the CBI annual conference that she understood that 'people don't want a cliff edge, they want to know with some certainty how things are going to go forward' and that there might be transitional withdrawal from the EU.

(The allegation that there was a need to avoid a 'cliff edge' was much repeated after the referendum. Lord Lawson rightly pointed out that there was no cliff edge. The allegation was simply a ruse to delay Brexit. Were there to be a transitional period, then there would be another cliff edge at the end of that, and so the argument would start again. The whole concept treats leaving the EU as something bad, with dire consequences, rather than something positive to be welcomed.)

Then, there was the outright opposition. On June 27, 2016, a petition calling for a second referendum was under investigation after it was disclosed that the 3.5million signatories included 40,000 residents of Vatican City, whose population is only 900, 25,000 British residents in North Korea, around 3,000 from South Georgia and the Sandwich Islands, and also almost 3,000 in Antarctica. One Remainer was advising people to use her postcode in order to claim to be a British citizen.

In November 2016, Sir John Major, a former Tory prime minister, said at dinner in Westminster: 'I hear the argument that the 48% of people who voted to stay should have no say in what happens. I find that very difficult to accept. The tyranny of the majority has never applied in a democracy and it should not apply in this particular democracy.' Sir John said that there was 'a perfectly credible case' for a second referendum. Meanwhile, Tony Blair told the New Statesman: 'It can be stopped if the British people decide that, having seen what it means, the pain-gain cost-benefit analysis doesn't stack up. I'm not saying it will, by the way, but it could.' Blair was revealed to have been in secret talks with the former Liberal Democrat leader Nick Clegg over how to keep Britain in the EU. The Liberal Democrats had ordered 90 camp beds so that peers could stay overnight for Brexit votes.

In February 2017, in a speech in which he urged Remainers to 'rise up' against Brexit, Tony Blair said:

> 'The people voted without knowledge of the true terms of Brexit. As these terms become clear, it is their right to change their mind. Our mission is to persuade them to do so. What was unfortunately only dim in our sight before the referendum is now in plain sight. The road we're going down is not simply Hard Brexit. It is Brexit at any cost.'

He continued: 'This is not the time for retreat, indifference or despair, but the time to rise up in defence of what we believe – calmly, patiently, winning the argument by the force of the argument, but without fear and with the conviction we act in the true interests of Britain.'

One wheeze adopted by the Remainers was to deny that the vote to leave the EU included leaving the Single Market. They claimed that leaving the Single Market was harmful and amounted to an extreme, hard Brexit. The BBC *Daily Politics Show* produced a video showing a number of senior Leave and Remain figures all saying that a Leave vote would include leaving the Single Market (for very obvious reasons). Even when Remainers were shown the video, they still denied that it had ever been the case that a Leave vote would mean leaving the Single Market. The Remainers lied, lied, and lied again. The truth had, in fact, even been stated by Cameron in the House of Commons during Prime Minister's Questions. Cameron was asked: 'Will he assure the House and the country that, whatever the result on 24 June, his Government will carry out the wishes of the British people – if the vote is to remain, we remain, but if it is to leave, which I hope it is, we leave?' Cameron replied:

> 'I am very happy to agree with my hon. Friend. "In" means we remain in a reformed EU; "out" means we come out. As the leave campaigners and others have said, "out" means out of the EU, out of the European Single Market, out of the Council of Ministers – out of all those things – and will then mean a process of delivering on it.'[1]

In November 2016, the OBR, which was fiercely in the Remain camp during the referendum, issued a report which claimed that because of the referendum vote, the government borrowing was set to increase by £58.7billion more than originally forecast. Philip Hammond announced that the government was abandoning its aim to balance its budget by 2020, saying that the aim now was to balance the budget 'as early as possible in the next parliament'. The government expected to see the national debt reach 90.2% of national income in 2017–18.

In December 2016, a number of court applications were made by pro-EU entities, including one in the Irish courts with a view to taking the matter to the EU judges, who, it was hoped, would rule that the Article 50 process could be reversed.

The foot-dragging was compounded by greed. In November 2016, the accountancy firm Deloitte, whose boss was David Sproul, a determined Remainer, leaked a memo that had not had government input which alleged that the government needed an extra 30,000 staff to deal with Brexit and that the Cabinet was split about the issue with the government having no plan. The memo was prominently reported on by the BBC until it emerged that its author had had no contact with No 10 and that the memo was unsolicited, had had no government input, and had no status whatsoever. Partners at Deloitte had been paid an average of £837,000 each in the previous year.

In November 2016, there was a confrontation between Tesco and Unilever when Unilever tried to impose high price increases on its products, blaming the fall in sterling and Brexit. Marmite, which was made in Britain, became unavailable in Tesco stores. Other companies, including PepsiCo, which make Walkers Crisps and Birds Eye, also were trying the same trick. Apple also tried it on. This was despite the fact that many of the products were actually made in Britain and not affected by the fall in sterling. The firms were dubbed 'Brexit Bandits'. Eventually, Unilever, whose managers were Remainers, backed down.

In January 2017, it was reported that civil servants were under such 'unsustainable' pressure due to Brexit that they wanted extra pay, as the challenges were 'unprecedented in peacetime', leaving them 'thoroughly dispirited and demotivated'. The First Division Association, whose members have an average salary of £77,000 and inflation-proofed pensions, had written to the Senior Salaries Review Body.

Those looking for easy money out of Brexit included the EU itself. In August 2016, it emerged, according to Felix Geradon, the deputy secretary-general of the Union Syndicale Bruxelles (the largest EU civil service union), that Britain faced demands to pay £4billion (8% of the total) to the EU towards its pension payments. This initial demand increased massively as the various EU entities warmed to their theme and as the May Government continued to dither.

In November 2016, Joseph Muscat, the Maltese prime minister, said: 'In giving a good deal to the UK, the EU will not want to jeopardise the Single Market. It won't be a situation when one side gains and the other side loses. We are all going to lose something but there will not be a situation when the UK will have a better deal than it has today. It simply cannot be.' Muscat stated that before there was any work done on a trade deal, Britain would be required to meet its financial obligations to the EU (ie would agree to pay £billions more into the future) and that any deal agreed on might be 'scuttled' by the MEPs, who have a veto.

In December 2016, at the end of a European Council summit, May was threatened with a £50billion demand for more money. The Czech minister, Tomas Prouza, told Sky News: 'We're talking about payments to the budget that the UK already voted for, pensions of British citizens working at the EU. This is only things the UK has already committed itself to paying,' and he added that this matter 'will be one of the first issues coming up on the table'.

In January 2017, of a transition period, Maltese Prime Minister Joseph Muscat said: 'It is not a transition period where British institutions take over, but it is a transition period where the European Court of Justice is still in charge of dishing out judgements and points of view.' Muscat also warned that the European Parliament should be directly involved in the negotiations or else it will 'sink' any deal reached no matter how 'good and fair' it was.

In January 2017, French MEP Sylvie Goulard said: 'We will develop a new relationship after [settling] the conditions of the divorce. We will make sure a country that is leaving is paying the bill.' MEPs were threatening to veto any deal unless Britain agreed to pay a 'divorce' bill of up to £60billion. Sir Ivan Rogers, who resigned as Britain's ambassador to the EU over disagreements with government policy and its 'muddled thinking', told MPs that negotiations were likely to descend into a 'fist fight', with the EU taking a 'hard line'. In February 2017, Sir Ivan Rogers said: 'We can expect a number of them to think, well, if the British want a future trade deal, and they want some form of transitional arrangement before a future trade deal – all big ifs – then this will come together at some gory European Council in the autumn of 2018 and it will come together with the money equation.' He further said that relying on WTO rules would be 'insane' and that it would take at least five years to make a trade deal.

Jean-Claude Junker told the German newspaper *Bild* in March 2017: 'Britain's example will make everyone realise that it's not worth leaving. On the contrary, the remaining member states will fall in love with each other again and renew their vows with the European Union.' He continued: 'Half membership and cherry-picking aren't possible. In Europe you eat what's on the table or you don't sit at the table.'

Koen Lenaerts, president of the European Court of Justice, said that he expected the court to be involved in the Brexit deal at some stage, as one party or another would go to the court.

In February 2017, Enda Kenny, the Irish prime minister, said: 'The British government and the Irish government agreed that there would be no return to the borders of the past', and he demanded that any Brexit agreement would allow Ulster to become a part of the Irish republic. In March 2017, regarding a divorce bill, Enda Kenny said: 'When you sign on for a contract you commit yourself to participation and obviously the extent of that level of money will be determined. It will have to be dealt with and it will be dealt with.'

By May, warming to their theme still further, regarding EU officials' pensions, a senior EU source said: 'Commitments have been made and this is not theoretical. These are commitments which exist and we need to make sure that the UK lives up to its part of these commitments.' The cost of the pensions for MEPs and Eurocrats was expected to reach £1.5billion per annum within ten years. Analysts calculated that Britain faced a demand of between £4.4billion and £5.7billion for the pensions and private health insurance.

These demands for future payments and a so-called divorce payment should be set against Britain's historic contributions. In December 2016, the Change Britain group calculated that Britain's gross contributions to the EU since joining in 1973 had been £527billion, with a net contribution of £175.69billion. A £60billion divorce bill would amount to one-third of the total net contribution paid since joining in 1973. Government lawyers advised that Britain was under no legal obligation to pay anything upon leaving the EU. There is no law are treaty obligation to do so. The House of Lords financial committee also concurred in its own report.

In February 2017, Treasury figures revealed that Britain's EU contributions were set to increase by one-third. By the summer of 2017, the EU's demands for money had reached £80billion to £90billion according to some reports and estimates of alleged liabilities.

In March 2017, May said:

> 'A number of MPs have used the term "divorce". I prefer not to use that term with regard to the European Union, because often, when people get divorced, they do not have a good relationship afterwards. MPs need to stop looking at this as simply coming out of the European Union and see the opportunity for building a new relationship with the European Union, as that is what we will be doing.'

Also in March 2017, in response to a question as to when free movement of people would end, May said: 'We want to have the agreements done in two years. There may then be a period when we are implementing those arrangements. What we will be able to do, as a result of leaving the EU, is to have control of our borders, is to set those rules for people coming from inside the European Union into the UK.'

In response to a question about the £50–£60billion demanded by the EU for leaving, May said: 'I am very clear about what people here in the UK expect, but I am also clear that we are a law-abiding nation, we will meet obligations we have.'

May's statement about free movement was not an isolated one. In April 2017, she reiterated it. Speaking while on a trip to the Middle East, May told reporters that there would be an 'implementation period' for British businesses to 'adjust' before free movement was ended.

Meanwhile, Lord Mandelson popped up, telling the German newspaper *Die Zeit*: 'Basically one can only advise the

Europeans one thing – forget Great Britain, and take care of your own interests.' He further stated:

> 'According to the Lisbon Treaty, the two sides are to reach agreement within two years on a trade agreement that covers all the smallest details of economic relations. This is absolutely impossible. Not just because the time just is not enough. It is much more serious that the British government is entering the negotiations with the wrong basic attitude.'

The Labour MP and chairman of Change Britain, Gisela Stuart, responded: 'It's deeply disappointing that he's putting his generous EU pension and interests before the needs of the British public ... whose side is he on?'

THE POLITICAL FALLOUT

It was not only the Tory Party that was thrown into turmoil by the Leave vote. UKIP's leader, Nigel Farage, decided to step down. UKIP, the principal anti-EU party, was therefore in a state of limbo. That state was worsened and more prolonged by UKIP's own internal wrangling and chronic infighting. The process for electing the new leader was lengthy. In the meantime, the MEPs did little to get Britain out. Farage himself focused on trying to get a seat at the Article 50 table rather than pushing for immediate withdrawal. In effect, UKIP endorsed the May Government's Article 50 strategy.

UKIP's new leader elected was Diane James, who was regarded as being in the Faragist wing of the party. However, she was a reluctant leader and had agreed to put her name forward when the favoured Faragist candidate, Steven Woolfe, ran into trouble due to irregularities and then failed to get his nomination papers in on time. Diane James showed some independence and tried to shut down the infighting. She ran into opposition from the party's National Executive Committee (NEC), which disagreed with the route down which she wanted to go. She was spat at while travelling by train by some leftie yobbo. Days later, she was subjected to very abusive bullying from the other UKIP MEPs. She resigned – first from the role as leader and then from the party itself – as the abuse from colleagues continued.

Farage bounced back as leader, claiming that there had been no change in leadership as the relevant papers had not been submitted to the Electoral Commission. The wider party accepted this. Another leadership contest commenced. This time, Woolfe was the favoured Faragist candidate again. However, it was then revealed that Woolfe had been in talks with the Tories with a view of defecting. In the EU parliament, there was a row between the UKIP MEPs, followed by 'an altercation'. Later, pictures were beamed around the world of Woolfe lying on the floor, flat on his face, after he had apparently fainted. He was hospitalized for a couple of days while an anxious Farage briefed the press. A UKIP NEC investigation was inconclusive as to what had happened outside the room and as to the exact nature of the 'altercation'. It was unclear as to whether a punch or punches had been thrown or whether it had been some pushing and shoving or 'handbags'.

Woolfe came in for much criticism and ridicule, and he withdrew from the leadership contest and then from the party. Three candidates contested. The Faragist came in last, and the winner was the former chairman and unity candidate Paul Nuttall. Soon afterwards, Nuttall put his name forward as the UKIP candidate for a parliamentary by-election in Stoke Central. Nuttall was subjected to relentless personal attacks on his character and as to the accuracy of his background – in particular as to his account of his presence at the Hillsborough football disaster, when many football supporters died. The UKIP vote in Stoke Central was poor, and the party only just managed to beat the Tories and hold onto second place. In addition, UKIP did badly in another parliamentary by-election in Copeland on the same day, with the Tories taking the seat.

Labour also experienced a leadership contest after much angst. Jeremy Corbyn, who had previously won the Labour leadership unexpectedly and with support from outside hard-left agencies, was accused of not doing enough to campaign to keep Britain in the EU. Corbyn was a longstanding critic of the EU.

The poison that had entered Labour politics was evident. At the end of June 2016, 46 Labour frontbenchers resigned in protest at Corbyn's leadership and his handling of the EU referendum. There were even mischievous rumours that Corbyn had voted Leave. Corbyn lost a vote of confidence among Labour MPs, who voted 172 to 40. Jack Straw, a former Labour foreign secretary, said that the Corbynistas were living a 'Trotskyite fantasy'. Corbyn attracted union support and refused to resign.

Labour's shadow chancellor was John McDonnell. McDonnell listed 'fermenting [sic] the overthrow of Capitalism' as a hobby in *Who's Who*. In a video, he proudly declared, 'I'm a Marxist,' and described the 2008 credit crunch as an event 'I've been waiting for a generation'. He had been sacked as financial director of the Greater London Council by Ken Livingstone (aka Red Ken) due to the capital being brought to the brink of bankruptcy by McDonnell's militancy.

One hundred thousand hard-left activists joined Labour in support of Corbyn. As his leadership was threatened, the Huffington Post reported in July 2016 that 60,000 had joined Labour in one week, with Labour's membership reaching 450,000. Membership subsequently exceeded more than 500,000. The Unite union had set up a telephone operation to boost support for Corbyn. Hard-left activists set up a 'Gimme 25' and a 'hardship fund' to pay subscriptions for new Corbyn supporters. The communist Momentum's founder, Jon Lansman, was even using a desk at Corbyn's Westminster office in June 2016.

At a meeting on the June 30 to launch an inquiry by Shami Chakrabarti into anti-Semitism and abuse in Labour, at which Corbyn was in attendance, a Momentum member, Mark Wadsworth, handed out press releases calling for certain MPs to be deselected, including Ruth Smeeth, who was denied a copy of the press release (she got one from a journalist). Corbyn took questions and then allowed Chakrabarti to speak. Chakrabarti invited Wadsworth to speak, and he said: 'Ruth Smeeth is working hand-in-hand with the Right-wing media to attack Jeremy.' Smeeth shouted, 'How dare you?' and the audience then shouted at Smeeth, who promptly walked out. Corbyn did nothing. After Smeeth issued a statement saying that Labour was no longer a safe place for Jewish people, Corbyn's office contacted her to say that Corbyn would contact her shortly. He did not until ten days later. Despite a meeting arranged by his office between the two of them, Smeeth showed up at the meeting while Corbyn did not.

Moderate female Labour MPs were the target of a campaign of abuse and threats. The campaign was not confined to women; notably, the Labour MP Andy Slaughter was targeted after he criticized Corbyn's fitness to be leader. He was threatened with deselection by local activists. In July 2016, Angela Eagle, who had contemplated standing against Corbyn for the leadership at one point before standing aside, had to cancel her constituency surgeries on police advice. At the time, Eagle was supporting Owen Smith's challenge to Corbyn. Eagle had previously had a brick thrown through the window of her local party's office and was receiving a multitude of threats from Corbyn's hard-left supporters.

Smeeth was subjected to campaign of abuse from Corbyn supporters, including being called a 'yid cunt', a 'CIA/MI5/Mossad informant', a 'dyke', a 'fucking traitor', as well as more than 25,000 other incidents of abuse, much of which was anti-Semitic, and even death threats. The counterterrorism police arrested two people. Smeeth had to rely on the police to organize her security arrangements.

Smeeth said: 'There are so many it's becoming difficult. I've just named half a dozen MPs without trying. It's the opposite of what we promised after Jo Cox was murdered.' Smeeth's complaints to Corbyn were consistently fobbed off with, Smeeth claimed, his response: 'I am anti racist, therefore it's not a problem.' In September 2016, Ruth Smeeth revealed that she had been given police protection and that counterterrorism officers were investigating one threat to hang her.

In any event, Corbyn won his second leadership contest easily, and his position was strengthened by the challenge.

One threat used during the EU referendum was that a Leave vote would weaken the unity of Britain. In particular, it was said that Scotland, which is more pro-EU and voted Remain, would object to leaving and that the SNP would exploit this for their own agenda. The SNP had almost wiped out the mainstream parties north of Hadrian's Wall.

After meeting with Nicola Sturgeon in Edinburgh in July 2016, May said: 'I've already said that I won't be triggering Article 50 until I think that we have a UK approach and objectives. It is important that we establish that before we trigger Article 50.' Even so, the SNP seized the opportunity to agitate for independence and sought to disrupt relations with the EU for their own purposes. The SNP tried to keep Scotland in the Single Market regardless. This daydream was steadily rebuffed by the EU, but the SNP used it to justify calls for another independence referendum.

The SNP did not allow economic reality to intrude on the independence agenda. In August 2016, it was disclosed that the tax revenues from North Sea oil had fallen to only £60million. This is compared to the £11billion received in 2011/2012 and compared to the £7.5billion previous forecast used to justify the SNP's case for Scottish independence. Scotland's deficit was £14.8billion in 2015, equivalent to 9.5% of GDP. In November 2016, Treasury figures revealed that government spending in Scotland was £56.6billion – £10,536 per man, woman and child; this is compared to only £8,816 in England.

In March 2017, a poll for the Glasgow-based *Herald* newspaper showed that, excluding the 'don't knows', 56% of Scottish people did not want another independence referendum and that only 44% did. Of the 57 polls conducted since the 2014 referendum, 44 showed a majority against Scottish independence.

SUMMARY

The Leave vote in the EU referendum came as a profound shock to the political elites across the West. They had been alert to the threat of a Brexit vote but had assumed that they would win. They had assumed that they could bully, threaten and frighten ordinary British people into voting as they were instructed to vote. Even Obama joined in. They were wrong. There was a rebellion. In particular, the English had had enough.

Lord Ashcroft, the pollster, immediately released an analysis of the result: 'How the United Kingdom voted on Thursday ... and why'. The report contained some fascinating revelations. Older voters were more likely to vote Leave, as were those who were either not working or retired. A majority of those in either full-time or part-time work voted to remain. Those with a university education were more likely to have voted Remain.

White voters voted to leave by 53% to 47%, while 67% of Asians and 73% of Black voters voted to remain. Of Christians, 58% voted to leave, whereas 70% of Muslims voted to remain. Of those who voted Tory in the 2015 general election, 58% voted to leave, while 63% of Labour voters and 70% of Liberal Democrat voters voted to remain.

Of those who voted Leave, 49% said their biggest reason for doing so was 'the principle that decisions about the UK should be taken in the UK', 33% said their main reason for leaving was that it 'offered the best chance for the UK to regain control over immigration and its own borders', and only 6% said their main reason was because 'when it comes to trade and the economy, the UK would benefit more from being outside the EU than from being part of it'.

For those who voted Remain, the most important reason cited by 43% was that 'the risks of voting to leave the EU looked too great when it came to things like the economy, jobs and prices', 31% believed that by remaining, Britain would have 'the best of both worlds', 17% cited that leaving would mean Britain would 'become more isolated from its friends and neighbours', and 9% cited their main reason as they held 'a strong attachment to the EU and its shared history, culture and traditions'. In other words, Project Fear worked – but not by enough.

Of those who regarded themselves as English and not British, 79% voted to leave, as did 66% of those who considered themselves more English than British and 51% of those who believed they were equally English and British. Only 37% of those who saw themselves as being more British than English voted to leave, as did only 40% of those who said they were British and not English.

Of those who voted Remain, 73% thought that life was better in Britain today than it was 30 years ago, whereas 58% of those who voted Leave said it was worse. Multiculturalism was regarded as a force for good by 71% of Remain voters and a force for ill by 81% of Leave voters. Feminism was regarded as a force for good by 60% of Remain voters and a force for ill by 74% of Leave voters. Globalization was seen as a force for good by 51% of Remain voters and a force for ill by 71% of Leave voters. Immigration was seen as a force for good by 79% of Remain voters and a force for ill by 80% of Leave voters. It is notable that Remain voters were split down the middle on the issue of globalization (51% to 49%), of which the EU is a part.

Three outcomes of the referendum would have an ongoing effect. First is the division in the Leave camp between Vote Leave and UKIP/Leave.eu. Vote Leave was the official organization for the Leave campaign, and the leadership was pro-Tory, with some anti-EU Labour allies – notably Gisela Stuart. The UKIP-backed Leave.eu failed to become the official campaign and instead tried to vie for attention with Vote Leave rather than supporting them. Leave.eu tried to form an alliance with the hard left, and George Galloway even spoke at a Leave.eu event. A UKIP/communist alliance as the official campaign would have been fatal to the Leave vote, and thankfully, Vote Leave predominated.

Some in UKIP supported Vote Leave, and some Tories, in particular David Davis, supported Leave.eu. Post-referendum, Vote Leave fell in behind the Tory Party, with the Labour element returning to Labour and all its problems. The Tory leadership election witnessed an unbelievable disorganization, with discord between Gove and Boris Johnson, and Leadsom striking out on her own. Critically, May, a Remainer, won the Tory leadership. The establishment retained control of the Tory Party, the majority of whose MPs were Remainers.

Meanwhile, UKIP descended into a backstabbing spiral of infighting. This culture has been a long-term UKIP weakness. What leadership there was in UKIP, sporadic as it was, endorsed May's approach to Brexit. All factions of UKIP supported the Article 50 negotiation process rather than arguing for leaving the EU at once. This allowed May to pose as being in favour of a genuine Brexit while she put together a series of sell-outs, fudges, interim deals, transition arrangements etc, all of which she intended to offer up to the EU. May's triumph was the second important outcome.

The third outcome was the economic case advanced during the referendum that tried to frighten voters to vote Remain. Neither Vote Leave nor UKIP/Leave.eu made a determined effort to answer the deluge of fabricated reports and lies spewed out by the Remain campaign. The Economists for Brexit had a virtual monopoly on making the economic case for leaving the EU, and they were *unilateral* free traders. The case for rebalancing trade between the EU and Britain was not put forth. Free trade without tariffs was deemed to be the only option and the path to prosperity. Tariff-free access to the Single Market was the primary Remain selling point. That the euro was damaging the British economy was not mentioned.

One can understand that Tory members of Vote Leave would not wish to attack their own government's economic policy, but UKIP should have had no such qualms. However, UKIP concentrated on immigration almost to the exclusion of everything else.

There is no point in winning an argument on immigration, vital though that issue is and even though the policy of mass immigration is one which English people have never wanted, if, on the left, there is a major flanking manoeuvre to the effect that an argument is advanced and won uncontested — the argument being that without membership in the Single Market, economic ruin would be unavoidable and so catastrophic that Britain must accept free movement no matter what the consequences of doing so are. The failure to contest the Single Market flanking manoeuvre was a failure of UKIP policy and strategic thinking.

As will be seen below, the economic arguments put forth by Remain continued to be advanced even by the May Government, this time in favour of tariff-free access to the Single Market. Many Remainers denied point blank that Britain had voted to leave the Single Market, despite the evidence. The May Government committed to leaving the Single Market but wanted a new partnership in its place and relied upon the Remain economic allegations to justify that.

Regarding leaving the EU, whoever wins the argument about the Single Market wins. By itself, the immigration issue is not enough.

PART TWO

BUSINESS AS USUAL

In both *The Ponzi Class* (in the chapter 'Ponzi Economics') and in *The Genesis of Political Correctness* (in the chapter 'Current Influence'), the current impact of Ponzi economics and political correctness is examined. Did the EU referendum outcome, with so many looking for a real change in how Britain is governed, change things? The answer is that not much has changed at all. It is business as usual. Despite the shenanigans across all the political parties, with new leaders and challengers popping up, it is still broadly politics as usual.

To give an overview, this book will examine seven topics: foreign aid, quality of life, trade policy, the Ponzi class and Ponzi economics, political correctness, race war politics, and immigration. A casual comparison of these issues shows that since the writing of *The Ponzi Class* and *The Genesis of Political Correctness*, the problems continue undisturbed.

FOREIGN AID

A contentious Ponzi Class pet project is foreign aid. Andrew Mitchell, the then Tory overseas development minister, even boasted that Britain was 'a development superpower' (see *The Ponzi Class*, page 320). At a time of a squeeze on government spending and low, if any, increases in incomes, many ordinary people object to their money simply being given away. These concerns have been resolutely dismissed by the Ponzi Class, who regard overseas aid as a sign of their moral superiority. It demonstrates how compassionate they are.

So enamoured with giving other people's money away was David Cameron that on his final day in office, he was reportedly urging May not to reduce the overseas aid budget, which he regarded as one of his greatest legacies. The May Government's incoming secretary of state for international development, Priti Patel, someone who was reputedly a critic, wrote in the *Daily Mail* in September 2016: 'The aid budget isn't my money, or the Government's money. It's taxpayers' money – your money. We politicians have a duty to spend it well, in ways that not only help the world's poorest, but also help us here at home. When people see aid being used properly they support it.' She added:

> 'But we need to face facts. Too much aid doesn't find its way through to those who really need it. And too often, money is spent without a proper focus on results and outcomes that allow the poorest to stand on their own two feet. Some participants in the aid debate are resistant to criticism and sometimes unwilling to understand or even acknowledge genuine concerns.'

It should be noted that Priti Patel did not question the size of the budget, only how it was spent. In any event, the money continued to flow out, and abuses continued to be reported.

In June 2017, Priti Patel told *The Guardian* during a trip to Somalia: 'Newspapers could twist up a story every day about UK aid, but to date there hasn't been one that's been 100% accurate. Part of my job has to be to demonstrate the value of UK aid.'

The largesse grew. New EU rules, which included adding prostitution and drug dealing to the GDP statistics, meant that the amount to be given away in foreign aid had likewise to be increased. The foreign aid budget rocketed to £13.3billion in 2016, more than double the amount spent in 2008. Of the increase, £685million was due to the EU rule change.

A sign of coming attractions was the so-called Ethiopian Spice Girls. Ethiopia has had an almost 10% growth rate per year for the past decade, a fact one might have thought to be more important than gimmicks and stunts from the British overseas aid lobby. However, Priti Patel described the donation to the Ethiopian Spice Girls (known as Yegna) as 'good value for money' that stopped teenage girls from getting pregnant. All five members of Yegna became mothers after joining the group. They earned £5,000 each for every radio series of eight episodes in a country where the average annual income is less than £500. The charity responsible for the formation of Yegna, Girl Effect, headed by a former senior civil servant, Howard Taylor, issued a statement:

> 'As the world becomes ever more connected, we leverage the power of insight, media and disruptive technology to enable change at scale. Our approach is to invest in girls as the world's biggest untapped resource. As girls rise, change becomes self-sustaining.
>
> Traditionally, development solutions that address poverty focus on supply side services – like schools or health clinics – things that we can see and touch. But all too often we treat the symptoms of poverty and overlook the cause.
>
> Our unique approach fills the gap of what is often unseen, to unlock a New Normal for girls. When the New Normal takes hold, girls become visible, vocal, connected and valued and are given the tools they need to become assets of change, not just recipients of aid.'

This babble is telling in how it reveals the wafer-thin rationale and the waste. But then, those involved are doing very well out of it. Even a communications 'expert' at Girl Effect got a salary of £40,000 and perks. Eventually, as the furore steadily increased, Priti Patel announced that funding for the project was to end.

But the waste in the budget continued. Sometimes it was minor, such as the £285million spent on an airport on St Helena that is useless due to 'wind shear', in which there is a sudden change of powerful wind direction. Although the wind conditions had been noted by Charles Darwin in 1836, apparently no one at the Department for International Development had bothered to do the necessary research.

Sometimes the waste was tinged with political correctness. For example, in December 2016, it was reported that Britain had given India £185million in the last year and was due to dole out another £54million. India was the world's fastest growing economy, with more billionaires than Britain and with an overseas aid budget of its own. The spending included a project to increase the political participation of tribal women, increasing awareness of sexual harassment for students, and a housebuilding project to help first-time homeowners. India has the ninth-largest economy and is expected to overtake Britain by 2050.

The waste could also be more extensive and more pointless. For example, In January 2017, Britain committed to increasing foreign aid to Pakistan by £100million despite Pakistan having its own space programme and nuclear weapons; it increased defence spending (excluding nuclear weapons) by 11% in 2016 to £6.7billion. Pakistan was already the largest recipient of Britain's overseas aid.

The waste could also be compounded by abuse. In December 2016, it was reported that Britain's aid to the world's most corrupt countries had soared by 30% in one year. A sum of £1.3billion had been given to the 20 most corrupt nations in 2015 (Afghanistan, Syria, South Sudan, Somalia, Myanmar, Zimbabwe, Yemen, Iraq, Sudan, Libya, Haiti, Cambodia, Uzbekistan, Venezuela, Angola, North Korea, Turkmenistan, Eritrea, Burundi and Guinea-Bissau). It should be noted that many of these countries have substantial oil wealth. It was further reported that despite promising to stop giving aid to China five years ago, another

£44million was given. The Chinese space programme intends to have astronauts on the moon by 2036.

It was reported in August 2016 that the Teachers Group, controlled by a 77-year-old Danish man who is wanted by Interpol and which claims to be a charity (others have described the outfit as a cult), had received British monies. Britain had donated £5.6million to an African charity called Development Aid People to People Malawi. The Department for International Development was forced to end funding for a supposed college that was being built amid reports that the building doubled as a recruitment centre for, and that funds were being syphoned off to, the Teachers Group, of which up to 700 workers were believed to be members.

In December 2016, a report from the Independent Commission for Aid Impact (ICAI) stated that a £238million programme that was supposed to educate girls in fact mostly funded boys and, in some cases, had 'abandoned targets for supporting girls altogether'. The programme in Pakistan involved the distribution of vouchers, only 43% of which were actually given to girls.

In January 2017, it was reported that the budget for cash handouts had escalated from £53million in 2005 to as much as £300million in 2016. Roughly 235,000 Pakistani families get wads of cash every three months in the Benazir Income Support Programme (BISP) to boost their incomes. The plan is to expand the scheme to 441,000 families by 2020. In August, the Pakistani press reported on a 'growing number of complaints about fake accounts and alleged corruption'. In September, Abdul Malik Baloch, the chief minister of one of Pakistan's four regions (Balochistan), complained of 'massive corruption' in the programme and that most of the money was being misappropriated: 'Undocumented people registered with the BISP do not know how to use the ATMS to draw the money. They are also deprived of the money at the post offices and the BISP offices by the staff.' There were reports of bribes being paid to get the Benazir bank cards.

In Yemen, a spokesman for the French charity Acted said: 'Cash transfers are an effective way to support vulnerable populations affected by humanitarian crises ... they are timely and they ensure aid is delivered swiftly. Not only do they benefit individuals, they support local markets and livelihoods. Most importantly, cash transfers preserve one's dignity.' Britain contributed 10% of the EU handouts in the Yemen.

In January 2017, the ICAI produced a report which highlighted that the cash handouts in Bangladesh were 'well known' to be going to the wrong people and that the Department for International Development (DFID) had not 'engaged directly with the problems'. In Rwanda the selection process for the handouts 'correlates only weakly with poverty levels'. In Nigeria, fake urine samples were used to get payments for pregnant women, and in Zimbabwe, 17% in a 'child-focused programme' did not have any children; the Zimbabwe government refused to remove the childless from the aid scheme.

In February 2017, the National Audit Office disclosed that fraud in the overseas aid budget had led to 102 investigations in 2010/11 and 429 investigations in 2015/16. It further warned that there had been 475 fraud investigations in the first nine months of 2016/17. It attributed the fourfold increase to the targeting of 'fragile' states with the determination to get the money spent in order to reach the target of 0.7% of GDP.

The overseas aid budget had become a mechanism for British state-sponsored organized crime. The fraud was not always the worst of it. In April 2017, Lord Carey, the former Archbishop of Canterbury, pointed out:

> 'In the run-up to Easter, British taxpayers will be appalled by this institutional bias against Christians by politically correct officials. In this the British Government is not just breaking its manifesto pledge to look after Christian refugees. It also appears to be breaking the law. The conflicts of the Middle East

have resulted in suffering and persecution of Christians. They have been killed or chased out of the birthplace of their faith.

The British Government has repeatedly promised to help persecuted Christians but has done nothing. Instead, Muslim officials have been put in charge of the billions of British taxpayer aid in the UNHCR camps. This is ensuring that help and aid rarely reaches the Christians.'

Approximately 10% of the population of Syria is Christian. John Pontifex of Aid to the Church in Need, a charity helping Christians in the Middle East, said: 'Unless Christians abide by Muslim customs they are not welcome.' The Christian population of Aleppo fell from 300,000 at the start of the civil war to around 30,000 by 2017.

Time and again, so desperate were the officials to reach the expenditure target that examples could be found of the aid budget being spent on any old thing. It was reported that Britain had 'dumped' £9billion of its aid budget in the World Bank over the previous five years. The World Bank had even charged £241million in administration charges to receive the money. In November 2016, it was reported that in 2015, Britain paid the EU £1.3billion to be spent on development in the Third World. More than half of the £12billion overseas aid budget was paid into international organizations such as the EU rather than being donated directly to poor countries. The EU had been recently criticized for spending much of its development budget in wealthy countries such as Russia, China and Brazil. In Brazil, the EU had spent £660,000 on the 'social integration of women living in fishing communities' and £120,000 on the 'integration of indigenous city dwellers'. In Georgia, the EU had spent £400,000 on the organization of 'sustainable energy days'. EU auditors had reported that large sums could not be accounted for.

In February 2017, it was reported that the British embassy in Beijing was promoting a new project for 'improving care in the community for elderly people in China'. British diplomats had held workshops to encourage applications for grants from a £1.3billion overseas aid fund. A government spokesman said:

> 'In a post-Brexit world, a more outward looking, global Britain investing and trading with the fastest growing markets is good for the UK and good for the world. Helping to build well-regulated, competitive markets is the right thing to do to deliver global prosperity, stability and security and help the poorest – 60 per cent of whom live in middle income countries – to stand on their own two feet and become our trading partners of the future. As ICAI acknowledges, the fund has made significant progress in a short time. '

It should be noted that the spokesman assumed that the May Government was motivated by its globalization agenda and the interests of China – not the interests of Britain – and was even prepared to cite Brexit to justify this agenda.

In December 2016, figures showed Britain donated £58million to reform foreign jails at a time when the British prison system was struggling to cope with major cuts in the number of prison officers. Recipient countries included China and Somalia.

In February 2017, it was revealed that more than £100million of overseas aid was spent on shopping malls and retail chains in a variety of Third World countries. The recipients included China's largest bra retailer, a Nigerian cinema chain, Vietnamese restaurants, wine merchants in Thailand, retail malls in Cameroon, Zambia, Nigeria and Mozambique, and a Costa Rican bookseller. The spending had been done via the Commonwealth Development Corporation.

Even Caribbean hotels expected to receive funds amounting to £17million from the overseas aid budget. The Tory MP Peter Bone said:

'Schemes like this really rankle with the public, who have enough trouble paying their own energy bills without being asked to subsidize the costs of luxury hotels. I am sure the operators of these resorts will be delighted to be getting a helping hand from the British taxpayer, but I cannot see how it is helping this country in any way. We have got to start looking to help people at home rather than wasting millions on useless projects abroad.'

In a new effort to find something to spend the overseas aid budget on, the Department for Digital, Culture, Media and Sport became involved in spending decisions. A range of 'cultural projects' in the Middle East were funded. Turkey, the world's 16th largest economy, was awarded £923,660 for a nationwide survey 'to map public perceptions' on their heritage. More than £1.2million was spent on two historical sites in Turkey, and a further £100,000 was given to the University of Liverpool to help preserve historical Turkish rock carvings.

And that was not all: £460,000 was spent on converting a former Saddam Hussein palace into a museum; £1.7million was given to up to 100 archaeologists in Egypt, Jordan, Lebanon, Iraq, Libya, Tunisia and the Palestinian Territories to attend training courses on how to use aerial images databases; £95,486 was spent on young nomadic Bedouin people in the Palestinian Territories for them to learn about their cultural heritage; and £99,713 was spent to compile a database of ancient pulpits in Cairo.

A culture department spokesman said: 'The Cultural Protection Fund is providing essential support to countries where heritage is threatened by conflict, including Syria, Egypt and Iraq. These projects are a first step to helping restore and preserve heritage of global significance.'

In March 2017, the ICAI found that £9million of British foreign aid was being used in Libya to fund migrant detention camps which had mostly fallen under the control of people smugglers.

Despite the high-minded rhetoric and moralising, the overseas aid budget has become a gravy train promoting corruption and organized crime. Sometimes this can be minor, such as when it was revealed in December 2016 that the British Channel 4 News presenter Krishnan Guru-Murphy had been paid £15,000 for a trip to Mexico by the Department for International Development. He had been accompanied by Zeinab Badawi and his trip had only involved a few hours of work chairing meetings at a two-day event organized by the Global Partnership for Effective Development. Guru-Murphy claimed not to have known the source of the payment and said that it would be donated to charity.

But the gravy train mentality is endemic. In December 2016, the latest figures showed the DFID had the highest salaries in Whitehall, with an average annual salary of £53,000. The department had also increased its staffing by 27% since 2010. Staffing costs increased from £95million to £133million between 2010 and 2016. The number of staff increased from 1,822 to 2,208. Half of the increase took place after Priti Patel took over. It was revealed that the payments to private contractors had increased to £1billion per year, with some consultants earning as much as £1,000 per day. At the Adam Smith International, which has been involved in the distribution of hundreds of billions of pounds of aid monies, four executives netted £43million in share payments and bonuses in the four years to 2016. In December 2016, one of those awarded a knighthood in the New Year's honours list was Mark Lowcock, who headed the DFID.

In April 2017, a report by MPs on the international development committee warned that private firms were overcharging for providing foreign aid services. It urged ministers to take action to stop contractors from 'getting rich' out of foreign aid. Adam Smith International, one of the largest contractors, had made multimillion-pound profits. Another contractor had charged double the true staffing cost of a project. DFID officials blamed the EU for not allowing them to take into account previous failures of contractors bidding for new contracts. International Development Secretary Priti Patel promised a crackdown on 'extensive profiteering'.

Only the USA and Germany gave more money in foreign aid than Britain, although, per capita, Britain donated £203.75 compared with £76.24 for the USA and £226.70 for Germany. Britain gave £13.3billion, the USA £24.9billion, Germany £18.3billion and France £7billion (£108.41 per capita). Britain gives £1 of every £8 of foreign aid from the developed world.

Priti Patel, someone who was once a critic of foreign aid, had gone completely native. In April 2017, she issued a 1,700-word statement setting out the alleged achievements of her department. Before acquiring her post, Patel had called for the department to be abolished. Now Patel said Britain should not 'compromise our commitment to being a global leader in international development' and that 'When we invest in stability, jobs and livelihoods, and sound governance, we address the root causes of problems that affect us here in the UK. It is not in our national interest to simply sit on our hands and wait until these problems reach breaking point or find their way to our doorstep.'

QUALITY OF LIFE

One of the most important aspects of Ponzi economics is the ability of the Ponzi Class to offload debts onto the general public and to diminish their quality of life by redirecting monies to pet projects (*The Ponzi Class*, pages 316 and 336). That has continued uninterrupted and, if anything, more brazenly. A new term has arisen to justify this economic mismanagement: 'intergenerational fairness'. This means that the falling living standards of younger people should be addressed by reducing the living standards of the elderly. Pensions are a key target.

In November 2016, Philip Hammond, the Chancellor of the Exchequer, announced a review of the pensions triple lock, which increases the state pension annually by the higher of inflation, wage growth or 2.5%. The Treasury later confirmed that the review was to assess the affordability of the lock. Hammond said that there would be no changes until after 2020 – ie after the next general election. Furthermore, in December 2016, Simon Stevens, the chief executive of the NHS, argued for an end to the triple lock on pensions, telling MPs:

> 'We need big changes and a conversation on a new deal for retirement security in this country. You've got to look at the full range of services and needs that people have. We should move beyond a triple lock for pensions to a triple guarantee on retirement security, which would include income but also being able to stay in your own home and getting the care you need.'

This shift was to have dire consequences during the 2017 general election. It is important to note that what became known as the dementia tax was not a sudden invention but had been an idea germinating for some time.

Despite having a ring-fenced budget that was immune to the supposed austerity, the NHS spent much of the winter of 2016/17 complaining that it was unable to cope. In October 2016, a BBC/CQC report showed that 1,500 care homes for the elderly had closed over the previous six years. This was a major factor in the number of so-called bed blockers in hospitals who could not be discharged, as there was nowhere to send them since they needed full-time care. The low level of council funding for those in care homes was a reason for the closure of so many. In January 2017, a report from the National Childbirth Trust said that mothers were being treated like 'cattle' or 'products on a conveyor belt'. Half had had poor care and some had been told not to visit 'extremely busy' maternity units. In January 2017, a study by the Health Service Journal showed that 96% of hospitals in October 2016 had failed to meet their own safe nurse-staffing levels for daytime shifts, and 85% had failed to meet the levels for the night-time shifts. In February 2017, in one week at the Royal Blackburn hospital in Lancashire, 95 seriously ill patients were queuing in a corridor for only 33 beds. The elderly lay on trolleys or sat in wheelchairs, and mothers with babies sat on the floor.

In March 2017, it was reported that £800million of funding for the NHS to help struggling GP surgeries and mental health care had been used to bail out hospitals, whose debts had increased as NHS trusts overspent by £900million. Even so, hospitals had reduced the number of beds by 15,000 in the last six years. This was the equivalent of 24 hospitals being closed and was a reduction of 10% in the number of beds. The NHS experienced a serious bed shortage in the winter of 2016/17.

One problem with elderly patients was the difficulty in discharging them from the hospital when the social care budgets, which had not been ring-fenced, had been cut. In February 2017, an Institute for Fiscal Studies (IFS) report disclosed that between 2009/10 and 2015/16, the budget for adult social care fell from £17billion to £16.4billion (while overseas aid spending increased from £8.5billion to £12.24billion).

In December 2016, it was reported that 45% of councils had stopped providing meals on wheels for vulnerable pensioners and another 20% had significantly increased their charges. In February 2017, in a survey by ITV news, councils disclosed that those pensioners who needed home care were having to wait for up to one year before that care could be provided. Social care had been cut by 6% in the previous year. In April 2017, it was revealed that more than 2,000 elderly people, living in their own homes, had died over the previous three years before care visits could be arranged. Some had been waiting for up to nine months.

In March 2017, the Commons Communities and Local Government Committee found that those pensioners in care homes who were 'self-funders' had to pay an average of 43% more than those funded by local councils for an identical service. The same committee recommended a new annual tax of £280 to fund social care.

In December 2016, a report from the IPPR warned that by 2030, there would be a £13billion shortfall in social care spending (estimated to reach £21billion), as the number of those aged over sixty-five increased from 11.6million to 15.4million. By comparison, Osborne, when chancellor in 2015, had said that the foreign aid budget would need to be increased to £15.6billion by 2020 and to a projected increase of £19billion by 2030. In January 2017, David Mowat told MPs that families needed to take more responsibility for looking after their elderly relatives and could no longer rely on the state to do so. According to the Local Government Association, another £2.6billlion would be needed for social care by 2020.

What care the elderly get from the NHS is far from perfect, and the NHS is not quite the envy of the world it claims to be. The number killed on the Liverpool Care Pathway (LCP) programme reached 130,000 per year. The programme involved withdrawal of treatment for very ill patients, curtailing, if not stopping, the provision of food and water, and heavy sedation. Half of those on the programme had not given their consent. Hospitals had been offered extra monies for all of those put on the programme. It was phased out in the 12 months following July 2013 after widespread complaints of abuse. In Wigan, before the abolition of the LCP, nearly one in two hospital deaths were of those on the programme.

The scrimping regarding the elderly continued in new ways. In June 2017, the Oxfordshire Clinical Commissioning Group health trust instructed family doctors to reassess all patients over the age of 70 who are especially frail or who have long-term conditions, to include 10% of all care home residents. The purpose of the reassessment was to reduce 'inappropriate' prescriptions, with half the cost saved being given to the doctors. The aim was to save £1.45million per year. Professor Helen Stokes-Lampard, chairman of the Royal College of GPs, said that the scheme 'will risk jeopardising the trust between doctors and their patients'.

In July 2017, on the same day that the BBC was at the top of the news headlines due to its pay revelations, and the day before the summer recess, the May Government announced that it intended to increase the retirement age to 68 seven years earlier than previously planned, although further consultations would be undertaken. The move would allegedly save £74billion and would affect six million people.

The government was even keen to target the elderly regarding the housing shortage. In August 2016, a report from the Resolution Foundation revealed that home ownership in England was at its lowest level in 30 years. The primary cause was low wage growth and rapidly increasing house prices. In November 2016, an ONS report showed that one in four people in their 20s and 30s were still living with their parents. In February 2017, Gavin Barwell, the housing minister, said: 'If we can make it easier for elderly people to move [into sheltered accommodation] it releases family homes that we're desperate for.'

Home ownership fell to its lowest level in 30 years, with only 62.9% of adults owning their homes. Private renting had doubled. In March 2017, figures showed that average property prices had reached 7.6 times average earnings in England and Wales, according to ONS figures. The figures were £215,000 for a property and annual earnings of £28,336. This is compared to figures of £59,950 for a property and annual earnings of £16,885, or 3.6 times earnings, 20 years ago, when the ONS started compiling the data. Between 1997 and 2016, the average house price had increase by 259%, while earnings had increased by only 68% (see also *The Ponzi Class*, pages 307–308).

A looming scandal was the rip-off of leasehold houses. In April 2017, figures from the Department for Communities and Local Government disclosed that since the introduction of the Government Help to Buy scheme four years ago, sales of houses with leaseholds leapt from 781 in 2013 to 4,832 in

2016, around 15% of the total. Some of the ground rents have been doubled every decade, meaning that the houses are almost impossible to sell and the house owners are being fleeced with large bills they have to pay.

In June 2017, figures from the Student Loans Company showed that the student loan debt had reached £100billlion – with an increase of 16.6% in the last year. The total owed was expected to double to £200billion within six years. In March 2012, the debt had only been £45.9billion.

In December 2016, changes were introduced to require new police recruits to either study policing at university or, if they have a degree in another subject, complete a conversion course, or do a three-year 'degree apprenticeship'. The change was expected to cost police forces £millions. In December 2016, the government hiked university tuition fees to £9,250 a year in England.

The Joseph Rowntree Foundation reported that 880,000 families with stay-at-home mothers and only a single-wage earner had an income below the 'just about managing' level, as described by May. Part of the problem was that a single-wage earner was taxed more highly. Figures from the Bank of England revealed that credit card debt increased by £39million in January. The total owed on credit cards reached £66.7billion – a £10billion increase in five years. There was a further £1.1billion increase in overdrafts, personal loans and car finance in the year to January. The total amount of unsecured debt reached £194billion – a 10.3% increase in a year. Meanwhile, in November 2016, it was reported that the amount owed on credit cards, loans and overdrafts had increased to £190billion. This was an increase of 11% compared to the previous year and was the fastest increase since October 2005 (see *The Ponzi Class*, page 202, regarding the rise in household debt).

The Consumer Prices Index increased by 1.8% in January, the highest increase since June 2014. This meant that the overwhelming majority of savings accounts were paying less than the inflation rate. Baroness Altmann said: 'Savers are now almost guaranteed to lose money. This has created a generation of young people who have seen successive policies to undermine the value of saving and encourage people to take on more debt.'

The Ponzi Class were keen to present the problem as one of intergenerational fairness. In November 2016, The Social Mobility Commission produced a report that warned 'The 20th century expectation that each generation would be better off than the one preceding is no longer being met' and that only one in eight children born in poorer households would achieve a well-paid job. The report said that middle class families were on a 'treadmill', with falling earnings and higher house prices, and that those born in the 1980s were the first generation since World War Two (WWII) not to start their careers on higher salaries than their parents had.

Work and Pensions Secretary Damien Green said in September 2016:

> 'I absolutely accept that we need to look over time at the area of intergenerational fairness. But I do think we should step back from this view that we're being too generous to pensioners, because all these things are very long term and if you look over the long term pensioner poverty in the 1980s was 40% of pensioners. It's now down to 14%. That's an enormous, beneficial social revolution.'

In February 2017, in response to a report from the Resolution Foundation, May's policy adviser, George Freeman MP, said: 'Intergenerational earnings and income fairness are a major issue for a 21st century sustainable political economy.' The executive chairman of the Resolution Foundation, Lord Willets, a former Tory cabinet minister, said: 'The triple lock is a very powerful ratchet pushing up pensions at a time when incomes of the less affluent half of working households are barely rising at all.'

TRADE POLICY

The Ponzi Class went into great detail as to the ongoing failure of Britain to adopt a sensible trade policy (see *The Ponzi Class*, the chapters 'List and the Classical School', 'Joseph Chamberlain and the Tariff Reform Campaign', 'The Inter-War Years', and 'Trade Policy and the Trade Deficit'). Britain's long-term economic decline can be attributed to the simplistic interpretation of 19th-century free-trade theories. That simplicity remains, as is evident from the May Government's approach to Brexit. A golden opportunity to put right the British economy, to bring the trade back into balance with both the EU and China, and to rebuild manufacturing industry has been squandered.

The Remain campaign centred their case on the supposedly desperate need to keep Britain in the Single Market. For Remainers, exiting the EU would lead to a catastrophic collapse in exports, as Britain would be supposedly denied free access to the EU markets. This was nonsense.

Within days of the referendum outcome, many countries were showing a keen interest in doing new trade deals with Britain, including the USA and Australia. Both New Zealand and Australia offered to lend their trade negotiators to Britain to help. Todd McClay, the New Zealand trade minister, described Britain as 'a long-standing friend'. In July 2016, Chrystia Freeland said: 'Canadian investors put about £45billion into the UK every year. We have a very robust relationship. We are not just friends, we are family.' The Canadian government indicated that it was keen for Britain to be a part of the new trade agreement with the EU, even after leaving. In July 2016, Hammond announced that Britain had already commenced trade negotiations with China. In September 2016, Australia, India and Singapore were all revealed to be keen to open trade talks with the Britain.

In July 2016, the ONS revealed that exports to the EU only accounted for 12.2% of British output. Exports to non-EU countries had reached 15.7% of national output. In August 2016, the fall in sterling had led to a two-year high in export orders according to the CBI. The fall in sterling was an important boost, and yet the British government shied away from addressing the negative impact of the euro on the British economy. Even President Trump's administration was more aware of the problem than the British. In February 2017, Peter Navarro, head of President Trump's National Trade Council and an economics professor, told *The Financial Times* that 'A big obstacle to viewing TTIP [Transatlantic Trade and Investment Partnership] as a bilateral deal is Germany, which continues to exploit other countries in the EU as well as the US with an "implicit Deutsche mark" that is grossly undervalued' and that there was a 'structural imbalance in trade with the rest of the EU and the US'. The Trump administration, even if the May Government did not, recognised the manner in which Germany was exploiting the euro for its own ends and the extent of the damage this selfishness was causing. It should be recalled that German reunification was the primary reason for the disintegration of the exchange rate mechanism and for the damage done to Britain's economy in the early 1990s (*The Ponzi Class*, pages 191–194). President Trump withdrew the USA from the Trans-Pacific Partnership and had little interest in TTIP. All references to TTIP were removed from the White House website within hours of President Trump's assuming the presidency. President Trump further notified Congress of his intention to renegotiate NAFTA (North American Free Trade Agreement – between the USA, Canada and Mexico). President Trump announced that if he was 'unable to make a fair deal', he would 'terminate NAFTA'.

For the May Government, it was business as usual with no preference given to British firms. In October 2016, the Ministry of Defence said that it would be awarding the contract to supply the steel to build the hulls of new submarines to a French firm, as British steel was not tough enough. Sir Michael Fallon said: 'There wasn't a British bid for that particular type of steel.' Fallon proceeded to say that 85% of the submarines would be built in Britain. Also in October 2016, the Spanish-owned Scottish Power awarded £150million of contracts to build the foundations for a new wind farm off East Anglia to a Spanish shipyard. Scottish Power would receive millions of pounds in government subsidies for the scheme

The takeover of the best of Britain's industry, if anything, accelerated. In December 2016, figures showed that around £70billion had been spent by foreign firms taking over British companies in the previous 180 days. The companies taken over included Innovia, Immediate Media, Host Europe Group, and ARM Holdings. ARM was Britain's sole-surviving technology firm, and it was sold to a Japanese company following a shareholder vote in August 2016. There was no government intervention. From the EU referendum to July 2017, British companies worth £122billion were taken over by foreign firms. Worldpay, a financial technology company responsible for 40% of card payments in Britain, was the latest major company to face a takeover bid, worth £9billion, from a US organization.

With the Hong Kong Mass Transit Railway taking over, along with FirstGroup, the South West Trains franchise, 75% of Britain's railways were now run by foreign companies. The operators include Arriva, German owned; c2c, Italian owned; Govia, French owned; Abellio, Dutch owned; and MTR, Chinese owned.

In June 2017, Chris Grayling, the transport secretary, announced that three groups were being considered to operate the West Coast Partnership franchise and hence would run the HS2 trains. Two of the groups were partnerships between a British company and foreign rail companies; the third was a Chinese consortium that has no British involvement. The Tory MP Andrew Bridgen said: 'This is the biggest infrastructure project ever undertaken in the UK. If it ends up being mainly build and operated by foreign companies this further diminishes the benefits to Britain.' The Tory MP Sir Bill Cash said: 'At this critical moment for our economy it is absolutely essential we give the maximum opportunities to UK engineers and manufacturers.'

However, the Deutsche Boerse takeover of the London Stock Exchange was cancelled following intervention from the EU competition commissioner, Margrethe Vestager. The May Government had raised no objections to the sell-off.

In February 2017, it was reported that Caffe Nero, despite making a profit of £25.5million, yet again paid no tax, claiming that its parent company had suffered a £24million loss. The company had paid no corporation tax since 2007 despite total sales of £1billion since then. The firm's controlling holding company is based in Luxembourg, with the ultimate holding company for the group being based in the Isle of Man.

In March 2017, figures showed one of the consequences of the foreign takeover of Britain's firms. Annually, in Britain: Caffe Nero had sales of £274million, a loss of £24.2million, corporation tax nil; Vodafone: sales £6.7billion, a loss of £486million, corporation tax nil; GAP: sales £426million, £163million loss, corporation tax nil; Waterstones: sales £395million, profit £10.9million, corporation tax nil; EE: sales £6.3billion, profit £416million, corporation tax nil; Topshop: sales not known, profit £200million, corporation tax £36million; Boots: sales not known, profit not known, corporation tax not known (it was a part of the US Walgreens Boots Alliance and its headquarters are in Illinois and the firm does not disclose the information); Apple: sales £1.12billion, profit £106million, corporation tax £12.9million; McDonald's: sales £1.53billion, profit £270million, corporation tax £56million; Vision Express: sales £255million, profit £7.3million, corporation tax £282,000; Starbucks: sales £406million, profit £34million, corporation tax £8.1million; Thomas Cook: sales £2.3billion, profit £152million, corporation tax £8million.

In March 2017, the Australian Macquarie investment bank sold off its remaining stake in Thames Water for around £1.3billion. Since being bought by Macquarie in December 2006, Thames had paid out more than £1.2billion in dividends, while its debts had escalated from £1.6billion to £10billion. It had paid only £100,000 in corporation tax, and it now had a pension fund deficit of £260million. Thames had been fined many times, most recently in January 2017 for repeatedly polluting the Grand Union Canal in Hertfordshire. In June 2017, Thames Water was fined £8.6million by Ofwat after allowing water to leak at a daily rate of 677million litres per day in the previous year. Thames Water paid out £100million in dividends in the same period.

Research showed that a number of foreign-owned banks were paying little or no tax on the profits they made in the City. In the year 2014/15 the Bank of America made a profit of £1.1billion and paid no tax; for BNP Paribas, the figures were £837.3million profit and £167.4million tax; Citibank had £78.7million profit and no tax; Commerz had £718million profit and £171.7million tax; Credit Agricole had £371.4million profit and £75.5million tax; Goldman Sachs had a profit of £3.9billion and £229.2million tax; JP Morgan had a profit of £2.9billion and tax of £131.9million; Societe Generale had a profit of £551.1million and tax of £92.9million; UBS had a profit of £350.9million and paid £21.6million in tax; and UBS had a £350.9million profit and paid £21.6million in tax. Total profits of these banks was £11.2billion, and the tax paid was £890million – an average tax rate of 8%. John Mann MP and a member of the Treasury Select Committee said: 'It is outrageous that these banks are still not paying their fair share of tax. The public will rightly find this shocking and ask, "When will they stop taking us for a ride"?' The banks were strongly in favour of Remain and have lobbied hard for free access to the Single Market.

In June 2017, it was revealed that low-cost Indian and Filipino shipping firms, as well as European ones employing Indian workers, were undercutting British firms for work servicing British oil and gas rigs in the North Sea. Ship owners called on the government to insist that the oil and gas companies use more British companies for work in British waters. Guy Platten, chief executive of UK Chamber of Shipping, said: 'We need to provide a level playing field so UK companies can compete.' About 70% of operating costs is accounted for by the cost of the crew.

China was a key beneficiary of Britain's weak trade policy. It was reported in August 2016 that despite falling oil prices, China had become the largest producer of oil in the North Sea. China National Offshore Oil Corporation (CNOOC) produced 10% of North Sea oil output and had the two largest oilfields. In 2012, CNOOC's then chief, Wang Yilin, stated: 'large scale deep-water rigs' were China's 'mobile national territory and a strategic weapon'.

At a G20 summit, May said in September 2016:

> 'A decision about Hinkley will be made later this month. But our relationship with China is about more than Hinkley. If you look at the investment that there has been from China in various other parts of the UK and other infrastructure in the EU, we have built a global strategic partnership with China. I've been clear we will be continuing that global strategic partnership with China. It is a golden era of relations between China and the UK.'

In September 2016, the May Government decided to proceed with the £18billion Hinkley Point nuclear power station. China's involvement was approved. The National Audit Office warned that the cost of the subsidies would be almost £30billion – £1,000 per household – over the 35-year life expectancy of the power station. Two power stations of the same type as Hinkley were already ten years behind schedule in France and Finland, amid problems over safety and cost overruns. The cost of the Finnish power station had already tripled from the original estimate.

In December 2016, Chinese buyers took a 49% stake in the technology firm Global Switch at a cost of £2.2billion. The Chinese were allowed to do this despite Global Switch hosting computer servers for companies and despite ongoing Chinese computer hacking.

China employed an estimated 1.5million computer hackers and was very active in industrial espionage. Susan Rice, Obama's national security adviser, described China's espionage as 'not a mild irritation, it's an economic and national security concern.' In August 2016, the Chinese state-owned firm China General Nuclear Power, which is involved in the Hinkley project, was accused of trying to steal US nuclear technology. China also benefited in other ways. In July 2017, it was announced by JLR that for the first time, a new model would be built exclusively abroad. The E-Pace Jaguar SUV would be produced in factories in Austria and China.

There was only one glimpse of reality from the government. In November 2016, regarding productivity, Philip Hammond said:

> 'We lag behind the US and Germany by some 30 percentage points. But we also lag France by over 20 and Italy by 8. Which means in the real world, it takes a German worker four days to produce what we make in five, which means, in turn, that too many British workers work longer hours for lower pay than their counterparts. That has to change if we are to build an economy that works for everyone. Raising productivity is essential for the high-wage, high-skill economy that will deliver higher living standards for working people.'

Treasury documents showed that raising productivity by 1% per year would increase GDP by £240billion in ten years – equivalent to £9,000 for every household.

Despite the dire threats of Project Fear, in the three months to January, export volumes rose by 8.7%, the fastest growth for a decade. Factory output also increased by 2.1% between November and January. Since the referendum in June 2016, sterling has fallen 18% against the dollar and 12% against the euro.

A good example of the daftness of government green policy, the cost of it and the harm done to Britain's competitiveness, was the Drax power station. In 2013, the station spent £700million, of which £450million was a subsidy paid for by consumers in the form of higher energy bills, to convert three of its six furnaces to burning wood pellets – or 'biomass'. This was because the EU decreed that burning biomass was carbon neutral due to new trees being planted to replace those cut down for burning. Drax was hitherto a coal-fired power station, with coal being the cheapest form of energy.

In a report for the Chatham House by Duncan Barrack, who used to work for Chris Huhne, the minister at the Department of Energy and Climate Change, it was disclosed that a new tree could take hundreds of years to absorb the carbon emitted by a burnt one, and so the allegation that burning wood pellets instead of coal would reduce climate change was bunkum. Furthermore, as burning wood is less heat efficient than burning coal, there is a 12% increase in carbon emissions per unit of electricity. The government had ignored the carbon emissions of actually burning the wood pellets in its calculations, as it was deemed carbon neutral.

Far from reducing carbon emissions, the conversion of Drax from coal to wood pellets for fuel actually increased them.

THE PONZI CLASS AND PONZI ECONOMICS

The contrast between the lifestyles of the Ponzi Class and the plight of ordinary people remained. The Brexit vote was a revolt against the establishment. That revolt changed nothing. The greed of the Ponzi Class and their determination to sustain their elevated standard of living can almost be admired for its audacity.

In August 2016, one police chief constable who had only done 16 months of work was paid £600,000 over three and a half years by the West Yorkshire Police and was further awarded a gold-plated pension. He had been suspended for more than two years due to misconduct and criminal complaints being made against him. Despite an attempted cover-up, it was further revealed that chief constables and other senior police officers were enjoying 'allowances' of up to £17,000 per annum in addition to their basic pay to cover daily spending and household bills, private medical insurance, chauffeurs, first-class travel and up to 64 days off on holiday annually.

In September 2016, the chief executive responsible for the HS2 rail scheme, who was being paid £750,000 per annum, quit. The civil servant had accepted a new job offer from Rolls Royce. The cost of the scheme had already increased from £40billion to £55billion without any construction being done. Some estimates have put the final cost as likely being £80billion.

In October 2016, it was revealed that the HMRC was investigating up to 100 BBC presenters over allegations of tax dodging. Twenty-three staff members were believed to have set up elaborate schemes to avoid tax liabilities. The BBC dismissed the matter as historic and an industrywide problem. The lavishness of the BBC was simply breathtaking. George Entwistle resigned as BBC director-general after only 54 days after assuming the post. His payoff totalled £450,000 (double the contractual entitlement), plus his legal costs in negotiating his pay-off, plus £107,000 for appearing as a witness in the Saville abuse inquiry, plus 12 months of medical insurance, plus £6,000 for PR costs. Sharon Baylay, the former director of marketing, ecommunications and audience was made redundant after 17 months; she received almost £400,000 redundancy plus £1,763 for BUPA health cover. Caroline Thomson received a payoff of £680,000 and £14,000 for lawyers when she was made redundant. John Smith, the chief executive of BBC Worldwide, despite being only 55 years old, was awarded a £212,000 pension payment per annum and a £1.6million severance payment. Pat Loughrey, director of nations and regions, received £866,000, including £300,000 in lieu of notice even though he had already worked his notice and had been paid to do so. Roly Keating, director of archive content, got a new job at the British Library before negotiating a payoff of £376,000 from the BBC – which he returned due to the public outcry. Mark Byford got a payoff of £1million when he was made redundant as deputy director-general.

In July 2017, after much opposition, the BBC was forced to disclose the names of all its staff who were paid more than £150,000 per year. Those who were being paid via third-party organizations were not included. The disclosures showed that the BBC's highest paid employee was Chris Evans, who got £2.25million. Gary Linekar got £1.8million. Even some fairly unknown and low-ranking presenters were getting more than £150,000. There was some friction between female and male presenters on the same show where the female presenter was being paid less. Women were deemed to be underrepresented, and the BBC was therefore accused of sexism.

Also on the BBC 'rich list' were more than 100 managers, including those with non-jobs such as analytics architect; identity architect; service architect; integration lead; technical project manager; head of strategic change, world service; chief architect; director audiences; head of network supply; and director future commissioning. The BBC director-general, Tony Hall, was paid £450,000 per year, and the head of BBC Worldwide, Tim Davies, was paid £682,000 per year. It further emerged that many of the BBC's biggest stars were still using personal service companies to avoid income tax despite previously saying that they would phase out the practice.

The BBC was not alone. Lord Grade, who was once chief executive of the publicly owned Channel 4, described its salaries as 'gobsmacking'. The current Channel 4 chief executive, David Abraham, had a salary of £957,000, and the creative director, Jay Hunt, had a salary of £683,000. There were other examples such as Dame Lin Homer, a disaster at both the HMRC and when running the immigration service, who, it was revealed in July 2016, pocketed a pension pot of £2.4million. She got a £125,000 index-linked pension payment per year.

Such extravagant salaries are harmful, not only due to the waste and the corrupting influence of the sense of entitlement, but also because they create a sense of superiority. Even politicians, who are paid far less, are subordinate to television journalists and presenters, for example. This is exacerbated by the detachment and lack of patriotism, as the salaries are paid due to the importance of the person and the importance of the organization paying that person, rather than because the country as a whole is successful. It is the organization's ability to plunder the country that creates the opportunities for fat salaries. This subversiveness reinforces the ideology of political correctness and fuels the snobbery of it.

In November 2016, it was reported that many charities, including Barnado's, the RSPB, and Cancer Research UK were using donations received to cover pension shortfalls. John Ralfe, a pensions expert, said: 'The people who give money to charities believe they are handing over their cash to further good work, not to plug black holes in organizations' pension funds. This is becoming a huge looming problem for charities.' Ros Altmann said: 'So many charities do not have enough cash to meet these pension liabilities ... they have to divert it from other causes.'

In December 2016, it was revealed that board members, consisting of businessmen and councillors, of Local Enterprise Partnerships (LEPs), which receive £7.3billion of taxpayers' monies to promote economic growth, had been awarding grants to themselves. One had even received £1million for a call centre; another received £550,000 for a zoo.

In December 2016, official figures showed that 58 quango chief executives earned more than £150,000, which is more than the prime minister. This is an increase from 42 since 2015. Despite so-called austerity, the number of quangos had only fallen from 468 to 463 over the past year. The highest paid was chief executive for HS2, who pocketed £750,000.

SSE awarded chief executive Alistair Phillips-Davies a 73% pay increase, to a salary of £2.9million. This compares with a salary of £4.6million for the head of the National Grid, a salary of £4.3million for the chief of Centrica (the owner of British Gas), £2.8million for the chief of United Utilities, and £2.4million for the chief of Severn Trent.

In April 2017, a report for the Taxpayer's Alliance disclosed that 539 Town Hall staff were paid at least £150,000 annually. This was a rise of 11% in one year. Another 2,314 council employees were getting £100,000 or more. The chief executive for the Sunderland Council was paid £625,570, and the director of finance £605,958. The chief executive of Liverpool Council was paid £461,823. The North Lanarkshire director of finance was paid £486,208.

In June 2017, the Department for Education disclosed that there had been an 8% increase in the number of head teachers earning £100,000 or more. The total exceeded 1,300. The average head teacher's salary had increased to £68,300. The highest-paid head teacher was getting £420,000 per annum.

University vice-chancellors' remuneration increased by more than 10% in 2015/16 in 23 universities, and by an average of 6.7%, with the highest salary being £451,000 and the average salary being £277,834. Fifty-five universities paid their vice-chancellors more than £300,000. Vice-chancellors also spent an average of £7,762 on flights and an average of £2,982 on hotels (with the University of Sheffield spending £24,433). A Russell Group spokesman said: 'Vice-chancellor pay is decided by official university remuneration committees which include expert representatives from outside the sector. These experts understand the importance of attracting and retaining experienced individuals who are capable of managing complex international institutions.'

In April 2017, figures showed that vice-chancellors, deans, and presidents at 40 universities, including Oxford and

Cambridge, in addition to salaries, were also having their council tax, utility bills, gardening costs and cleaning costs being met in their grace-and-favour accommodations. Some even enjoyed the services of housekeepers to do washing and ironing. The University and College Union described the perks as 'embarrassing largesse'.

Dame Glynis Breakwell, vice-chancellor of the University of Bath, who was paid £451,000, enjoyed a grace-and-favour five-bedroom house and £8,738 in cleaning costs with a housekeeper 'responsible for bed linen, washing and ironing' in addition to her council tax and utilities being covered. Louise Richardson, the University of Oxford vice-chancellor, was paid £384,000 (including a pension contribution), with council tax, utilities, cleaning and gardening costs being covered at a rent-free house (estimated to be worth £3.75million). Sir David Eastwood, vice-chancellor of the University of Birmingham, got £425,000 with council tax and utilities being covered. Sir Leszek Borysiewicz was paid £353,000, with council tax and utilities being covered at his vice-chancellor's lodge.

In July 2017, figures from the University and College Union showed that 22 universities each paid more than 100 staff more than £100,000 salaries. The top earner was Dame Glynis Breakwell of the University of Bath, one of the smaller universities, who was awarded an 11% pay increase to take her salary to no less than £451,000; the university had 67 staff earning at least £100,000. Oxford University had more than 451 staff earning at least £100,000. University College London had 444, and Cambridge University had 409.

In reference to figures showing how universities had cut the number of British students admitted while increasing the number of wealthy non-EU foreign students, who are charged more, Chris McGovern, Chairman of the Campaign for Real Education, remarked:

> 'Universities have increasingly become a racket and their central focus has become making money rather than on education. We need to put our own country

> and own young people first, rather than favouring overseas students because they bring in more cash ... Universities putting their own financial needs over the needs of the country need to be held to account.'

Despite a 17% increase in applications since 2008, the Russell Group of universities had cut the number of British students. For example, Cambridge University had cut the number of British undergraduates by 29% while increasing the number of non-EU undergraduates by 18%.

In January 2017, figures showed that the number of NHS bureaucrats earning more than £150,000 more than doubled in three years.

Even the judges got in on the act. In February 2017, a 'judicial attitude survey' carried out by academics and endorsed by Lord Chief Justice Lord Thomas, who said that he would forward the findings on to the Senior Salaries Review Body, found that two-thirds of judges considered themselves to be underpaid and that their pensions were inadequate. A Court of Appeal judge enjoyed a salary of £204,695. Lord Thomas said: 'In the light of the substantially greater remuneration available to the most able practitioners in private practice, these matters are vital to our ability to attract candidates and retain judges of the highest calibre.' The judges were quietly awarded an 11% pay rise – almost an extra £20,000 per annum for a High Court judge and more than £22,500 extra for a Court of Appeal judge.

In March 2017, Lord Hope, a crossbench peer, complained that the £300-per-day tax-free allowance for attendance at the House of Lords was inadequate. Baroness D'Souza, who had spent months investigating peers who clocked in to claim their £300-per day-allowance before disappearing, discontinued her probe to avoid 'naming and shaming' those involved. She said:

> 'What I wanted to find out ... was who was attending and what they were claiming, and even though it is

very difficult to quantify, there are some who make no contribution whatsoever but who nevertheless claim the full amount. This is not a daycare centre or a club – it is actually a legislative house and I do firmly believe that the people who attend ought to be able to be in a position to contribute. I abandoned this research because it would have involved a degree of naming and shaming, which I certainly didn't want to do. But also, that would in turn have provoked some kind of a press storm which clearly, you know, I didn't want to do.'

Baroness Boothroyd, the former Commons speaker, complained: 'Tony Blair in ten years appointed 374 new peers. Cameron was in office for six years. He created 244 new peers at a faster rate than any other prime minister. I think quite frankly it's a disgrace.'

Despite losing the referendum, Cameron handed a multitude of honours to his chums, including peerages, CBEs, OBEs and knighthoods to a stylist, press spokesmen, speechwriters, donors, general flunkies and even Osborne. In January 2017, Osborne became a senior adviser to BlackRock Investment Institute. However, George 'six jobs' Osborne faced the prospect of no less than five inquiries into his jobs. This followed his appointment as editor of the *Evening Standard* as well as his appointment to work one day a week at Blackrock on £650,000 per annum. Osborne did not stand for re-election in the 2017 general election.

Lawyers continued to get rich. One couple who was married only five months spent 30 months in divorce proceedings. The wife, a model, had spent £230,000 in legal fees trying to get a share of an alleged £20million fortune despite the former husband having declared himself bankrupt.

There was one problem on the horizon for some lawyers, however, relating to the looming scandal of the sale of leasehold houses. These lawyers were facing a bill of an estimated £500million relating to the sale of leasehold houses, where the ground rent could be increased ruinously, making the properties unsaleable. To save fees and time, and at the behest of the developers, the lawyers had been used by both parties in the original sale and had not warned the buyers of the potential charges. There was a conflict of interest.

However, in May 2017, it was reported that the bosses of the ten largest building firms had enjoyed a £170million pay increase since the introduction of the government's Help to Buy scheme four years before. Close to one-third of the 405,000 houses built since 2013 have been bought under the scheme.

The contrast with ordinary people was stark. In July 2016, figures from the Higher Education Statistics Agency disclosed that 50,000 recent graduates were working in menial jobs not requiring degrees. Many students were graduating with debts of more than £40,000.

In September 2016, the Centre for Economics and Business Research reported that most students would be unable to repay their student loans, and that only doctors and lawyers would be able to do so before the debts were written off after 30 years: 'Many of the other professions, including the relatively well-paid ones, never manage to pay off the loan because it can easily rise at a faster rate than salaries.' It was also reported that nearly every university would increase tuition fees to £9,250 per year.

Even so, in October 2016, the Department for Education announced that EU students would continue to be given student loans even after Brexit and despite the fact that increasing numbers are not repaying the loans. Jo Johnson, the Universities Minister, said:

> 'We know that the result of the referendum brought with it some uncertainties for our higher education sector. International students make an important contribution to our world-class universities, and we want that to continue. This latest assurance ... will

provide important stability for both universities and students.'

Despite the Leave vote, nothing was to change. It was business as usual.

In July 2016, hospitals admitted that foreign patients were being given priority for cataract surgery over British NHS patients. Rationing of cataract operations had been introduced for British patients due to demand.

In December 2016, the National Audit Office highlighted that schools needed to make cuts of £3billion over the next three years despite their budgets being stretched due to rising numbers of schoolchildren. Schools had been having to accommodate an extra 470,000 since 2009, and there was a need for yet another increase of 750,000 new places in England by 2025. Approximately 700,000 schoolchildren have at least one parent who has foreign citizenship.

In December 2016, it was reported by the CQC that care home fees had increased by 23% in the last year. It was now costing almost £35,000 per year for an elderly person to be in a care home.

The BBC was exposed for paying £59million per year to a firm of debt collectors, Capita, to get licence fees. Capita's boss is paid £2.7million per year. Capita's field agents have a target of 28 non-payers a week and get a bonus of £15,000 a year. Capita has been accused of underhanded and aggressive tactics in dealing with the general public.

The banks continued to flourish. In July 2016, it was reported that they were charging more for an overdraft than payday lenders were charging for loans. Banks were charging £90 in a month for an unplanned overdraft of £100, which was four times the amount allowed for a payday loan for the same amount. In August 2016, despite another cut in interest rates, most of the banks refused to immediately pass that cut on to their borrowers, if they passed it on at all, and many banks proceeded to cut their savings rates by more than the 0.25% rate reduction. For example, Scottish Widows, owned by Lloyds Bank, cut its rate on an e-cash

ISA from 1% to 0.6%. RBS, owned by the taxpayers, actually introduced negative interest rates.

A report from the Financial Conduct Authority in June 2017 revealed that City fund managers were charging large fees, with profit margins of an average of 36%, for little benefit to their savers, who would do better to simply track the stock market. 90% of the actively managed funds underperformed the stock market according to research from S&P.

Yet another mis-selling scandal seemed to be brewing. In June 2017, the Financial Ombudsman Service reported a 64% rise in complaints about loans to buy cars. In March alone, the lending amounted to £3.6billion. Most of the deals involved the buyers not buying the car outright.

In September 2016, the amount paid into the Bank of England final salary pension scheme had doubled since 2011. This was against a background of continuing quantitative easing measures which have decimated private pensions, with another £60billion of printed money being recently pumped into the economy.

Despite its open dishonesty, and despite undertaking to recompense those small business people who were victims of their fraud, RBS was accused in December 2016 of only offering a token amount. In February 2017, RBS announced a loss of £7billion in the last year, bringing its losses to a total of £58billion since being bailed out with taxpayers' money. RBS staff bonuses totalled £343million in 2016.

RBS was not the only bank that had acted fraudulently. HBOS, which was taken over by Lloyds Bank, actually experienced the embarrassment of criminal convictions after many years of swindling their business customers. This is a good example of the malpractice of Britain's banks (see also *The Ponzi Class*, pages 337–340).

Between 2002 and 2007, small businesses were transferred to the HBOS Reading HQ and classified as 'high risk' even though many had never missed making a repayment. Lynden Scourfield was in charge of HBOS's Impaired Assets Division, and he required business owners to appoint Quayside Corporate Services (QCS) as advisers in return for continued HBOS support. QCS was run by David Mills and Michael Bancroft. QCS would then increase the business borrowings, often against the owners wishes, which HBOS would grant. QCS then siphoned off funds by invoicing inflated fees of up to £30,000 per month each. QCS, in return, arranged for Scourfield to have free trips to Barbados and Cannes and for him to receive cash, Rolex watches, drugs and use of prostitutes. The businesses were asset stripped by QCS and bankrupted or sold on to favoured buyers for a token payment, and even to sham buyers owned by members of QCS.

Despite increasing levels of complaints in 2007, a 2009 BBC Radio 4 programme, and even a debate in parliament that detailed allegations of cash payments and prostitutes, it was not until 2010 that the police investigated. In 2016, the matters were brought to trial.

Business owners lost their livelihoods, their pensions, their savings and their homes. Small businesses were estimated to have lost up to £1billion. HBOS, which owned the Halifax and the Bank of Scotland, was taken over by Lloyds Bank. The bank received a £20.5billion taxpayer-funded bailout to cover bad debts caused by excessive lending. Although HBOS finally revealed that Scourfield had been making unsanctioned loans in 2007, the bank denied responsibility for the small businesses being forced into ruin. Former Tory Minister Sir James Paice said the chief of HBOS 'flatly denied' the lender had done anything wrong even after Scourfield was finally sacked.

One victim, Joanne Dove, lost her business, home and marriage as a result of the fraud. She said:

> 'I can only liken my experience of dealing with HBOS appointed executives to how I would imagine dealing with the Mafia would be. It was financial rape ... I lost everything, my reputation, all our money, all our pension schemes. My children lost their father in their lives and the idyllic childhood they previously had. Our

family was devastated ... they robbed me of my life's work.'

Miss Dove's business, Cotton Bottoms, needed £400,000 to expand. The loan was granted on the condition that Michael Bancroft from QCS was appointed to the board as a non-executive director. QCS quickly plundered the business, stirred up division between husband and wife by secretly offering the husband a deal to buy out the firm and giving him a new position, and eventually forcing Miss Dove to sell the business at a sixth of its true value. At one point, when pregnant with her fourth child, Miss Dove was locked in a room by Bancroft as he demanded a controlling interest. Miss Dove said: 'I felt like a hostage. It was like having a huge parasite implanted in the guts of the business.'

Andrew Reade, who lost £250,000 after his company, Keenets, was plundered by QCS, wrote to Victor Blank, the then chairman of Lloyds TSB, at the time of its takeover of HBOS in 2008, outlining the facts in extensive detail. He attached a dossier describing how many companies had suffered because of what he described as a 'huge fraud' involving Scourfield and QCS. Sir Victor Blank was advised that a response from him would 'not be appropriate'.

One couple, the Turners, had their accounts frozen and were forced to sell jewellery to fund investigations into the fraud. They repeatedly complained to the bank, regulators, the police and even to MPs. The bank denied any wrongdoing and attempted to repossess the Turners' home; there were 22 eviction hearings. Mr Turner said: 'It was a complete cover-up. The bank repeatedly attempted to mislead us, the other victims, our MPs and other authorities.' Mrs Turner added: 'What happened at HBOS Reading was fraud on an industrial scale.' The Turners managed to retain their home.

Regarding Lynden Scourfield, Anthony Stansfield of the Thames Valley Police said:

'The cover-up went on for ten years. An internal email in February 2008 within the risk department of HBOS clearly says that a major fraud had taken place within the Reading branch of HBOS, and that at least £200million had been defrauded from HBOS customers. Yet despite this evidence, the board of Lloyds ... continued to refuse to accept that a fraud had taken place and pursued the victims.'

This crookedness of the banks is because they know that the judges, who have crafted the banking laws, will aid and abet them and that the establishment will cover up for them. The banks have remained defiant.

The tolerance of crooked bankers by the government was routine. A glaring example was HSBC, about which the US senator Elizabeth Warren quizzed a member of the US Treasury Department in March 2013, when she said:

'In December, HSBC admitted to money laundering; to laundering 881million dollars that we know of, for Mexican and Columbian drug cartels; and also admitted to violating our sanctions for Iran, Libya, Cuba, Burma, The Sudan. And they didn't do it just one time. There wasn't a mistake. They did it over and over and over again across a period of years. And they were caught doing it, warned not to do it, and kept right on doing it. And evidently, making profits doing it. Now HSBC paid a fine. But no one individual went to trial. No individual was banned from banking. And there was no hearing to consider shutting down HSBC's activities here in the United States.

So what I'd like is – you're the experts on money laundering – I'd like your opinion. What does it take? How many billions of dollars do you have to launder for drug lords and how many economic sanctions do you have to violate, before someone will consider shutting down a financial institution these days?'

The Treasury official did not enlighten Elizabeth Warren, who explained:

> 'If you are caught with an ounce of cocaine, the chances are you are going to go to jail. If it happens repeatedly, you may go to jail for the rest of your life. But evidently, if you launder nearly a billion dollars for drug cartels and violate our international sanctions, your company pays a fine and you go home and sleep in your own bed at night. Every single individual associated with this. I think that is fundamentally wrong.'

HSBC benefited from lobbying by the British government. Its drug-money laundering did not preclude it from benefiting from the various amounts of QE (printed money given to the banks) nor its interests from being given priority in Brexit over the national interest and views of ordinary English people (see *The Ponzi Class*, pages 222, 224 and 297 for the consequences of QE on private pensions).

Within 24 hours of the budget, the government backed away from a proposed £2billion increase in National Insurance payments from the self-employed. The required legislation was delayed until the autumn after a backbench revolt over a clear breach of the Tory election manifesto. May announced that the proposed increase would be packaged together with an increase in new rights (such as maternity pay) for the self-employed after a review over the summer by Matthew Taylor, a former adviser to Tony Blair and Labour activist. May insisted that the increased payments were necessary, as the rise in self-employment was 'eroding the tax base'.

It was the proposed new rights to the self-employed that the May Government cited to justify their £2billion raid. In *The Ponzi Class*, there is the parable of Gangle Land (to supersede the Keynes banana plantation parable), where a financial minister was known as 'Fingers'. 'Fingers' helped himself to people's monies in return for issuing IOUs. Yet now, in the real world, 'Fingers Phil' was doing exactly the same, except that he was already intending to reduce pensions even as he was issuing the IOUs. He was issuing promises of rights to be honoured by some future government (ie IOUs) in return for helping himself to hard cash belonging to the self-employed.

It did not stop there. 'Fingers Phil' had struck again. Hammond had also sneaked a major increase in probate charges into his budget – a move expected to raise £1.5billion over five years. Instead of a set fee of either £215 or £155 for a solicitor, the government's new scheme would increase fees based on the value of the estate and would reach as high as £20,000. Analysis revealed that many might need to borrow to meet the new fees. In any event, this proposal attracted widespread Tory backbench opposition and fell by the wayside.

Britain's economy continued to depend on consumer spending and credit. In April 2017, Bank of England figures showed that the amount owed on credit card debt jumped by £520million in one month, bringing the total owed by families to £67.3billion. Meanwhile, the proportion of household income saved fell to its lowest level ever at 3.3% in the last quarter of 2016. The majority of credit card companies did not have a minimum income requirement to get a new card. The credit binge continued, and by June, Bank of England figures showed that the amount owed on credit cards increased by £600million in May to a record £68.1billion. This is an average of £2,500 per household.

In July 2017, it was revealed that the national debt had reached £1.75trillion, £65,000 per household, after a £4.6billion increase in government spending in June (including an extra £1.2billion payments in debt interest caused by higher inflation). Before the financial crisis, the national debt had been £540billion.

Ominously, in May 2017, the Bank of England predicted an inflation rate of 2.8% for 2017, while wages would only grow by 2%. This would be the first time since since 2014 that inflation would be at a higher rate than wage increases. In consequence, living standards were forecast to fall. Carney said: 'This is going to be a more challenging time for British households. Wages won't keep up with prices.' Carney did not explain the inflationary consequences of the recent £60billion of QE printed money he had recently lavished on the banks. In June, the ONS reported that inflation had reached 2.9%.

POLITICAL CORRECTNESS

The morality of the Ponzi Class is political correctness. A full analysis of this creed is contained in *The Genesis of Political Correctness*, as are examples of its damaging impact. One such example has been the persecution of British troops, in particular by so-called human rights lawyers. Although some justice has finally prevailed, the persecution continues.

Sir Michael Fallon said: 'IHAT (Iraqi Historical Investigations Team) was established in order to prevent this country being hauled in front of the International Criminal Court. We have to investigate these allegations.' The proper solution to that is not to sign up to such silly treaties that allegedly oblige Britain to persecute its own troops, not to hand over control of such matters to bureaucrats on foreign quangos, but to withdraw from such treaties if they have been corrupted and are being exploited by the enemies of the West.

That the government's approach to its own armed forces was starting to crack was apparent in August 2016, when the firm Public Interest Lawyers (PIL) were stripped of the right to be paid legal aid following breaches of the legal aid rules. In September 2016, amidst the scandal of the persecution of British soldiers and talk of a need for a union to protect their interests, May held a meeting with the armed services top brass. This meeting proved a photo opportunity and allowed the May Government to claim to have stepped in to help the beleaguered soldiers, 200 of whom were threatening a judicial review and legal action against the government. Investigators had turned up at soldiers' homes or barracks and demanded information and threatened arrest. In one case, they arrived at an ex-girlfriend's home to question her as to whether her former partner was abusive, had tattoos or spoke in his sleep. Six soldiers had even been arrested. The closure of PIL made likely that more than 1,000 cases would be dismissed, but more than 650 cases had arisen from the British involvement in Afghanistan. A spokesman said that the prime minister wanted 'every effort made to prevent any abuse of the legal system, and restated her determination to protect the armed forces against any instances of vexatious complaints'. The costs of the IHAT were predicted to reach £57million by 2019.

A typical example of what was going on was highlighted in October 2016, when the Supreme Court was told that a Taliban commander, who was suing the Ministry of Defence over his detention, had been covered in bomb dust when he had been detained. Serdar Mohammed had been convicted in Afghanistan of making roadside bombs. He alleged that his human rights had been breached when he had been detained for 110 days in 2010.

In December 2016, Phil Shiner, of the now defunct law firm PIL, pleaded guilty to a series of misconduct charges relating to abuse claims made against British soldiers in Iraq. PIL was responsible for the vast majority of the 3,000 abuse claims submitted to the IHAT, even alleging murder and mistreatment. Iraqi agents were being paid large sums of money to secure allegations, the majority of which were obviously bogus. IHAT had been set up as a consequence of the Human Rights Act. PIL pocketed many millions of pounds of taxpayers' money in legal aid. PIL also forwarded files on British troops to the International Criminal Court. Shiner was hauled before the Solicitors Disciplinary Tribunal despite the fact that in 2007, Shiner had been named solicitor of the year by the Law Society. In February 2017, deciding that the IHAT 'as a separate unit should end', Sir Michael Fallon wrote:

> 'Mr Shiner's downfall will have been painful to behold for those in the human rights lobby who lionised him. But as is often the case with charismatic conmen, it was not just naive campaigners whom he fooled.
>
> For too long he and others were able to exploit vulnerabilities in our legal system, exacerbated by the seemingly relentless rulings that expanded the reach of the European Convention of Human Rights into combat zones and fuelled by legal aid.
>
> ... Mr Shiner's allegations were on an industrial scale. Thousands had to be examined and in some cases investigated, under unprecedented scrutiny by the High Court and the International Criminal Court. Let me be clear – there was no alternative.'

In March 2017, Phil Shiner was declared bankrupt, a move that could mean he avoided actually paying at least £4million relating to baseless claims against British troops. It was also revealed that prior to being struck off as a solicitor, he had transferred ownership of his £330,000 house to his daughters.

Theresa May had said: 'We will never again let human rights lawyers harass the bravest of the brave.' However, in December 2016, the Police Service of Northern Ireland was exposed as re-examining every killing by the British army during the Troubles. The Legacy Investigation Branch was investigating 238 'fatal incidents' in which the army had been involved.

In December 2016, a Chelsea Pensioner who had terminal kidney failure was interrogated for four hours over the death of an IRA terrorist in an ambush in Armagh in 1974. Dennis Hutchings, a 75-year-old former soldier and great-grandfather, was charged with attempted murder by the Legacy Investigation Branch (LIB). Despite being previously told by the Historical Enquiries Team in 2011 that the matter was closed, Hutchings was charged and was due to stand trial in 2017. Hutchings said: 'I feel anger, totally, totally let down. I feel hung out to dry. That's what has happened to all of us. We are being thrown to the wolves.'

In May 2017, it was reported that 18 former soldiers of the parachute regiment could face trial over the killing of 13 people during Bloody Sunday riots in 1972. After a 12-year inquiry by Lord Saville, the killings were described as 'unjustified and unjustifiable'. The potential charges included murder, attempted murder, wounding and perjury.

In December 2016, Assistant Chief Constable Mark Hamilton, who was in charge of the LIB, said that the government would be proposing a bill for a new inquiries unit which would aim to complete its investigations within five years, but 'If there is no political decision, it will take many, many, many years for the Police Service of Northern Ireland with the 70 detectives it has. We have made it very clear that we are neither resourced nor funded for the scale of the legacy task we are required to carry out.' In December 2016, Kris Hopkins, the Northern Ireland Minister, said that there would be no reinvestigation into the murders of 185 British troops by Irish terrorists.

In January 2017, the witch hunt against British troops arising out of Iraq and Afghanistan was held responsible for the shortfall in army recruitment. The army had only managed to take on 6,910 cadets against a target of 9,850. The army was 4% below its planned strength of 82,000. Even so, Britain deployed 120 troops to Estonia in March 2017 in a show of strength against Russia. Three hundred vehicles were also deployed, including tanks and artillery, and more troops, bringing the total deployment to around 800 soldiers. Sir Michael Fallon said that the aim was 'standing up to Russian aggression'.

Some were not impressed with Britain's token military capability. In May 2017, a report entitled *Dealing with Allies in Decline* from the US Center for Strategic and Budgetary Assessments said that Britain was no longer able to deploy even one division due to the scale of the cuts to the army.

The report said that Britain would struggle to sustain a brigade (6,500 troops) in an overseas war. A division is comprised of several brigades and amounts to between 25,000 and 50,000 troops. The report stated: 'America's most important NATO allies have been gutting their military capabilities over the past quarter century. Indeed, the decline of UK military capabilities offers a particularly stark national example of the overall European trend.' The report also stated: 'Significant reductions in mechanized capabilities and Army end strength mean that for the next several years, the UK will probably be able to deploy and sustain no more than a brigade (around 6,500 troops) in overseas combat missions.' The report further warned of the lack of aircraft for the Royal Navy's two new aircraft carriers and of the shrinking RAF. (This should be compared to the subsequent Tory manifesto which said: 'We will maintain the overall size of the armed forces, including an army that is capable of fielding a war-fighting division.')

Despite the problems caused by abstract theories about human rights, in December 2016, the May Government abandoned supposed plans to scrap the Human Rights Act. The Tory 2005 manifesto pledged to 'review' the Act, and the 2010 manifesto pledged to 'replace the Human Rights Act with a UK Bill of Rights'.

But the lies about how awful British troops were supposed to be were not unique. Demonizing people for supposed wrongs is a key part of political correctness. Those who are deemed oppressed are then encouraged to hate their own country. One such group is women, although those women who are not ardent feminists are ignored. In fact, women are doing very well compared to the rest of society and are not oppressed.

Education is a good example. In August 2016, the latest results showed that girls continued to outperform boys at school, with 71.3% of girls getting at least a C grade compared to 62.4% of boys. In September 2016, figures from the Department for Education disclosed that 53.5% of women aged between 17 to 30 were in higher education compared to only 43.4% of men. This difference is the highest on record. Figures from the OECD warned of the 'downward social mobility' for British people and that immigrant children were more likely to have degrees.

But the attempts to foment hatred continued. In January 2017, despite girls being more likely to go to university than boys, Shami Chakrabarti launched a new fund of £500,000 for Essex University to provide bursaries for girls. Essex University already had more female than male students. Chakrabarti said:

> 'Gender injustice is so embedded in our society and our world, that sometimes we stop seeing it. We accept the rows of men sitting in parliaments or the latest gender health, education or pay gap figures with a shrug and a sigh. It's time to wake up, give ourselves a shake and confront those content with the status quo.'

At times, the attempt to portray women as victims became ludicrous. In August 2016, the TUC claimed that 52% of women had been sexually harassed at work and demanded new laws. In response, the CBI declared that there should be zero tolerance of sexual harassment. The findings had been compiled by YouGov. The figure of 52% was achieved only by including any claimed harassment over previous years, and only a fraction had occurred in the past year. The main kind of harassment was 'hearing colleagues making comments of a sexual nature about another woman or women in general', which was claimed by 39% of those who responded, and only 11% claimed it had happened in the last year. The survey questioned 3,524 adults but only included answers from 1,533 women who were willing to be asked about harassment.

In November 2016, a teaching guide condemned *Beauty and the Beast* as saying that 'if a woman is pretty and sweet natured she can change an abusive man into a kind and gentle man. In other words, it is the woman's fault if her man abuses her. And of course, the Beast turns into a handsome prince because ugly people cannot be happy.' The teaching guide condemned other Disney films and was targeted for children as young as 11 years old. An episode of *Coronation Street* was reported to Ofcom for racism after a character quipped that her hair had 'more roots than Kunta Kinte'.

In January 2017, a lawyer who got drunk at the London Rowing Club Christmas party and slapped a woman's bottom and called her an 'Australian slut' was convicted of a racially aggravated assault. A more high-profile example was when, in February 2017, John Bercow said in the House of Commons:

> 'Before the imposition of the migrant ban I would myself have been strongly opposed to an address by Mr Trump in Westminster Hall. After the imposition of the migrant ban by President Trump I am even more strongly opposed to an address by President Trump in Westminster Hall. We value our relationship with the US ... However, as far as this place is concerned, I feel very strongly that our opposition to racism, and to sexism, and our support for equality before the law and an independent judiciary are important considerations in the House of Commons.'

Bercow had had no such qualms when dealing with the emir of Kuwait, when he said: 'Your Highness, it is my privilege to welcome you here to our Parliament for this important stage of your state visit. Your presence here today is a welcome reminder of the many intimate ties that exist between our nations and our peoples.' Kuwait does not concern itself with women's rights, and homosexuality is illegal. Nor did Bercow object to other state visits from dubious leaders, including from China.

The concept of who can be allegedly offended grew. The transgendered now became victims. In August 2016, Oxford City Council decided to add the term 'Mx' (pronounced 'mix') as an option and was also considering phasing out the terms 'Mr' and 'Mrs', claiming that they might cause offence. The recommended change was produced by a panel of councillors. In the NHS, doctors were told to stop referring to pregnant women as 'expectant mothers'. They were told to use the term 'pregnant people' to avoid offending those in the process of changing gender.

Shamefully, even children were dragged in. Dr Joanna Williams, an education expert, said: 'We are increasingly reminded that schools are struggling financially. Yet the time, effort, and money that goes into producing on monitoring transgender policies is out of all proportion to the tiny number of trans children currently in British schools.' Dr Williams also said: 'Children might start school knowing the difference between boys and girls – but they are quickly encouraged to unlearn this knowledge.' Dr Williams pointed out:

> 'When we cut through the metaphors, the challenge not just to stereotypical gender roles but to the attitudes of parents is clear. However politically well intentioned teachers may be, criticising the views and values of home vastly alters the remit of the school away from educational and towards the promotion of a distinct political outlook. The role of the teacher becomes policing the values, thoughts and language of children to bring them in line with one particular ideological position.'

More than 120 schools adopted gender-neutral uniforms, allowing both boys and girls to wear skirts or trousers. In April, the National Union of Teachers voted in favour of teaching children as young as two years old about transgender lifestyles. They claimed it would be a measure against hate crime. Some charities provided workshops for primary schools about trans awareness and gender issues.

In May 2017, Northamptonshire Police announced that they would abandon traditional police helmets in favour of 'gender neutral' baseball caps. In addition to the baseball caps being less expensive and allegedly more comfortable, the force also claimed that the unisex caps would appeal to the 'non-binary transgender community', who might find 'gender-based headgear ... a barrier'. A force spokesman said that the force did not know how many 'non-binary transgender' officers it had.

In December 2016, new rules adopted by Bafta mean that starting in 2019, films in two categories will be subject to new criteria to show that they have increased the representation of ethnic minorities, the disabled, women, lesbians, gays, bisexuals, and the transgendered. This will include on-screen characters and plots and is an attempt to appeal to allegedly underrepresented audiences.

The Advertising Standards Authority (ASA) announced in July 2017 that it would ban adverts that had gender stereotypes. Guy Parker, the ASA's chief executive said:

> 'Portrayals which reinforce outdated and stereotypical views on gender roles in society can play their part in driving unfair outcomes. Tougher advertising standards can play an important role in tackling inequalities and improving outcomes for individuals, the economy and society as a whole.'

The obsession with quotas remained. In October 2016, ONS figures showed that only 1.1% of the population described themselves as either gay or lesbian, and only 0.6% described themselves as bisexual. The BBC had a target to have 8% of its staff be gay, lesbian or bisexual by 2020. In September 2016, the BBC set a target quota of 15% for non-whites. That the BBC was out of touch was revealed in June 2016, when, just after the referendum vote, a memo leaked that had been written for the BBC by David Cowling, a former special adviser to a Labour cabinet minister in the 1970s and the former head of the BBC's political research unit. The memo stated:

'It seems to me that the London bubble has to burst if there is to be any prospect of addressing the issues that have brought us to our current situation. There are many millions of people in the UK who do not enthuse about diversity and do not embrace metropolitan values yet do not consider themselves lesser human beings for all that. Until their values and opinions are acknowledged and respected, rather than ignored and despised, our present discord will persist.

Because these discontents run very wide and very deep and the metropolitan political class, confronted by them, seems completely bewildered and at a loss about how to respond ("who are these ghastly people and where do they come from?" doesn't really hack it).

The 2016 EU referendum has witnessed the cashing in of some very bitter bankable grudges but I believe that, throughout this 2016 campaign, Europe has been the shadow not the substance.'

In July 2016, The National Police Chiefs Council recorded a rise in reported hate crimes since the referendum. Nottinghamshire Police were revealed to have now classified wolf-whistling as a hate crime; misogyny, defined as 'behaviour targeted towards a woman by men simply because they are a woman', was now a crime. Specialist officers were now available to council victims. In November 2016, the Essex Police admitted that it was including offences against red-haired people as a hate crime. A hate crime officer (apparently there is such a thing) said: 'Hate crime is often a matter of perception.' It also emerged that schools and universities were to be discouraged from showing pictures of white men in science lessons, as it might put off ethnic minorities. Dr Damian Spiteri of York University called for more 'multicultural' images.

There was a determined attempt to demonize Brexit supporters as hateful or racist and to prevent them from celebrating the referendum victory or having freedom of speech. In September 2016, writing in *The Guardian*, Sir Nicholas Kenyon, a former director of BBC Proms and a Remain campaigner, argued:

> 'As the annual ritual of the Last Night of the Proms approaches in the year of the Brexit referendum, there may be a sense of foreboding that this most British of occasions might be hijacked to celebrate the triumph of Little England, to reinforce the message of a land of hope and glory in which Britons never shall be slaves – to the EU or anyone else. How wrong that would be.'

In November 2016, Milo Yiannopoulos, a journalist and supporter of President Trump, was banned from speaking to sixth-formers at his old school. Simon Langton Grammar School for Boys in Canterbury imposed the ban citing 'safety and security' following threats of protests. There was also one complaint to counterterrorism officials. One parent remarked that Yiannopoulos's talk was banned 'thanks to a handful of busybodies with no connection to the school' and said:

> 'We are all very disappointed. My sons are no Milo fans – they wanted to be able to challenge Milo's views. Langton's sixth-formers would have been more than a match for him. Banning bad ideas does not make them go away. The censors have granted Milo more publicity than he would have got if his talk had gone ahead.'

Yiannopoulos wrote on Facebook:

> 'Who even knew the DfE had a counter-terrorism unit? And that it wasn't set up to combat terrorism but rather to punish gays with the wrong opinions? Perhaps if I'd called my talk "Muslims are Awesome!",

the NUT and the Department of Education would have been cool with me speaking. Disgusted.'

In April 2017, Dame Jenni Murray was subjected to a demonstration from students at Oxford University, where she had gone to speak about her new book, *A History of Britain in 21 Women*. The demonstrators accused Dame Murray of 'transphobia' and held up placards saying: 'Trans women are real women.' Dame Murray had written that those who had once lived as men 'do not have the experience of growing up female' and so were not real women. Dame Murray said that she was 'not the slightest bit surprised' at the demonstration' and 'Attempts at "no platforming" have happened to a number of women who have discussed this issue.'

In March 2017, Oxford University declared that it would be displaying 20 portraits of women, ethnic minorities, lefties, gays, lesbians and the disabled. The declaration followed complaints that the current portraits had too many white males. Trudy Coe, the university's head of equality, told the BBC: 'The portraits have been almost exclusively men. We're just beginning to redress the balance. It's sending a signal to a wider range of students that they belong here.'

Hull University warned that a failure to use 'gender-sensitive' terminology in essays would lead to lower marks 'on a case-by-case basis'. Gender-sensitive language avoids using masculine pronouns, such as 'he' or 'him' and avoids using words containing 'man', such as 'manpower'. A senior lecturer said: 'Language is powerful and we place a high emphasis on gender-neutral language on courses.' Another lecturer warned students that 'Failure to use gender-sensitive language will impact your mark.'

In June 2017, Dr Lucy Delap, deputy director of history and policy at Cambridge University, told colleagues that they should no longer use terms such as 'brilliance', 'genius' and 'flair' on the grounds that they 'carry assumptions of gender inequality and also of class and ethnicity inequalities.' The Canterbury Christ Church student union's 'lesbian, gay, bisexual and transgender officer' refused to share a platform with Peter Tatchell (a prominent LGBT campaigner who had twice been roughed up when trying to make a citizen's arrest on Robert Mugabe of Zimbabwe in 1999 and 2001) because Tatchell had signed an open letter criticizing the increase in the practice of no-platforming. By doing so, Tatchell was accused of 'incitement of violence against transgender people'.

In June 2017, Oxford University decided to allow students to take an exam at home in order to help women get better results. The university was accused of being 'under the tyranny of feminism'. The move was prompted by figures showing that 32% of women achieved a first in history compared with 37% of men. The move was described by the university as providing 'greater equity for students in terms of performance by gender'.

Parliament Square was to have a statue of Millicent Fawcett, who began the campaign for votes for women in 1866. Of the statue, May said: 'The example Millicent Fawcett set during the struggle for equality continues to inspire the battle against the burning injustices of today. Her statue will stand as a reminder of how politics only has value if it works for everyone in society.'

May adopted a similarly apologetic and politically-correct stance in an article for PinkNews about the decriminalization of homosexuality 50-odd years ago:

> 'I am proud of the role my party has played in recent years in advocating a Britain which seeks to end discrimination on the grounds of sexuality or gender identity, but I acknowledge where we have been wrong on these issues in the past. There will justifiably be scepticism about the positions taken and votes cast down through the years by the Conservative Party, and by me, compared to where we are now. But like the country we serve, my party and I have come a long way.'

May further wrote that there was 'much more to do' in pursuit of homosexual equality. Once again, May was encouraging a sense of victimhood amongst a supposedly oppressed minority. Once again, she was stirring up hatred.

In April 2017, the Commons Business Committee put forward proposals to force listed companies to have a 50% quota for women for all new board appointments. The companies would be forced to explain to shareholders if they failed to meet this target.

Under new government rules revealed in February 2017, universities, which have already been expected to increase the number of ethnic minority students attending to 20% by 2020, would also be required to declare how many ethnic minority students obtain either a first or 2.1 degree. Universities Minister Jo Johnson said that the government intended to 'strengthen the opportunities for those students from disadvantaged or non-traditional backgrounds to fulfil their potential'.

Sentencing Council guidelines to apply from June 1, 2017, told judges and magistrates that when passing sentence, they are to take into account 'experience of abuse and/or neglect, negative influences from peer associates and the misuse of drugs and/or alcohol' and also said: 'There is also no evidence to suggest that black and minority ethnic children and young people are over-represented in the youth justice system.' One cause of this, the guidelines stated, was that there

> 'may be the experience of such children and young people in terms of discrimination and negative experiences of authority. When having regard to welfare of the child or young person to be sentenced, the particular factors which arise in the case of black and minority ethnic children and young people need to be taken into account.'

A spokesman for the Sentencing Council said: 'The guidelines recognise that black and ethnic minority children are over-represented in the care system, and children in care are more likely to end up in the criminal justice system. Children should not be blamed for factors beyond their control.' In other words, society was to blame for an alleged high rate of ethnic minority crime rate and not the criminals themselves.

In April 2017, knife crime reached a five-year high following curbs on police stop-and-search measures. Offences increased by 14% to 32,448 in 2016. David Wilson, an ex-prison governor and now criminology professor at Birmingham City University, said: 'The reduction in stop and search is undoubtedly one factor in a cocktail that has led to an increase in people carrying knives. If people feel less likely to get stopped, they will feel emboldened to go out with a knife.'

Those in the Ponzi Class did not confine their political correctness to Britain, nor did they allow themselves to be confined by consistency. In April 2017, Matthew Rycroft, Britain's ambassador at the UN, said that Britain was 'committed to the promotion and protection of human rights worldwide', as 'this is the right thing to do, [and] also because it is cornerstone of peace, stability and a tool for conflict prevention.' Hours later, Britain supported Saudi Arabia becoming a member of the UN women's rights commission, which was intended to 'shape global standards on gender equality and the empowerment of women'. Rycroft also backed Saudi Arabia keeping its seat on the UN Human Rights Council.

RACE WAR POLITICS

The most dangerous aspect of political correctness is race war politics. The aim is to encourage a hatred of the West in general, white people, and, for Britain, a hatred of the English. Being English is deemed racist. The English do not even have their own parliament as the other British nations do. The English are treated as second-class citizens in England. Sometimes this is a sneering disregard for English people, such as when, in August 2016, David Hoare, the chairman of Ofsted, said at a teacher's conference: '[The Isle of Wight] is shocking. It's a ghetto; there has been inbreeding. There is a mass of crime, drug problems, huge unemployment.' Would he have dared say anything like this about black people?

There is the steady repopulation policy. Islamic culture in particular is promoted. An example is in Luton, where the taxpayer-funded Inspire Sports Village had introduced men-only swimming for Muslims and also women-only swimming later in the evening. A spokesman for Active Luton said: 'We aim to provide everyone in our community, regardless of age, ability or ethnicity, with affordable and accessible opportunities to get active in ways which suit their wide-ranging needs and lifestyles.'

This promotion of radical Islam is not in the British national interest. For example, in December 2016, Baroness Deech, a former education adjudicator, warned: 'Many universities are in receipt of or are chasing very large donations from Saudi Arabia and the Gulf states and so on, and maybe they are frightened of offending them. I don't know why they aren't doing anything about it. It really is a bad situation.' She further said: 'Amongst Jewish students, there is a gradually a feeling that there are certain universities that you should avoid. Definitely Soas (the School of Oriental and African Studies in London). Manchester I think is now not so popular because of things that have happened there. Southampton, Exeter and so on.'

Anti-Semitism was not confined to academia nor the Labour Party. A leadership battle for control of the Unite union provoked a police investigation after the rival candidate to the present leadership incumbent, Len McCluskey, who is a close supporter of Corbyn, was the target of an anti-Semitic campaign. Gerard Coyne, who is not Jewish, was trolled by McCluskey supporters with allegations such as having backing from the Jewish Mafia and that he was pandering to the Jewish community. One tweet said: 'His anti anybody who isn't Jewish is exposed' and alleged he had 'shadowy backers'. Another tweet alleged that Coyne was 'cosying up to powerful Jewish conservative supporters of Zionism and ready to sell his soul'. The McCluskey campaign condemned the messages, and McCluskey himself stated that there 'was no crisis of anti-Semitism in the Labour Party'.

It is hatred that is being promoted – not tolerance. There is even the ridiculous situation where, in July 2016, cribbing a radical protest movement in the USA set up in response to police shootings, a Black Lives Matter movement sprang up in Britain to hold protests and marches in London, Bristol and Liverpool. In August 2016, chanting, 'No justice, no peace,' a bunch of Black Lives Matter protestors chained themselves together on approach roads to Heathrow and Birmingham airports. The police arrested ten. Natalie Jeffers, the leader of Black Lives Matter, was funded by taxpayers to tour the world and make speeches about feminism. While a number of white colleagues were demonstrating in September, Jeffers was on her way to a £200-per-night hotel in Brazil. She gave a speech on 'the state of our feminist movements' at a black feminist forum event of the Association for Women's Rights in Development. Her income came from the overseas aid budget. Given the size and largesse of British overseas aid, it is hardly surprising that those in the hard left are determined to milk it. They will be attracted to it like flies to a cow's backside.

In another example, in June 2017, 14 police officers were injured in a riot in East London after fake news stories were circulated about the death of Edir 'Edson' Frederico Da Costa, who died in hospital six days after being stopped by police. Da Costa's cousin, Larissa Dos Santos, claimed on Facebook:

> 'He was brutally beaten to death and left in the hospital nameless and in a coma. Little did we know the extent of the damage until we received the list of

injuries he sustained, which included a fractured skull, a fallen voice box and a ruptured bladder to name a few. Up till now we still don't have the names of the arresting office [sic] that murdered my cousin.'

The police claimed that Da Costa fell ill because he had 'swallowed a large quantity of drugs' after being stopped. The IPCC issued a statement saying that a pathologist had found 'no injuries to suggest severe force was used', and they denied that Da Costa had suffered spinal injuries, a broken neck, or bleeding to the brain.

However, protesters from Black Lives Matter and the Socialist Workers Party mounted a demonstration that turned violent. Black Lives Matter had claimed online that the police were 'guilty of murder' and posted on Twitter that 'Riot police inflicting even more violence and brutality on the community. They pushed a pregnant woman on the ground and dragged her. Forestgate trending coz the police beat up a black man so bad he lost his life.' The Socialist Workers Party newspaper said: 'At Grenfell Tower we saw many, many people killed because the people at the top treat poor people and black people as unworthy. Here they treated Edson as unworthy. It is the same thing. You only get change when you fight.'

Joshua Virasami, a leading member of Black Lives Matter, posted on Twitter: 'They killed Edson in his car. They beat him to death and now they are terrorising his people on road. Fuck the police.' Another leading member, Amina Gichinga, who is also a leader of the group Take Back the City, posted online: 'The grief, rage, turmoil that I saw at the #JusticeforEdson protest today ... this is a community hurting and fighting for justice ... People ... fail to address the rage of officers who killed Edson.'

Although the attempt to remove a statue of Cecil Rhodes failed (set out in *The Genesis of Political Correctness*, page 164), still the agitation continued. In January 2017, it was reported that one of the leading organisers of the campaign Rhodes Must Fall had been awarded £40,000 as a Rhodes scholar. Joshua Nott, who was privately educated, from Johannesburg, boasted that he would 'never toast Cecil John Rhodes'. He further objected to the statue of Rhodes outside Oxford's Oriel College. In the campaign to remove a statue of Rhodes in Cape Town, Nott said: 'I think protests should not be degraded ... But you can only get your voice heard if you engage in extreme or violent protests. I use the Rhodes scholarship to defeat the very ideals of what it originally stood for.' A Rhodes Trust spokesman said: 'We pick young people of enormous ability without regard to any particular political affiliation.' Those actively stirring up anti-English hatred are being showered with money to come to Britain instead of being kept out. It is sad that the Rhodes Trust has been taken over by the politically correct, who are using its funds to besmirch Cecil Rhodes and his legacy.

Rhodes was not the only target. For example, in April 2017, officials caved in to pressure and agreed to rename the Colston Hall in Bristol due to his links with the slave trade. The 150-year-old venue was named after Edward Colston, who was one of Bristol's most generous benefactors.

The campaign was one-sided. A hostility to English people and British culture was tolerated. Only white people were deemed to be racist. In September 2016, Javaria Saeed, a Muslim and a former counterterrorism officer said: 'My experiences were that Muslim officers being racist towards my views, also, in private, holding racist views against white officers and sexist views against females. If such views were expressed by white officers, they would be fired.' She further said: 'Racism in the Met is not from white officers in my case, but from Muslim officers who the service refused to properly investigate because they were afraid of being called Islamophobic and racist.' She claimed that some Muslim men regarded FGM as a 'clean and honourable practice' that 'shouldn't be criminalized'. Her complaints to senior officers were ignored.

The details of the Trojan Horse plot by Muslims to take over schools was set out in *The Genesis of Political*

Correctness (page 156). At the time of writing, it seemed that the plot had been thwarted, although some friction remained. But the extremism continued. Four schools, Jamia Al-Hudaa (Nottingham), Darul Uloom (Birmingham), Darul Uloom (Leicester), and Jamia Al-Hudaa (Sheffield), which were ordered to close due to extremism, in fact continued to operate after they lodged appeals against those orders. One girl at the Nottingham school had been expelled simply for owning a disposable camera (she was accused of 'narcissism').

In November 2016, a judge ruled that a ban on the identification of a school put into special measures be maintained after it launched a judicial review. Ofsted had intervened earlier in 2016 out of concerns of the treatment of segregated girl pupils. The ban was imposed to prevent a 'media storm' and 'tensions and fears for parents'.

In November 2016, it was revealed that a private Islamic school in Leicester required girls to wear the niqab (a long black gown that covers the whole body, having only slits for the eyes). The full-time school utilizes a building that is also used by another five part-time schools, mainly evenings and on weekends.

It was reported in February 2017 that Trish O'Donnell, head of the Clarksfield Primary School in Oldham, received death threats along with 'harassment and intimidation' from Muslim fundamentalists. O'Donnell sent an email to Oldham Council saying that there were 'very strong reasons to believe that ... a "Trojan Horse" agenda [is] being played out' and that her position was increasingly untenable. The intimidation included a physical assault, threats to blow up her car and verbal abuse. The majority of children at the school were of Pakistani origin.

Another Oldham school, Horton Mill, was also subject to concerns from a counter-extremism official after it hosted a speaker who had justified the killing of British troops.

Five Birmingham wards (Hodge Hill, Washwood Heath, Bordesley Green, Sparkbrook, and Springfield) with high Muslim populations had produced 26 of Britain's 269 known jihadists, according to a Henry Jackson Society report. Sparkbrook Ward was one of only two areas outside London with a foreign-born population higher than 30%; it also has a large number of residents who do not speak English, and it has 22 mosques. Birmingham has a large number of immigrants from war-torn Kashmir and was the centre of the Trojan Horse scandal.

Understandably, not all parents are enamoured with Islam. Not that officialdom has any sympathy. In April 2017, Derek Holloway, the CofE school inspection chief said:

> 'Through RE teacher forums and feedback from our RE advisers, I am aware that some parents have sought to exploit the right to withdraw children from RE lessons. This is seemingly because they do not want their children exposed to other faiths and world views, in particular Islam. Anecdotally, there have also been some cases in different parts of the country of parents with fundamentalist religious beliefs also taking a similar course. Sadly, and dangerously, the right of withdrawal from RE is now being exploited by a range of interest groups often using a dubious interpretation of human rights legislation.'

The contempt towards English girls was not confined to schools. There remained the ongoing problem of child-grooming gangs. For example, in November 2016, three Somalis who had plied young girls with drinks and drugs before raping and trafficking them were jailed for a total of 32 years. The three were part of a gang of 13 Somalis, most of whom had entered Britain claiming to be refugees. The nine girls were as young as 11 years old, and the abuse occurred between 2009 and 2013. A report showed that the gang members were free to abuse the children due to a failure of doctors and social services and a delay in the police investigation. For example, in November 2016, Sageer Hussain, one of four brothers who led a grooming gang abusing English girls, was jailed for 19 years. He had once said that 'All white girls are good for is sex and they are just slags.' The brothers will collectively serve 98 years in jail. One 13-year-old girl was raped 13 times and told that her mother would be gang-raped if she went to the police. The brothers were said to have 'ruled Rotherham' and had a reputation for violence. For example, in February 2017, at the Sheffield Crown Court, six Asian men were jailed for abusing two young girls, one of whom became pregnant when only 12 years old. Two of the men shouted, 'Allahu Akbar,' as they were led away.

In May 2017, a report for the Greater Manchester Police revealed that the children who were victims of grooming had increased from 146 in 2013 to 714 in 2016. The report admitted that grooming was underreported and that the latest figure could be the 'tip of the iceberg'. The report did not identify the ethnicity of the offenders other than to conclude: 'A small minority of British Pakistani men are criminal sex offenders as in other communities.' In June 2017, figures disclosed that between 2013 and 2016 there was a fivefold increase in child sex offences in Greater Manchester. In 2017, there were 1,732 children who were victims or at risk; this was three-times the number in 2015.

However, recent trials involving grooming street gangs involved high numbers of Pakistani men. There have been 14 such trials in Rochdale, Rotherham, Derby, Leeds, Aylesbury, Telford, Banbury, Middlesbrough, Dewsbury, Carlisle, Burnley and Blackpool. An ongoing enquiry in Rotherham has identified 300 'predominantly' Asian suspects.

Liz Thirsk, of the Rochdale-based Parents Against Grooming and a former Liberal Democrat councillor, said: 'The bottom line is that this is still going on. It hasn't stopped and in my opinion it is not going to be stopped as long as we choose to be politically correct and refuse to admit that we have got a cultural issue here with some Pakistani men.' Many of the convicted paedophiles in Rochdale were considered to be pillars of the community and active in the local mosque (see also *The Genesis of Political Correctness*, pages 159 to 160).

Nazir Afzal, the former Crown Prosecution Service chief for the North West, took the decision to prosecute some of the paedophiles. He consequently faced quiet hostility from some in the Asian community. Events where he was speaking had smaller audiences. He said: 'Some boycotted me by not turning up at events. They said that I had picked a subject which was a stick to beat the Muslim community. Some even accused me of being a coconut.'

Within days of the referendum vote, in response to claims of an increase in hate incidents, Cameron told MPs, 'We have a fundamental responsibility to bring our country together ... we will not stand for hate crime or these kinds of attacks.' The National Police Chiefs Council claimed that there had been 85 reported incidents to a website from Thursday to Sunday and that this was a 57% increase from the previous year. In August 2016, the UN Committee on the Elimination of Racial Discrimination accused Leave campaigners of 'creating prejudice' due to their 'divisive, anti-immigrant and xenophobic rhetoric' during the referendum and further blamed them for the reported increase in so-called 'hate crimes'.

The supposed post-referendum 57% increase in hate crimes was based on a press release from the National Police Chiefs Council on June 27, 2016, four days after the referendum vote. Although the press release stated that there had been 'no major spikes in tensions' since the vote, a footnote said a website called True Vision had had 85 people alleging hate incidents during the four days, which was an increase from 54 from the same four days the previous month. The press release advised: 'This should not be read as a national increase in hate crime of 57% but an increase in reporting through one mechanism' over four days. This caveat was instantly and totally ignored.

On appointment as Home Secretary, Amber Rudd quickly launched a 'hate crime action plan'. In October, there was a 'hate crime awareness week' promoted by the Government, costing £2.4million. The Met set up a £1.7million 'crime hub' to target internet 'trolls'. A number of universities set up centres for 'hate crime studies', and charities were funded to 'combat' or 'monitor' hate crime. The CPS appointed a 'hate crime coordinator' in every region in addition to 'area-based Equality, Diversity and Community Engagement Managers' who 'contribute to the delivery of the Hate Crime Assurance Scheme'. A perception by the victim that an incident is a hate crime is sufficient to make it so; intent is irrelevant.

In July 2016, the government's 'anti-hate crime action plan' required head teachers to log every alleged anti-Muslim, anti-Semitic, homophobic, racist incident. Amber Rudd said:

> 'Those who practise hatred send out a message that it's OK to abuse and attack others because of their nationality, ethnicity or religious background; that it's OK to disregard our shared values and promote the intolerance that causes enormous harm to communities and individuals. Well, I have a very clear message for them: we will not stand for it. Hatred has no place whatsoever in a 21st-century Great Britain that works for everyone. We are Great Britain because we are united by values such as democracy, free speech, mutual respect and opportunity for all. We are the sum of all our parts – a proud, diverse society. Hatred does not get a seat at the table, and we will do everything we can to stamp it out.'

Rudd did not expect immigrants to accept the national culture and focused on abstract theories. She did not defend English or British culture.

In August 2016, the Equalities and Human Rights Commission chairman, David Isaac, said: '[some people] were able to legitimise their feelings about race following the referendum result' and that 'We must redouble our efforts to tackle race inequality urgently or risk the divisions in our society growing and racial tensions increasing. If you are black or an ethnic minority in modern Britain, it can often still feel like you're living in a different world, never mind being part of a one nation society.'

Dianne Abbott told a fringe meeting at the Labour Party conference in September 2016:

> 'The Brexit vote, whatever you think of that vote, has added another turn of the screw to rising racism. The Brexit vote and the Leave people winning seems to have given far too many people permission to racially abuse and attack people all over the country. People, not just East Europeans, but people of all colours, are being attacked and assaulted by people who talk about Brexit ... There has been this upsurge after this Brexit vote in horrible, horrible attacks.'

She also said that 'The people who complain about freedom of movement will not be satisfied because what they want is to see less foreign-looking people on their street and that's not going to happen.'

This was not Abbott's first anti-British, anti-White bile. In 1984, she said that Ireland 'is our struggle – every defeat of the British state is a victory for all of us' and 'Though I was born here in London, I couldn't identify as British' and described Northern Ireland as 'an enclave of white supremacist ideologies'. In 1988, she told a US audience that Britain had 'invented racism' and that Parliament was 'the heart of darkness, in the belly of the beast'. In 1989, she described the Home Office as 'a fundamentally racist organization'. Shortly before 9/11, she voted against the banning of a number of terrorist organizations such as Al-Qaeda, Egyptian Islamic Jihad, the Armed Islamic Group, Harakat-ul-Mujahideen, the Palestinian Islamic Jihad, and the Islamic Army of Aden. She claimed that some of the groups were 'not terrorist organizations, but dissident organizations'. In 2012, she tweeted: 'White people love playing "divide and rule". We should not play their game.' In 2015, she said: 'On balance, Chairman Mao did more good than harm ... he led his country from feudalism.' Mao was responsible for the deaths of 45million people.

In April 2017, an attack on an Iranian asylum seeker in Croydon, London, led to Dianne Abbott claiming:

> 'Sadly, this is not an isolated incident but part of a sustained increase in hate crimes that this Tory Government is yet to offer any effective response to. With right-wing politicians across the world scapegoating migrants, refugees and others for their economic problems, we are seeing a deeply worrying rise in the politics of hate. We must make clear that there is no place for anti-foreigner myths, racism and hate in our society.'

She continued to tell Sky News: 'I'm not surprised in the attack because we have seen a rise in hate crime and anti-migrant feeling, particularly since Brexit. Much of the Brexit campaign was around fear of migrants, this now is being reflected in the rise in hate crimes.'

The tolerance towards Abbott might be contrasted with the extreme intolerance shown to Marie Morris, the Tory MP for Newton Abbot, who, in July 2017, was suspended from the Tory Party after she used the term 'nigger in the woodpile'. The suspension occurred within hours, and she was further threatened with disciplinary action. May said: 'I was shocked to hear of those remarks, which are completely unacceptable. I immediately asked the Chief Whip to suspend the party whip. Language like this has absolutely no place in politics or in today's society.' A recording of what Marie Morris said was circulated to the Huffington Post.

Marie Morris immediately issued an apology saying that the comment was 'entirely unintentional' and that 'I apologise unreservedly.' Tim Farron of the Liberal Democrats said: 'I am utterly shocked that this person represents the good people of Newton Abbot. Even if she misspoke, this is the nastiest thing I've heard an MP utter since Lord Dixon-Smith uttered the same awful phrase a few years ago.' The Tory

MP Heidi Allen said: 'I'm afraid an apology is not good enough – we must show zero tolerance for racism. MPs must lead by example.'

The term was once very commonly used and originated from America. It was once in mainstream use, even up to the end of the 20th century, and even was used in an Agatha Christie novel. In the 21st century, the word 'nigger' is used frequently in films and in rap songs by black people themselves.

In January 2017, David Isaac, chairman of the Equality and Human Rights Commission, a former chief executive of Stonewall, alleged: 'One of the things that concerns us greatly is the position in relation to the spike in hate crimes since June 23.' He also said:

> 'We are hugely concerned about what might happen in relation to an increase in hate crimes when Article 50 is triggered ... We are meeting with groups, we are seeking to ensure that there is as much police protection and understanding in relation to hate crimes as possible ... Britain needs guidance in relation to huge anxiety that reside, not just in relation to non-UK citizens and our visitors, but actually many of our own citizens.'

Isaac receives £500 per day at the EHRC for one or two days' work a week; he is also a partner in the Law firm Pinsent Masons.

Amber Rudd was, laughably, hoisted by her own petard. In January 2017, a speech given by Amber Rudd at the Tory conference in October was recorded by the police as a 'hate incident'. Professor Silver, a physicist, had made a complaint. In a television interview, Professor Silver, who admitted that he had not heard the speech, said that it had 'discriminated against foreigners' and so he had complained to the West Midlands Police.

In contrast to the demonization of the British or English (in particular), a very different approach was evident regarding jihadists. For example, it was revealed that Ronald Fiddler, who had been a Guantanamo Bay detainee for two years, who had been awarded £1million from the British government after denying that he had any terrorist involvement (with monies from newspapers in addition), and who used the name Abu Zakariya al-Britani, had been killed in an Islamic State suicide mission in Iraq near Mosul. ISIS issued a statement praising their 'martyrdom-seeking brother' along with a grinning picture of him in his suicide truck, laden with explosives.

Around £20million was paid by the British Government to around 16 ex-detainees of Guantanamo Bay, with the details being kept confidential. An estimated one-third of those released from Guantanamo Bay had returned to jihadist activity according to the Office of the Director of National Intelligence in Washington.

In March 2017, after another terrorist attack by Khalid Masood, May told the House of Commons:

> 'We meet here, in the oldest of all Parliaments, because we know that democracy – and the values it entails – will always prevail. Those values – free speech, liberty, human rights and the rule of law – are embodied here in this place, but they are shared by free people around the world.'

May's bald assertion that democracy would 'always prevail' did not match the reality of growing division that was increasingly resulting in bloodshed and violence. She did not explain why she thought democracy would survive Britain becoming a Muslim majority country, as, ultimately, the policy of mass immigration would entail.

Khalid Masood, born Adrian Elms, had committed a number of various crimes, including GBH, and had served two prison sentences. He was allegedly radicalized in prison, where he converted to Islam. He used a number of aliases.

May's supposedly determined stance did not match policy. In July 2017, the Home Office published only a brief summary of a report into the funding of Islamist extremism in Britain. The suppression of the full report was believed to be motivated by a desire to hide the involvement of Saudi Arabia. The Home Office investigation discovered that extreme Islamist groups were raising hundreds of thousands of pounds in donations by pretending to be charities. They were also believed to be obtaining further funds from charitable foundations. In addition, the report said that a 'small number' of extremist organizations were getting a 'significant source of income' from overseas.

The Henry Jackson Society revealed that hard-line mosques in Britain were being funded by Saudi Arabian government-linked groups. Tom Wilson said: 'There is a clear and growing link between foreign funding of Islamist extremism and violent terrorism in the UK and Europe. While entities across the Gulf have been guilty of advancing extremism, those in Saudi Arabia are undoubtedly at the top of the list.'

IMMIGRATION

At the heart of Ponzi economics is the policy of mass immigration: more immigrants are needed to create the illusion of growth (as long as the immigrants do something or other, then that extra output is logged as growth) and to provide extra tax revenues to pay for the state's ever-expanding activities.

An ageing population is often cited to justify mass immigration. This excuse is nonsense, as immigrants age themselves, and increasing the numbers of immigrants does not pay for an ageing population. And as in any Ponzi scheme, the immigrants must keep pouring in at an ever-faster rate to keep the scheme going, which is impossible, and so the scheme collapses, leaving a mountain of debts and unpaid bills (*The Ponzi Class*, the chapter 'Ponzi Economics').

The issue of mass immigration has been cited as a main reason – if not the main reason – for the Leave vote. Anna Soubry said that the Remain campaign was in error 'to keep on about the economy' and that 'It was like we kind of made and won that argument, so then the vacuum appeared and then bang, in they came with their killer card, which was immigration and we refused to engage in it.' Ordinary people are angry that their country is being taken away from them and angry that the country is being ruined financially. One might, therefore, have expected a commitment to end mass immigration would be a central part of Brexit. It was not. There was much talk of regaining control of our borders, combined with much talk about the need to avoid a 'cliff edge' and of providing workers for businesses, students for universities etc. There was no talk of the costs of immigration.

In September 2016, Boris Johnson told Andrew Marr: 'For 25 years, UK businesses and industry has been mainlining immigration like a kind of drug without actually investing enough or caring enough, frankly, about the skills and the training of young people in our country, and that's what Theresa May and the new Government want to focus on.' To illustrate, 80% of Pret A Manger workers are immigrants. Malmaison Hotels has a figure of 60%. Bernard Matthews has a figure of 30% for its 2,000 workers. Greencore Group has been positively recruiting from Eastern Europe, claiming it cannot find British workers. A Resolution Foundation report calculated that skilled workers (such as electricians, plumbers and bricklayers) are paid on average £436.40 per year less due to mass immigration.

However, in October 2016, Sajid Javid, the communities secretary, regarding visas, said that 'The Government is determined to get a good deal for Britain. Whether it's construction or any other sector, we don't want to make it any more difficult for those industries than it is.'

In November 2016, the ONS disclosed that the number of people working had reached a record high of 31.8million, of which 2.3million were EU immigrants, a net increase of

221,000 in the year to September. Of these, 276,000 were from Bulgaria and Romania, an increase of 58,000 in one year. The number of non-EU immigrant workers reached 3.2million, an increase of 199,000 in one year. The 2.3million figure for EU workers is an increase of 1.5million from 2004 and an increase of 1million from 2010. More than 1million were from the A8 Eastern European countries (Poland, Czech Republic, Estonia, Hungary, Latvia, Lithuania, Slovakia and Slovenia).

The number of Eastern Europeans in Britain increased from 170,000 in 2004 to 1.24million in 2013. In the 1970s and 1980s, birth and death rates were broadly in balance. In 2013–2014 the population increased by 491,000. Foreign-born women were responsible for 27% of all births in England and Wales in 2014, and 33% of all births had at least one immigrant parent. Immigration was responsible for 85% of the population increase between 2001 and 2012. According to the ONS, the population will increase from 65million to at least 70million within 11 years and will reach 77 million by 2050 and 80million by 2060. The ONS assumptions are modest; if immigration continues at the 2014 level, then the population will reach 80million just after 2040 and 90million just after 2060. However, the new National Insurance numbers issued to EU migrants amounted to 2,234,000 between 2011 and 2015, which greatly exceeded the numbers reported as arriving from the EU. The ONS claimed that the apparent undercount of 1.2million was due to NI numbers being issued to short-term immigrants, who are excluded from the immigration figures. Since 2004, 126,000 children from the European Economic Area have come to Britain.

In December 2016, it was revealed that the number of asylum applications in the year to September had reached 41,280, a surge of 14% and the highest figure for a decade, and there was another 4,162 who had been allowed in under a resettlement scheme. In April 2017, it was reported that with a backlog of 26,879 failed asylum seekers 'subject to removal action' at the end of December, Home Office figures showed that the number removed had fallen by two-thirds since 2010 and that only 3,500 had been deported in 2016. The number of EU immigrants given permanent residency had doubled in one year, to 37,638. The total number of immigrants had reached 650,000, with net migration at 335,000. In October 2016, it was revealed that Britain had issued more visas than any other EU country.

Since the government refused to enact Brexit, the immigrants kept pouring in at record levels. There was only talk of reducing the number after leaving the EU, and that that will only happen in the long term, as there is a need for interim deals and extensive negotiations. In October 2016, Hammond was reported to have blocked proposals for new visa rules to restrict unskilled workers. The Treasury was reportedly in favour of a 'transitional' exit, where Britain would still submit to EU laws and make payments to the EU while a long-term trading relationship was discussed.

Of the 2.7million EU nationals in Britain, 390,000 are either unemployed or deemed to be inactive, figures from the ONS revealed in April 2017. Britain had 4,600 EU nationals in prison, costing £167million per annum.

The EU is a major problem. As set out in *The Ponzi Class*, Eurocrats do not see anything wrong with mass immigration, nor with the immigrant invasion organized by the various people smugglers. The southern countries of the Eurozone remained in economic doldrums with high levels of unemployment. In September 2016, those under 25 and out of work had increased to 50.3% in Greece and to 37.3% in Italy; it was 43.9% in Spain and was 21.1% in the euro area as a whole. These unemployed, of course, see Britain as an attractive destination and are likely to continue doing so, especially if the Eurozone takes a turn for the worse.

In August 2016, Jean-Claude Junker said: 'Borders are the worst invention ever made by politicians' and that 'We have to fight against nationalism, we have the duty not to follow populists but to block the avenue of populists.' Far from trying to stem the flow of illegal immigrants, the Royal Navy was used to encourage and facilitate it with its operations collecting and transporting illegal immigrants across the Mediterranean. The flow across the Mediterranean has been substantial (see *The Genesis of Political Correctness*, page 145, where the EU policy is contrasted with that of Australia).

In May 2017, a report leaked to the German *Bild* newspaper warned that 6.6million migrants were massing in countries on the Mediterranean Sea, ready to get into Europe. Of these, 2.5million were from North Africa, with 1million in Libya. Turkey had 3.3million, of which 3million were Syrians, with the remainder being from Afghanistan and Iraq, according to UNICEF. Another 1million were in Egypt, 430,000 in Algeria, 160,000 in Tunisia and 50,000 in Morocco. Others were in transit countries, with up to 720,000 in Jordan.

There is no good reason why Europe should be accepting immigrants from Africa, which is many times larger than Europe. Libya, which is the centre of the people smuggling, is larger than France, Germany, Spain and Italy put together. Nor is there any justification for other European countries to be sending immigrants on to Britain, which is both very densely populated and only less than half the size of France.

President Trump, during his election campaign, advocated safe havens to accommodate refugees and immigrants. A responsible policy would be to put that idea into effect and create a substantial safe haven in Libya where all immigrants and refugees could be accommodated in safety and indefinitely, thus ending permanently the idea that Third World immigrants can get into Europe. Such a policy would put an end to people smuggling and stop the traffic, with the attendant fatalities, across the Mediterranean. The UN Convention on Refugees would be redundant. Libya, which has a relatively small population, is a failed state that has split apart. The creation of a safe haven would help stabilize the region. Another safe haven might be created for similar reasons in Somalia – another failed state.

In 2015, the EU launched Operation Sophia, with naval vessels deployed to pick up immigrants in the Mediterranean and to bring them into Europe. These immigrants were deemed to have been rescued. Knowing that the various EU navies were now transporting the immigrants found in the sea to Europe, the people smugglers were even more inclined to put the immigrants out to sea in more and more vessels – seaworthy or not. Colonel Reda of the Libyan coastguard said: 'The goals of the operation are good, but the idea is all wrong. The only good it does is create more migrants. It's like Europe is saying: "Come and hurry to get here – we will pick you up and make you safe." It makes my job impossible.'

Mohammed al-Ganedi of the Libyan intelligence warned of the danger posed by ISIS, who had infiltrated into Libya: 'They are training people in camps, brainwashing them, and sending them with the migrants into Europe.' He continued:

> 'The terrorists we are fighting come from Mali, Sudan, Chad, Somalia ... the same people as the migrants ... These are poor, uneducated people. They get offered up to 3,000 dinar just to join – about £1,500 – which is a fortune to them. The leaders brainwash them at their camps and send money back to their families. These ordinary Africans are now among the most ferocious fighters, and are led by foreign fighters from all over the Middle East. They become fanatics.'

In one reported incident, a people smuggler was offered £40,000 to smuggle 25 ISIS fighters to Europe from Libya, and in another example, 40 Tunisian ISIS fighters tried to leave Sirte in Libya by ship. People smuggling and arms trafficking are the most lucrative sources of income in Libya, with a boatload of migrants generating earnings of £100,000. In September 2016, one people smuggler told a reporter that he could pocket £5million 'in a good season' and that: 'Everybody knows what is going on, but nobody sees anything. If you say anything, you will die.' Mohammed

Kahloon, an official in a government detention centre, complained: 'There is no government, no law, criminals everywhere – how can we stop it? We can't. It's impossible. You have all sorts among the migrants – extremists, criminals, ordinary people – a huge mix of humanity. All are here and all want to get to Europe. We simply cannot cope.'

On October 6, 2016, 11,000 immigrants were rescued in the Mediterranean in two days. Of these, 4,655 were rescued just 12 miles off the Libyan coast. By this time in 2016, 142,000 had reached Italy, compared to 154,000 for the whole of 2015. A House of Lords report stated: 'The mission does not ... in any meaningful way deter the flow of migrants, disrupt the smugglers' networks, or impede the business of people smuggling on the central Mediterranean route.' Boats have been launched in the Mediterranean with only enough fuel to get them into international waters, with some then even telephoning the naval vessels to ask for help. The immigrants are then taken to Italy.

In April 2017, the Foreign Office admitted that destroying the people smugglers' boats had led them to use even flimsier vessels. Frontex, the EU's border agency, complained that charities operating in the Mediterranean were working with the people smugglers. Frontex said that the people smugglers were being given 'clear indications before departure on the precise direction to be followed in order to reach the NGOs' boats', with the NGOs then transporting the immigrants to Italy.

By May 2017, the numbers of immigrants crossing the Mediterranean had increased by 42% so far in 2017; 44,222 had reached Italy compared to 31,205 over the same period in 2016. Immigrants claimed that in Libya, women were being routinely raped by armed gangs and that those deemed unfit to travel would be killed. They were being held as slaves. In Sicily, where most of the immigrants were put ashore, the Mafia was reportedly siphoning off huge sums of public monies.

Britain, which once had the largest navy in the world, was no longer capable of defending its own coast from illegal immigrants and people smugglers. In August 2016, the Commons Home Affairs Committee issued a report, *Migration Crisis*, which stated:

> 'Border Force needs to be given all the necessary equipment, including vessels, to enable it to carry out its responsibilities effectively. The number of Border Force vessels in operation appears to be worryingly low. Royal Navy vessels should be made available to Border Force to make up for shortfalls, where necessary.'

The report criticised the existence of only three Border Force vessels to protect 7,000 miles of Britain's coastline as 'worryingly low', it accused the former Foreign Secretary, Philip Hammond, of complacency regarding the immigrants massing in Libya and intending to invade Europe (the committee believed there were half a million, although UNICEF estimated there were as many as one million in Libya – see above), and it criticised the EU for dealing with the 'colossal' immigration crisis and of doing 'too little too late'.

That Britain, an island off the northwest European coast, might need to defend itself against illegal immigrants invading by boat had hitherto been unthinkable. However, this was now a problem. In August 2016, five Iranian illegal immigrants were arrested on the coast of East Sussex after they had landed in an inflatable dinghy. In October 2016, people smugglers were reported to have increased their fees to £13,500 to get immigrants across the English Channel.

In July 2016, the number of illegal immigrants caught trying to get into Britain had trebled in the last year. A report by the Home Affairs Select Committee disclosed that one-third of the fines imposed on HGVs for carrying illegal immigrants were not even collected, and that 3,600 stowaways had been found in Dover over the three months of the previous summer.

In December 2016, it was disclosed that the latest immigration scam involved immigrants marrying women pregnant with another man's child in order to stay in Britain. In the ten months to February 2015, more than 1,200 Eastern European women were involved in sham marriages to partners, mainly from Nigeria, Ghana and Pakistan. The men were prepared to pay more if the bride was already pregnant, believing that it would increase their human rights claim to a family life.

In May 2017, yet another immigration scam emerged. Albert Awaku, a Ghanaian who had married his German wife (of Ghanaian descent) in Ghana in a proxy procedure at which neither was present won the right to live in Britain by citing his human rights to a family life. At the Appeal Court, Lord Justice Lloyd James said: 'The law of England and Wales recognises proxy marriage if valid by the lex loci celebrations (law of the land). Accordingly a spouse of an EU national who has concluded such a marriage will qualify as a family member.' The ruling followed a decision by Amber Rudd, the home secretary, who 'changed her position' and invited the judges to allow the appeal. The Ghanaian had been fighting for four years for the right to come to Britain and was represented by a human rights lawyer and a solicitor, Jennifer Owusu-Barnieh, who specialised in proxy marriages. A blog post for the solicitors stated that a proxy marriage was 'a process where a couple can get married with their consent but without being present at the ceremony' and advised:

> 'The Home Office has through policy banned illegal immigrants from getting married in the United Kingdom. Proxy marriage became their next challenge ... A Ghanaian and a British or European can have a proxy marriage in Ghana. The proxy marriage is then registered and a certificate is issued. The couple can then make an application to the Home Office to obtain leave to be in the UK.'

A partner at the firm, who has been on Ghanaian radio wrote: 'BOOM! The Home Office is receiving marriage certificates from people that through government policy ... could not get married in the UK.'

As ever, the authorities did little to stop the criminality of illegal immigration, and human rights laws were a useful excuse for politically correct snobbery and stupidity. In July 2016, an Iraqi people smuggler accused of controlling one of Britain's largest networks was granted legal aid to fight extradition to France. Rekawt Kayani was believed to be responsible for smuggling hundreds of illegal immigrants into Britain. He was given asylum in 2003 and British citizenship in 2011. His lawyers argued that the 'real harm' was to Britain and not France and so extradition to France should be refused. In September 2016, one gangster, Twana Jamal, an Iraqi Kurd who had smuggled hundreds of illegal immigrants into Britain and had been jailed for five years, was believed to have made up to £4million per year in profits. Immigrants had been charged £4,500 each.

Four Syrians were allowed into Britain under human rights laws on the basis that they wished to join relatives in Britain and had a right to family life. Even though the Court of Appeal ruled that they should not have been allowed to enter Britain, the Home Office decided that it would not deport them anyway. Two had been given refugee status.

In June 2017, a Jordanian illegal immigrant who was convicted of six counts of possessing material for a purpose connected with terrorism was awarded £250,000 in legal aid to fight deportation. The man's claim for asylum was refused, and he was believed to be a 'sleeper agent' for a group linked to Al-Qaeda. The legal aid was, of course, payable to his lawyers.

In an example of the lengths to which immigrants would go to stay in Britain, in April 2017, the Court of Appeal ruled that one asylum seeker had allowed himself to be burned with iron bars in 'self-infliction by proxy' in an attempt to stay in Britain. The man was from Sri Lanka.

In September 2016, the National Audit Office estimated that the cost of relocating 20,000 Syrian refugees to Britain would cost £1.7billion – £85,000 per refugee. Additionally, the first year's costs would come from the Overseas Aid budget and would amount to £420million. In October 2016, councils complained that they could not cope with any more immigrants – even though there were receiving £40,000 per year per young immigrant from the Home Office. The councils alleged that the total cost could be up to £133,000. Nevertheless, a demonstration at Parliament Square laid 2,500 used life jackets on the grass to symbolise those refugees who had died getting to Europe. All of the life jackets had been worn by refugees crossing from Turkey to the Greek island of Chios. The stunt was organized by the International Rescue Commission's president, David Milliband, a leading member of the Limousine Left, and it had special permission from Mayor Khan as it breached the normal three-hour limit.

The Ponzi class in general fixated upon those children claiming to be refugees in Europe. The resolve was that these 'child refugees' should be brought into Britain. In October 2016, Amber Rudd, the home secretary, admitted that the government had agreed to pay £36million to help close the so-called 'Jungle' camp of illegal immigrants at Calais, and promised to take more child refugees: 'The UK Government agreed to contribute up to £36million to maintain the security of these controls, to support the camp clearance and to ensure in the long term that the camp is kept closed. This funding would also be used to help keep children safe in France.'

The issue of child refugees was given great publicity when, in October 2016, Shamsher Sherin, who claimed to be 13 years old, arrived in Britain to join his father. The singer Lily Allen tweeted: 'So happy to see that Shamsher made it to the UK safely and won't be risking his life jumping on to moving vehicles.' Allen had previously visited the Calais camp, met Sherin and tearfully told him: 'The English in particular have put you in danger' and 'We've bombed your country, put you in the hands of the Taliban and now put you in danger of risking your life to get into our country. I apologise on behalf of my country. I'm sorry for what we have put you through.' Sherin's father, who was 49 years old and now lived in Birmingham, claimed to be a former commander of the Islamist group Hezb-e-Islami.

Sherin's father had been smuggled into Britain in the back of a lorry. The father said: 'I knew I had to escape to build a better future for my family' and that he had gone to Pakistan and then paid £6,000 to people smugglers to move to Britain. He was granted indefinite leave to remain in 2012. Despite claiming asylum because his life was supposed to be in danger, he went back on a three-month holiday to Afghanistan in 2016, when he visited his wife.

A new scheme, the Dubs scheme, was introduced to seek out 'child refugees', despite the fact that Home Office data showed that half of those claiming to be child refugees over the last decade were in fact over 18. Court documents recorded that some had broken voices, grey hairs and even moustaches. In Norway, dental checks were used to identify the true ages of immigrant 'children', and 90% were discovered to be over 18. In Britain, according to the Home Office, around two-thirds were believed to be adults. In the *Daily Mail*, Harriet Sergeant wrote that, of the 'child' 'refugees', one immigration officer told her that:

> 'Ninety per cent of them are not orphans. Their coming here is very well worked out. Their families have paid the people-traffickers to bring them here. The intention is for the families to follow shortly after. For the most part, they are not fleeing for their lives. For years we have had adult Pakistani males arriving in this country maintaining they are Afghan teenagers. They claim to be 13 or 14 but they are clearly over 20, with good facial hair.'

Pictures in the press showed 'children' who were adult males, if not middle-aged males. One social worker remarked that: 'The first thing they want is a razor. It's a dead giveaway.' A charity had to issue an apology after claiming that one 'child' 'refugee' was an aid worker. It was subsequently exposed that he had entered Britain as one of the alleged minors. The authorities responded by hiding the 'children's' faces under blankets to conceal their ages.

In October 2016, even the former Labour home secretary Jack Straw demanded age tests for immigrant 'children'. David Simmonds of the Local Government Association said:

> 'What we don't know yet is the process of verification the Home Office may have undertaken to establish the age of people. We know a significant proportion of people who come to the UK under existing arrangements, claiming to be children, turn out to be over the age of 18 which has been a big problem for councils.'

Councils, who have to stand the cost of lone child immigrants, were threatening to withdraw support for those found to be over 18.

In November 2016, it was revealed that the number of lone child refugees in council care in England had more than doubled in two years. There were now 4,210 unaccompanied children seeking asylum in England. Councils complained that they were struggling to cope. In December 2016, despite already having taken 750 'children' after the closure of the camps near Calais, schools were warned that even more, 'in the high hundreds', would need to be found places in the New Year. The Dubs scheme was ended in February 2017 after local councils said that they could not manage. Only 350 'children' had been admitted against a target of 3,000. Britain would, however, still continue to take refugees from the camps in the Middle East. In May 2017, Eurostat disclosed that of the 3,175 supposed unaccompanied children who lodged asylum claims in Britain, 405 were from Albania.

In bygone years, a government was expected to defend its citizens from foreign threats. In bygone years, women were expected to protect children, and more women MPs were welcomed as making parliament more representative of women's concerns. Now, with a large number of female MPs, mature men from countries with very different attitudes towards women are brought in to mix with British children. We are supposed to believe that these mature men do not pose a threat to our children and that they just want to be friendly. What sort of women are these MPs?

In September 2016, up to 135 war criminals were believed to be living in Britain. There was also a tolerance of outright criminality of immigrants once they got into Britain. For example, the Afghan illegal immigrant Mehdi Midani attacked eight women in ten days shortly after getting into Britain. The attacks were done on cocaine and alcohol. On one day, he attacked four women in four hours. He was jailed for eight years.

In July 2016, a Somali illegal immigrant was in court after impersonating a police officer in order to kidnap children. He was supposed to have been deported after serving a sentence for rape. He had grabbed and raped a woman in 2008. He appealed the deportation order on human rights grounds. He had further convictions for robbery, theft and possession of cannabis.

In August 2016, it was reported that Elias Hussain Mahmud, an Ethiopian illegal immigrant, raped a woman twice within months of being granted asylum in Britain. The woman, who was walking to work, was attacked from behind and knocked to the ground before being raped twice.

In August 2016, it was reported that an Armenian one-eyed illegal immigrant who had been refused asylum had committed 31 armed robberies over 18 months. He targeted women cashiers. He was sentenced to 16 years in jail. He had previously not been deported despite a number of shoplifting offences.

In August 2016, Sivarajah Suganthan, a Sri Lankan asylum seeker whose claim for asylum was refused but who benefited from a campaign to allow him to stay in Britain after he had fathered two children, was convicted of a sex attack.

It was reported in March 2017 that Paulo Antonio, an immigrant armed robber of uncertain nationality, received legal aid to fight deportation. He had been jailed for nine years for armed robbery in June 2005. In September 2010, he was put on a plane to Portugal, but the Portuguese refused to accept him, saying he was not Portuguese. He was detained in 2013 for 293 days while the authorities tried to establish his true nationality. He had previously claimed to have two different dates of birth, three different father's names and two names for his mother, who at first was alive and then dead. He sued for damages for his detention and was awarded £50,000.

Hassan Massoum Ravandy, an Iranian illegal immigrant, was awarded £40,000 after he claimed to have been unlawfully detained for 17 months. Judge Heather Baucher described the £40,000 as an 'appropriate award'. Despite a deportation order, he had remained in Britain for 15 years, during which he had committed a number of crimes including shoplifting, possession of drugs and burglary.

In 2016, a total of £4million was paid to immigrants who claimed to have been unlawfully detained, including those who had committed serious sex crimes. In another example, in July 2017, a Moroccan immigrant, Khalid Belfken, was awarded £40,000 in compensation after a judge ruled that he had been wrongly held in detention. The judge decided that the authorities should have released him when there was 'no reasonable prospect' of deporting him. This was the second time Belfken had received damages for unlawful detention.

Belfken entered Britain at the age of 15 in March 2005. He claimed asylum, and this was refused, although he was granted a visa to remain until his 18th birthday. He instantly began a crime spree. In October 2005, he was convicted of theft and burglary. Subsequent offences involved him possessing offensive weapons, and he attacked police officers twice. He repeatedly returned to his crime spree despite being locked up on four times. His most recent offences were for burglary while armed with a weapon. He has been subject to a deportation order since 2008. Attempts to deport him were hampered by his lying about his age, name, place of birth, and by Morocco's refusal to take him back or even provide him with travel documents. Consequently, the judge ruled that because Britain had difficulties deporting him, he should not have been detained: 'the right to liberty is of fundamental importance'. He had been detained as he was considered to be a serious danger to the public pending his deportation.

This absurd problem of deportation was far from unique. For example, in June 2017, two Romanian crooks could not be deported because the High Court judges ruled that the jails in Romania were not big enough. The judges, citing human rights, said that the prisoners would not have sufficient 'personal space', although the crooks, who the Romanian government was trying to extradite having been convicted of burglary and drugs offences, would be sent to semi-open prisons where they would be allowed into unlocked walking areas, access to phones, and up to ten hours of visits per month, and would only be confined to their cells for meals and evening roll call.

Another good example is the saga of Gilbert Deya, the self-styled 'Archbishop of Peckham', who laid bare the absurdity of Britain's human rights laws. Deya had been subject to many orders that he be deported back to Kenya, and yet he had remained in Britain.

In December 2006, Deya was arrested in Britain under a Kenyan international arrest warrant, accused of the theft of five children. In November 2007, an application that his human rights would be breached were he to be sent back to Kenya was rejected by a judge. In December 2007, Jacqui Smith, the home secretary, ordered Deya's extradition. In October 2008, the High Court dismissed an application that Deya's human rights would be broken due to his allegation that he faced punishment for his political views. In

December 2008, Deya claimed that guards beat inmates at the Kamiti prison in Nairobi where he was to be sent. In August 2009, Alan Johnson, the then home secretary, refused to investigate the jail's conditions and upheld the extradition order. In October 2009, Deya claimed to have anonymous statements from prison guards at Kamiti that contradicted statements from the Kenyan authorities. In June 2011, Kenya rejected the affidavits as forgeries. In September 2011, Theresa May, the then home secretary, upheld the extradition order. In November 2013, Lord Ramsbotham visited Kamiti and declared the prison to be satisfactory. In October 2015, May once again upheld the extradition order. In 2016, Deya gave the High Court 'a certified copy' of a Kenyan order allegedly halting the case against him and cancelling the arrest warrant; the document was unsigned, and Kenya rejected it as a fake.

On the July 14, 2017, a High Court judge declared:

> 'The delay in this matter is truly alarming. The claimant was initially arrested in December 2006. It is little short of scandalous that the proceedings have taken until now to resolve. It is essential that cases such as this are firmly "gripped" by the [secretary of state for the Home Department] to guard against incremental and massive slippage of this nature. The Court will be more than willing to play its part.'

The judges dismissed yet another human rights application made on behalf of Deya by his lawyers. An application for judicial review was also dismissed.

The Charity Commission launched an investigation into the Gilbert Deya Ministries which had received £865,620 in donations in 2014 and had £1million in savings and a £2milllion property portfolio. After the latest court ruling, sources said the Deya had made more representations to May, as the former home secretary, which she was supposedly 'obliged' to consider due to the Human Rights Act. Deya was said by a 'pastor' of the Gilbert Deya

Ministries to be at a 'mission' in Manchester and was not contactable by mobile phone. In any event, he was finally deported to Kenya three weeks later and was remanded in custody at Kamiti prison pending trial.

In June 2017, the European Court of Human Rights ruled that Britain had breached the human rights of an illegal immigrant from Zimbabwe when he had been detained pending eviction. The man had committed a series of crimes, including assaulting a police officer and possession of Class A drugs with intent to supply, for which he was jailed for three years. The man had originally entered Britain on a six-month visa and simply stayed on. He made an application for asylum which was refused, and then he applied again, alleging that he had been tortured in Zimbabwe. He was detained following his release from prison, and he was then granted asylum by senior immigration judges. The man then complained to the ECHR about his detention.

In June 2017, the Supreme Court ruled that two drug dealers should not have been deported until they had had the chance to appeal. The Immigration Act of 2014 had introduced a 'deport first, appeal later' system. The judges claimed that the system had breached the drug dealers' human rights:

> 'The proper analysis is that the Home Secretary has failed to establish that it is fair. For their appeals to be effective, they would need at least to be afforded the opportunity to give live evidence. They would almost certainly not be able to do so in person. The question is: as a second best, would they be able to do so on screen? The evidence of the Home Secretary is that in such appeals applications to give evidence from abroad are very rare. Why? Is it because an appellant has no interest in giving oral evidence in support of his appeal? I think not. It is because the financial and logistical barriers to his giving evidence on screen are almost insurmountable.'

In August 2016, it was reported that Amin Husseine, a Somali immigrant who had committed at least 20 crimes over seven years, could not be deported despite his crimes and despite his asylum application being rejected, because Somalia was deemed too dangerous. The crimes committed by Husseine included four sex assaults. His latest was an attempt to abduct a ten-year-old child from a supermarket for 'sexual or violent' reasons. When detained by Tesco security guards, he threatened: 'When I get back to Somalia I will kill every British person I see and come back and abduct another child.' He was jailed for only two and half years.

The hostility expressed by Husseine is far from unique. In July 2016, it was revealed that there were 2,000 extremists in Britain. Only one was subject to the Terrorism Prevention and Investigation Measures Act. In December 2016, Air Chief Marshal Sir Stuart Peach, chief of the Defence staff, warned that 'We face a potential network of combat experienced terrorists' because '[ISIS] are losing territory rapidly, foreign fighters are being killed and displaced but they are moving in migrant flows, hiding in plain sight.' He pointed out that 'How we manage identity in a world where people are deliberately trying to destroy their identity documents and move in migrant flows – it is a very important subject.'

Another example was reported in June 2017. Tarik Chadlioui, a Moroccan imam with a Belgian passport who urged Muslims to wage jihad against 'infidels', cited human rights laws to prevent his extradition to Spain on charges of supporting ISIS with propaganda and incitement. According to the Spanish police, 'He produced audio-visual material for the recruitment of jihadis on his YouTube channel for indoctrination and posted symbols and banners for Islamic State on social media.' The Spanish police had recently arrested four men in connection to the jihadist network. Chadlioui was accused of radicalising Omar Mostefai, a suicide bomber who killed 89 at the Bataclan theatre in Paris in 2015.

A variety of estimates concluded that between 1,000 and 2,000 Muslims went to join ISIS from Britain. Around 400 of those are believed to have returned. Only ten of those 400 have faced the law. According to Andrew Parker, director general of MI5, there are at least 3,000 known Islamists in Britain. Subsequently, in May 2017 after yet more terrorist attacks, MI5 revealed that 23,000 suspects had been investigated for terrorism. 3,000 jihadists were under investigation, with around 500 active terror investigations.

Reportedly, it takes 30 officers to provide 24-hour surveillance of one suspect. MI5 has resources to monitor only 50 suspects, with around 3,000 active jihadis in Britain and more returning from Iraq and Syria as ISIS is defeated. At least 13 terrorist attacks had been foiled over the previous four years. Europol reported that it believed that the wives and children of the jihadis also posed a threat due to being radicalised and their being desensitised to extreme violence.

In May 2017, it was reported that *for the first time*, laws to ban jihadists returning to Britain had been used. Temporary Exclusion Orders had been introduced in 2015 but had never been used despite the number of jihadists popping back to Britain. Tarique Ghaffur, a Muslim who was assistant commissioner at Scotland Yard at the time of the July 7 terrorist bombings advocated internment for the 3,000 jihadists in Britain:

> 'These would be community-based centres where the extremists would be risk-assessed. Then the extremists would be made to go through a deradicalisation programme, using the expertise of imams, charity workers and counter-terrorism officers. These centres would have oversight from vetted Muslim and other community leaders, who would ensure they stayed within the law.'

This view contradicted that of Lord Blair, the ex-chief of Scotland Yard, who said such a move would be counterproductive.

In one example of liberal values colliding with reality, in June 2017, Lynn Barber, a journalist, took a so-called asylum seeker into her own home. She had lived alone following her husband's death. Mohammed claimed to have been a refugee from Khartoum. He had entered Britain illegally after spending five months at Calais trying to do so. The experience did not turn out well. Mohammed was polite at first, but then he became untidy, took drugs, downloaded pornography, and was disrespectful towards women and non-Muslims. In one argument, he said: 'I am not a refugee. My family are very rich! We could buy you up like that! Do you want money? Is that why you write this filth? I get you money. You first world women are all the same: you are heartless. You have no feelings. You Christians are all racists.'

He was given asylum, and he has a wife in the Sudan who is studying pharmacology and who also intends to come to Britain once she has completed those studies. Lynn Barber declared that she intended to take in another refugee.

In June 2017, ONS figures showed that Britain's population jumped by 538,000 in the year to June 2016. Almost two-thirds of this increase was accounted for by net migration. The population of England increased to 65,648,000. Also in June 2017, a report, *The Politics of Fantasy*, published by Civitas exposed that the Home Office was hiding the true illegal immigration figures, which were that 150,000 illegal immigrants were entering Britain every year. Part of the reason for the large scale of illegal immigration was that the border controls were seriously underfunded. The report further warned: 'Without effective enforcement of immigration laws and regulations, the result of Brexit won't be that we "take back control" of our borders, as the Prime Minister has promised. It will be a surge in illegal immigration.'

The scale of illegal immigration should not be underestimated. Apart from the abuse of the asylum system (if one can even call it that), and apart from the practice of illegal immigrants being granted permission to stay under the 14-year rule (where immigrants can stay if they have been in Britain that length of time), MigrationWatch UK reported in June 2014 that the total number of illegal immigrants was estimated to be as high as two million. This two-million figure is likely to be true given earlier government and other estimates, and given that the illegal immigrants keep pouring in (see *The Ponzi Class*, page 302).

One of the greatest costs of mass immigration is the impact on housing. In February 2017, Lord Green, told the House of Lords that 'The difference between high and zero migration is 110,000 households formed every year. That is 300 every day. To put the point slightly more dramatically, that would mean building a home every five minutes, night and day, for new arrivals until such time as we get those numbers down.' Lord Bourne stated: 'Net migration will probably fall as a result of Brexit, but it will be some time before that happens.' Lord Bourne said that an estimated 45% of the growth in new households was due to net migration. This meant that almost half of the new houses being built would be taken by new immigrant families.

The cost of housing immigrants is not cheap. For example, in November 2016, it was reported that the Sube family, immigrants from France who were originally from Cameroon, had just moved into a new £425,000 detached property at taxpayer's expense after they had complained about their previous house being too small. They had already turned down the offer of a five-bed council house, saying it was too small. The Subes, a family of ten (eight children), were estimated to be receiving £44,000 in various welfare payments and state income. The Subes had moved to France 15 years ago and become EU citizens, and so were qualified to be able to move to Britain and receive British welfare.

In October 2016, ONS data showed that despite people moving out of London, due to high housing costs, the scale of immigration meant that the capital's population was increasing by 120,000 per year. In December 2016, the ONS disclosed figures which showed that 70% of the children born in London had at least one parent born abroad and that the figure had reached 33% for England and Wales, up from 21.2% in 2000, with 230,811 with at least one parent born abroad out of a total of 697,000 births. London's population increased by 480,000 between 2011 and 2015 (a 5.7% increase) and was set to reach 9.8million by 2025. London was the only city in Britain to experience a fall in the numbers of those 19–21 years old after 2011. Also, for people 45 and older, 90,000 more moved away than arrived. English flight and the repopulation of London continued apace.

In February 2017, Labour's deputy leader, Tom Watson, said:

> 'You can actually say London requires more liberal immigration policies but there are other parts of the country where immigration may be putting pressure on public services like schools and hospitals. That's why I think when we come out of the EU we can have an immigration policy that maybe addresses both those issues. These are nascent ideas, we're not ready to make them robust in a manifesto yet but they're certainly the debate that is going on in the Labour Party right now and in wider circles.'

In January 2017, Eurostat estimated that the population of Britain would exceed that of France by 2030 despite France being more than twice the size of Britain, and would exceed that of Germany by 2050. Immigration was cited as being the main reason for the rapid population growth.

The EU was not the only entity pushing to determine who lives in Britain, and there is a clear danger that a weak government desperate for free-trade treaties will cave in to foreign bullying. On a three-day trade visit to India, in November 2016, May was pressured by the Indian prime minister, Narendra Modi, into increasing the visas available to Indians. Modi wanted to see more Indians migrating to the UK and specifically mentioned students. May responded that she was prepared to consider this, but she said that she wanted India to make it easier for Britain to return overstayers back to India. As home secretary, May had made changes to the visa system to restrict the ability of students to take jobs in Britain once their studies had ended.

The Brexit vote made little difference to government policy. In February 2017, speaking in Estonia about ending low-skilled immigration, David Davis said:

> 'In the hospitality sector, hotels and restaurants, in the social-care sector, working in agriculture, it will take time. It will be years and years before we get British citizens to do those jobs. Don't expect just because we're changing who makes the decision on the policy the door will suddenly shut – it won't.'

It was revealed by the Home Office that in the last three months of 2016, 32,481 European Economic Area citizens and their families were given the right to stay in Britain. This was seven times the 4,924 for the same period in 2015. In 2016, 65,195 EEA citizens and their families were given the right to stay in Britain, compared to a figure of 18,064 in 2015; this was the highest figure since records began in 2006.

ONS figures showed that the number of immigrant workers in Britain had increased by 431,000 in the year to December. Meanwhile, the number of British-born workers fell by 120,000. Of the 31.8million workforce, 5.5million were immigrants, of whom 3.2million were from outside the EU.

It was disclosed in February 2017 that for the first time, more than half the immigrants arriving in Britain in 2016 had come from the EU. That year, 268,000 EU citizens and 275,000 non-EU citizens immigrated into Britain. Of these,

180,000 of the EU immigrants had come looking for work. In June 2017, OECD figures revealed that 13.9% of the population of Britain, 8,988,000 people, had been born abroad. This was higher than the USA, where 13.5% of the population had been born abroad – 43,290,000 people. In July 2017, the latest ONS figures showed that 28.2% of births in Britain were to foreign mothers. This is compared to a figure of 11.6% in 1990. Alp Mehmet of Migration Watch UK warned: 'At this rate, we will have to provide for another five million people by 2027, largely due to immigration.'

The abuse of the immigration system grew. In March 2017, the Europol European Migrant Smuggling Centre (EMSC), which was set up in February 2016, said that it had uncovered an additional 17,400 people smugglers operating in Europe and that 90% of immigrants had paid such gangs to reach Europe in a £3billion trade. It was feared that embassy officials were being bribed. The people smugglers were advertising a list of services on social media, including transportation, fake passports, false work permits, sham marriages, and false travel documents. Frontex revealed that 11,000 immigrants in the EU had been found to have forged documents in 2016.

The May Government's approach to controlling immigration remained half-hearted. In July 2017, a report from Independent Chief Inspector of Borders and Immigration David Bolt criticised the Home Office for its lackadaisical approach to students who were staying in Britain illegally. Originally, 25,000 had been identified as 'unaccounted for', but the Home Office had whittled the figure down to 16,000. However, in addition, a further 24,145 had been identified as needing their visas withdrawn. Moreover, no 'enforcement activity' had been taken against those in Britain illegally.

In March 2017, UN officials warned in a report for UNICEF about the flow of immigrants crossing the Mediterranean from Libya:

> 'It is not only a risky route taken by desperate people, but also a billion-dollar business route controlled by

criminal networks. The central Mediterranean route has become a massive people smuggling operation, which has grown out of control for the lack of safe and alternative migration systems. It exploits porous and corrupt border security and the vacuum created by the Libyan conflict.'

In July 2017, the UNHCR said that 70% of the immigrants crossing the Mediterranean were not refugees, but were economic migrants. In June 2017, in less than one week, 9,000 immigrants were plucked from their boats in the Mediterranean. Around 83,000 such immigrants reached Italy in the first six months of 2017. Another 5,082 reached Spain.

Fabrice Leggerie, the chief of Frontex, EU's border agency, condemned charity-operated rescue boats, which he said made people smuggling more likely, and he said:

'We must avoid supporting the business of criminal networks and traffickers in Libya through European vessels picking up migrants ever closer to the Libyan coast. This leads traffickers to force even more migrants on to unseaworthy boats with insufficient water and fuel.'

Antonio Tajani, the European Parliament president, suggested EU-backed detention centres in Libya and said: 'We either act now or 20million Africans will come to Europe in the coming years.'

Sir Michael Fallon claimed in February 2017 that Afghan forces were struggling to beat the Taliban and said:

'If this country collapses, we here will feel the consequences, very directly. There could be three to four million young Afghan men sent out by their villages to migrate westwards, and there are heading here. There are heading to Germany or Britain and that could be the consequence if this entire country collapses.'

The problem of failed states and bloody extremism is closer than Afghanistan. Countries along North Africa and in the Middle East are at least as bad as Afghanistan. Many of the immigrants and terrorists who have entered Britain come from Libya.

In May 2017, after a recent Islamist terrorist atrocity, John R. Bradley wrote in the *Daily Mail*:

> 'For those of us who had studied the history and lived in the region, it was obvious that, despite their internal divisions and rivalries, all those disparate jihadist groups in Libya had one overriding and very dark ambition: to replace Gaddafi's secular regime with one based on their own mercilessly hardline interpretation of Sharia law, before seizing the country's oilfields and finally cutting all ties with Western countries they openly despised. For this reason, the groups had been banned and their members ruthlessly persecuted by Gaddafi and other secular Arab leaders ... The British government welcomed Salman Abedi's [an Islamist terrorist] father Ramadan into our country with open arms in 1993 as part of a reckless liberal policy of granting political sanctuary to Islamist activists from Libya and other Arab nations.
>
> The misguided belief was that they would warm to the host nation that offered them sanctuary, and modify their opinions through the new experience of living in an open democracy. Instead, many of them not only continued stirring up rebellion in the countries they came from, but called openly for Islamist rule in their adopted homeland. Successive British governments turned a blind eye to this treachery.'

The Associated Press claimed that after the fall of Gaddafi, Salman Abedi's father fought in Libya in the 1990s with a group, the Libyan Islamic Fighting Group, linked to Al-Qaeda. Furthermore, his brother was connected to ISIS. Salman Abedi was able to take advantage of a 'jihadi corridor' to move between Libya and Syria. His British passport then allowed him to return to Britain to commit his atrocity.

Ignoring the EU referendum vote and people's concerns about mass immigration, the government's response was not to keep the extremists out by securing the borders and disallowing criminals and extremists the entry or deporting them if they did get entry. The government responded by trying to control the views of the extremists, most obviously by the Prevent programme. This has been mired in political correctness and has had mixed success. For example, one of the London Bridge terrorists (an attack on London Bridge by three Islamists who drove a white van into pedestrians and then jumped out armed with knives and attacked people – see below), Khurum Butt, had a brother, Saad Butt, who set up the Young Muslim Advisory Group that was funded by the Prevent programme. Saad Butt met regularly with members of the last Labour government in Whitehall to discuss how to tackle extremism.

The Prevent programme's budget was estimated to be around £40million per annum; the government refused to publish the data, citing 'national security'. An investigation by the *Daily Mail* found that recipients of Prevent funding included: the Tapestry theatre group in Birmingham, which toured schools to give presentations about 'Right-wing and Al Qaeda inspired ideology' comparing the 'recruitment methods from both groups'; the Banbury Fair Trade Society for a 'multicultural food festival'; Bedford's Faith in Queen's Park group for 'fusion youth singing' and cricket and basketball clubs; a Muslim scout group in Bristol received funds for camping equipment; and in Barking, a local mosque got £50,000 in 2007/08 and more money subsequently for rap 'workshops', lunches, a boxing club, and a five-a-side 'kickball' tournament. Lord Carlisle had previously condemned the Labour government for the use of Prevent funds for 'sports and recreation activities'.

The Home Office claimed that in 2016, 42,000 had attended 142 Prevent activities and that in excess of 150 trips to Syria had been stopped.

Between 2015 and 2016, more than 7,500 people were reported as being vulnerable to radicalization. The majority of those making the reports were 'specially trained' council officials and schools. A quarter of all those reported were accused of being far right. Instead of targeting the problem, radical Islam, the focus was to avoid the particular threat posed by this creed. The terrorist threat grew, and the acts of terrorism became more frequent. The 2017 general election was disrupted by vicious acts of terrorism and several more minor incidents. Mass immigration and the refusal to secure the borders was a major factor in this.

In May 2017, it was reported that Abu Rayah, a Bangladeshi who had had his British passport cancelled, nevertheless was employed in Britain delivering Just Eat takeaways. This was after he had returned from Syria and despite his previous association with Muslims Against Crusades, which celebrated 9/11 and set fire to poppies.

In June 2017, it was revealed that Youssef Zaghba, a Moroccan with Italian citizenship and one of the London Bridge terrorists, had been allowed into Britain despite him being on an international watch list. Italian authorities warned the British security services that he had told them: 'I'm going to be a terrorist.' In March 2016, Zaghba had been stopped at Bologna Airport while attempting to get to Istanbul on his way to Syria. British Government officials denied the Italian claims: 'The Italians have made a mistake on their own patch and now they are desperate to cover their own backs.'

Khuram Butt, the ringleader, had already been cautioned for extremism. He was a Pakistani immigrant. He had longstanding links to extremists and extremist organizations such as Anjem Choudary and had even appeared on a television documentary, *The Jihadis Next Door*, where he was filmed unfurling an ISIS flag in London. He had further been offering children sweets and trying to lure them to become Muslims. One mother who had challenged him said that he had replied: 'Your people, all of you, Americans, Europeans, going in our countries and killing our innocent children. In the name of Allah I'm ready even to kill my mother', and he had then gone on to excuse the killers of Lee Rigby and the Charlie Hebdo terrorists in Paris. The mother said: 'He was so angry with me I thought he was going to take my life that day when I confronted him. I'm lucky I'm still alive.' Even one of his friends reported him to the anti-terrorism hotline, but the authorities did nothing.

The third terrorist in the London attack was a failed asylum seeker who had changed his name and then married a British woman in Dublin. Rachid Redouane was Moroccan and also an associate of Anjem Choudary. After marrying, he applied for an Irish visa to join his wife in London. An Irish security source described him as having 'extensive immigration history related to the UK.'

In April 2017, the police stopped two terrorist plots in London. In one operation, an unarmed woman was shot in a police raid to prevent what was described as an 'immanent' bomb attack. In another operation, a terrorist carrying a backpack full of knives was arrested a short distance from Downing Street. The jihadist, a Somali man, had spent several years in Afghanistan and had been under police surveillance following a tip-off from his family.

It was announced in April 2017 that up to 28 Muslim extremists were to be confined in 'separation centres' within prisons. The move was designed to stop them radicalising other prisoners. The prisons minister Sam Gyimah said: 'These centres are a crucial part of our wider strategy to help tackle extremism in prisons and ensure the safety and security of our prisons and the public.'

As with other countries and has had been the practice with the child-grooming gangs, there was an instinct to cover up. In June 2017, just after an act of terrorism, CNN was caught staging an anti-ISIS demonstration by a handful of Muslim women. The CNN reporter described the 'demonstration' as a 'poignant scene' of women holding up signs saying 'turn to love' and 'ISIS will lose'. However, the scene was captured on a mobile and showed the CNN reporter positioning the demonstrators. The footage was circulated with the caption 'CNN creating the narrative #FakeNews'. CNN denied the allegation.

Days later, a nursery worker was left with broken ribs and a knife wound after being attacked by three Asian women who had shouted Koranic phrases and 'Allah'. The attackers, who were all dressed in black, had attacked from behind, pulling the victim to the ground and kicking her before attacking with the knife. The attackers fled when a passer-by intervened. A nearby school was put into lockdown as police searched in vain for the attackers. The police did not class this as a terrorist incident.

Nazir Afzal wrote:

> 'A major problem is that, at times like this, the Home Office seeks help from our so-called "community leaders". These men with long beards sermonising in mosques are no more representative of the communities these days than Mickey Mouse is. They haven't produced many answers to Islamist extremism in the past and are unlikely to produce any in the future. This is partly because they are invariably professional and middle class – but the majority of Muslims in the UK are under 25 and come from low-income backgrounds. The "community leaders" don't understand who we are dealing with when it comes to extremism.'

A good indication of the Ponzi class's attitude to immigration was revealed in the All Party Parliamentary Group (APPG) on Social Integration, which published its *Interim Report into the Integration of Immigrants*. The APPG report was a good example of the Ponzi class's politically correct group think. It was also the product of the pro-immigration lobby, and 'the social integration charity The Challenge ... provides the secretariat to this APPG', although this lobby was described as being made up of 'independent experts who have contributed to our work to date'.

The forward was written by the Labour MP Chuka Umunna, who asserted that 'we argue endlessly' about immigration but that too little attention is focused on the integration of immigrants. He further asserted that:

> 'Very few of the individuals we have met during visits to Boston in Lincolnshire and Halifax in Yorkshire were hostile to immigration. Indeed, most shared the view that it has been fantastic for our economy and for the cultural life of our country. It is clear, however, that demographic and cultural change has threatened people's sense of security, identity, and belonging within their communities and—in some instances—put pressure on local public services.'

This assertion is mind-boggling in its bias. One cannot but wonder to whom the APPG has been speaking. The fact is that the English, in particular, have been consistently opposed to the policy of mass immigration for many decades. They have never voted for it, and the British governments have foisted this policy upon Britain, England in particular, against the wishes of the people.

Umunna continued to allege that different communities were 'leading parallel rather than interconnected lives', which he urged 'we must confront'. He said this was necessary, as the lack of integration had 'left a vacuum for extremists and peddlers of hate on all sides to exploit' and that 'it is all too easy to blame "the other" for all our problems'. Umunna believed that 'it is possible to craft a middle way between the laissez-faire multiculturalism favoured by successive British governments — of different political persuasions — and the assimilationist politics of the French Burkini ban' and even invoked Brexit as requiring 'a new approach to immigration' (see *The Genesis of Political Correctness*, page 115).

The report set out six principles: 'PRINCIPLE ONE: The government must develop a comprehensive and proactive national strategy for the integration of immigrants'; 'PRINCIPLE TWO: Local authorities must be required to draw up and implement local integration action plans'; 'PRINCIPLE THREE: Government must reassess its current "one size fits all" approach to immigration policy'; 'PRINCIPLE FOUR: For new immigrants, integration should begin upon arrival in the UK'; 'PRINCIPLE FIVE: We need more and better data on the integration of immigrants'; and 'PRINCIPLE SIX: The government should demonstrate strong political leadership on immigration in order to build public confidence and facilitate successful integration of new arrivals at a regional and local level.' This principle is about extolling the wonders of mass immigration.

The report defined integration as being 'to mean the extent to which people conform to shared norms and values and lead shared lives'. Importantly, it should be noted that the idea of 'shared norms and values' etc is not the same as British culture. The report did not expect immigrants to adopt or even accept British culture. Furthermore, an immigrant is deemed to 'refer to economic migrants, as opposed to refugees or asylum seekers', which 'includes both recent immigrants and those who have resided in the country legally for a number of years, but do not have British citizenship'. According to this logic, immigrants cease to be so once they have British citizenship, and those who claim to be asylum seekers or refugees are not immigrants.

Regarding principle one, the report mentioned the failure to accurately predict the scale of immigration from the new EU accession countries. It regarded integration as 'ensuring that people of different faiths, ethnicities, sexual orientations, social backgrounds, origins, and generations do not just tolerate one another or live side by side but meet, mix and forge relationships' and that 'Civic integration is understood by the APPG as an awareness of and respect for the host country's laws, traditions, and culture, as well as knowledge of national languages and participation in democracy and political life.' This principle ignored the opinions and interests of the English and focuses on immigrants. It stated:

> 'The new national immigrant integration strategy should differentiate between, and include, policies shaped to reflect the needs and circumstances of different categories of immigrants. These categories may include, but are not limited to: long- term and short-term immigrants, economic migrants, skilled and unskilled workers, and immigrants coming in under the family reunion scheme, students, child immigrants, new immigrants, elderly immigrants, and immigrants who have lived in the UK for some time. It should also recognise the gendered experiences of immigration, whether as sponsors, actors, or dependants.'

The principle unashamedly wanted the state to monitor and interfere with very private aspects of people's lives. It further made the state responsible for whether or not immigrants integrate, rather than expect immigrants to take this responsibility themselves.

With Principle Two, the report highlighted the different impact of immigration on different parts of England, with London being more tolerant of more immigration, allegedly, while other places, such as Boston and Halifax, had a different view. In Halifax, there was judged to be an 'entrenched ethnic division' not caused by new immigrants. The report advocated not only a 'Controlling Migration Fund' but also an 'Integration Impact Fund' which 'should be used by local authorities to fund programmes promoting English language learning and social mixing between immigrant and host communities'. The report simply assumed that there is money for all this.

Principle three condemned the one-size-fits-all 'immigration systems where new immigrants move to 'areas with high immigrant concentrations' due to chain immigration and said that 'this prevents some regions from benefiting from the economic advantages of immigration'. The report stated that a geographical dispersal of immigrants aids integration. The report placed emphasis on Scotland's alleged need for more immigrants. The report stated that 'The APPG calls on the government to seriously consider devolving a degree of control over immigration policy powers to the constituent nations and regions of the UK.' By regions, the report meant the English regions and that the English nation should have no say in the matter. Furthermore, it stated:

> 'Shaping immigration criteria to address nation or region-specific economic and cultural needs might instil confidence among members of the public that the immigration system works for their area; whilst enabling nations and regions to set regional immigration quotas would create new incentives for politicians to actively make the case for immigration in their area.'

This is simply a mechanism to circumvent English opposition to mass immigration. In short, to use their own language, this is anti-English racism.

Principle four stated that integration of immigrants should begin upon arrival and that the state is responsible for this. The report advocated 'compulsory ESOL classes upon arrival' for those who do not already speak English and that the government should 'markedly increase ESOL funding'. The report further demanded that 'the Home Office investigate whether new immigrants could be placed on pathways to citizenship automatically upon their arrival to the UK' and that there should be a reduction in 'naturalisation fees'.

Principle five called for better data. Once again, the state should become more intrusive.

Principle six was a demand for the state to positively advocate continued mass immigration. The report drew a comparison with Australia without taking into account the fact that Australia is sparsely populated and a country that has required immigration to develop, whereas Britain is naturally an emigrant country and one of the most densely populated in the world. The report even alleged that geographically, Britain would find it harder to control its borders than Australia. Being an offshore European island is a handicap! The report stated:

> 'The government's consistent failure to meet its own immigration targets has only served to undermine public confidence in the ability of government to manage immigration effectively and encouraged populist resentment. The government must consider the impact on social integration of any post-Brexit immigration policy announcements to ensure that it does not create further social division and disadvantage among those communities already grappling with rapid social change.'

The report advocated that employers who employed immigrants be involved in promoting the benefits of mass immigration. In its conclusion, the report demanded a 'government comprehensive integration strategy', as 'Brexit has been the wake-up call: globalization has not delivered for all and now more than ever, we need political leadership to prioritise integration in order to address the deep societal divisions that were exposed on June 23rd.'

The idea that those employers who were employing immigrants should actually pay the full cost of immigration did not enter the dignified considerations of the APPG. That a failure to expect employers to pay those costs might cause resentment among those who are saddled with the consequences was beyond the APPG's mental capacity. If some tax-dodging multinational organization chooses to save on wages and training costs by importing immigrants, then let that tax-dodging multinational pay to the government the full cost of a house for each and every one of those immigrants – likewise for any other organization, tax-dodging or not. Then there are all the other costs.

In June 2016, Corbyn complained that coalition government had abolished the 'Migrant Impact Fund', which he described as 'a national fund to manage the short term impacts of migration on local communities'. He condemned the Cameron-led coalition for undermining 'the proper preparation and investment that communities need to adapt'. In other words, the central government should pay the costs of immigration so that local communities can advocate mass immigration with impunity, as they will not pay the costs of it. The APPG report has called it the 'Integration Impact Fund'.

Both *The Ponzi Class* and *The Genesis of Political Correctness* highlight the 'We' argument, that 'we' need to spend all kinds of money on a variety of worthy causes. By 'we', what is meant is English taxpayers' money. Those making these demands have no intention of forking out themselves. *The Ponzi Class* and *The Genesis of Political Correctness* both advocate the need for a solidarity tax that would enable those who loudly demand and squander large sums of other peoples' money to contribute to the costs of their schemes and show solidarity with those whose money has been squandered.

Those who are on lower wages, who have suffered unemployment, whose pensions have been decimated by the collapsed annuity rates, who cannot own their home, or who have their homes seized if they are taken into care, as well as many others, all have lost out financially due to the extravagance of the Ponzi class and their political correctness. By levying a solidarity tax on the Ponzi class, their supporters and the politically correct, substantial monies could be raised to meet the government's spending deficit and, hopefully, to compensate those who have been fleeced. *The Genesis of Political Correctness* lists potential target groups and ideas for implementation, including the importance of a solidarity audit so that those importing immigrants can be targeted to pay to house those immigrants, rather than blithely assuming that ordinary English people will be made to pay.

Talk of an Integration/Migrant Impact Fund will simply allow those who want more mass immigration to help themselves to yet more of other people's money to pay for that mass immigration. That is the opposite of what is needed. We need a solidarity tax: 'To put it into language that might appeal to the Left, what is needed is an irreversible transfer of wealth from those who advocate political correctness to the victims of political correctness. A Solidarity Tax is a means by which such transfer might be achieved' (*The Genesis of Political Correctness*, page 193).

SUMMARY

As can be seen, put simply, ordinary people continued to see their living standards eroded and continued to have politically correct ideology foisted upon them. The Ponzi class continued to enjoy unrestricted access to public monies to spend on themselves and their pet projects. The EU referendum Leave vote changed nothing. Even regarding the EU, the monies continued to flow out, the immigrants continued to flow in, the trade deficit continued, and a ton of insults and abuse was thrown at those who dared to vote Leave. This was against a backdrop of escalating Islamist terrorism and violence.

A few Tories huffed and puffed about the foreign aid budget, but they did not do anything about it even when they were put in charge of it. Priti Patel once criticized foreign aid, but now that she was responsible for it, she saw nothing wrong with it. Money was no object. She went native. So the gravy train continued, and the corruption and organized crime flourished. Foreign aid flowed out even though our social care system was struggling, even though the armed forces had a shortage of equipment and troops, and even though the government was eyeing up pensioners for any money they could get.

People's quality of life was subject to steady erosion – be they pensioners, young people, or anyone else – apart from the Ponzi class themselves. In a case of divide and rule, a new term has emerged: 'intergenerational fairness'. This was a Tory concept, and aggressively promoted by the May Government. In fact, it had nothing to do with fairness and was simply a ruse to try and take money away from pensioners and to blame them for the fall in living standards of younger people rather than the real causes such as tuition fees, the housing shortage or falling wages.

More recently, inflation was once again on the rise, and due to stagnant wages, people's incomes were being squeezed. Once again, people were borrowing more to fund their standards of living.

The Ponzi class, in their entirety, ignored the trade deficit and the consequences of it. Assets continued to be sold off to fund that deficit. The manufacturing boost that the fall in the value of sterling prompted did not prompt the Ponzi class to grasp the damage being done to Britain by the euro, or the opportunity offered by the Brexit vote to deal with that.

Meanwhile, the Ponzi class enjoyed the high life, with lots of taxpayer's monies for their pet projects. Police officers, BBC bigwigs, quangocrats, the academic jet set, judges, lawyers, and bankers all continued to do very nicely as they wallowed in political correctness and talked down their noses at the rest of us. That so many of these people are lefties should not be a surprise. Communist revolutions have routinely shown that once the champions of the masses get into power, they soon get their slice of toast firmly wedged in the caviar.

Political correctness remained the basis of morality. Not even a patriotic event such as Brexit disrupted the advance of this Marxist creed: soldiers were persecuted; so-called human rights remained an alternative to common sense; militant feminism engulfed society in general and education in particular; quotas were the aim; intolerance of free speech got worse; British history and historical figures were increasingly condemned.

Despite the escalating level of Islamist terrorism, race war politics remained as venomous as it was incendiary. A contempt of the English was considered normal and moral. Despite all the blather about tolerance, it was hatred that was being promoted. Allegations of so-called hate crimes were routinely inflated and invented. The real damage done to certain groups, a prime example being those girls subjected to grooming gangs, was glossed over and allowed to continue. In contrast, jihadists and immigrant criminals were tolerated and even given money.

Immigration remained a horror story. Despite the importance of immigration as an issue that prompted the Leave vote, Britain's borders remained open. Mass immigration continued with even jihadists being able to pop back to Britain if they got bored of their activities in ISIS-controlled areas. Not even a token gesture was made to stem the flow. The APPG report proved how keen the MPs were to justify mass immigration, even going so far as advocate an end to a national immigration policy, the break-up of England, and for those areas supposedly favourable to immigration to be able to bring in immigrants at will. For the Ponzi class, it was business as usual.

A shameful part of that business could be described accurately as judge-backed organized crime. Be it the fraud and malpractice of lawyers prosecuting British soldiers stemming from legal-aid-funded phoney allegations, the people smuggling industry funded by English taxpayer's monies via an avalanche of ridiculous judgements, or the looting of small businesses by bankers and their cohorts, the judges were responsible for the growth of organized crime. This *is* organized crime.

Far from being reined in, the judges continued to be fawned over. As the high priests of political correctness, they retained their monopoly of the definition of the holiest of holy words: 'human rights'. The Ponzi class therefore afforded the judges due deference. In reality, the judges were no different than primitive tribesmen in loincloths and fancy dress, dancing and whooping around a fire in the middle of the night and worshipping the moon god. Like many high priests, they were crooked and guarded their social status zealously.

Political correctness is not the definition of human rights. It should not be the basis of morality. There is no moon god, and the high priests need to be put in their place. They are just a self-serving vested interest group. Britain has remained a lawyers' dictatorship.

PART THREE

MAYISM

In *The Ponzi Class*, the case is made that the ideology of the ruling class is Ponzi economics, a corrupted version of free trade and Keynesianism, and political correctness. For the Ponzi class, political correctness is the basis of morality. The true nature of political correctness is examined in *The Genesis of Political Correctness*; in fact, the creed is a version of communism and is a false morality. The purpose of political correctness is to do harm.

The West generally is dominated by politically correct ideology. Despite the creed's lack of support in the general public or its complete lack of democratic legitimacy (no government has been elected with a commitment to introduce the creed), it has nevertheless swept unchallenged across Western societies, capturing control of the state and charity sectors with ease.

The Tory Party in Britain abandoned conservatism long ago. Given that Thatcher was economically as much a classical liberal as a conservative, a case could be made that true conservatism was abandoned by the Tories in the 1960s, if not the 1950s. What is undoubted is that the Cameron Tory Party was a keen adherent to political correctness and economically a keen adherent to Ponzi economics. But what of the May Government? To what extent is the May Government a separate entity from the Cameron administration out of which May and her colleagues emerged?

In assessing Mayism, or a lack of it, one can take into account three factors: May's previous political activity, her track record as Home Secretary and her influence on the Tory Party. One can take account of her handling of Brexit and how she seeks to carry it out – or not – and the direction she intends to take both the Tories and Britain in the future. May has already said that Britain will be defined by what it makes of Brexit, but a more telling point is that May will be defined by it.

May was the first female chairman of the Tory Party. In her speech to the Tory conference in 2002, she said: 'You know what people call us? The Nasty Party.' Prior to becoming prime minister, May had enjoyed a long time as home secretary. She had done nothing notable in this role other than to do little to effectively stem the tide of legal and illegal immigration. Up until 2012, she had also been minister for equalities (this is important and should not be overlooked).

A problem of assessing Mayism, is that the May Government has done very little. Decisions have been taken to avoid action, such as to delay the triggering of Article 50 and to make no effort to repeal the so-called Human Rights Act. This foot dragging is as telling as positive action. Even so, May and key ministers set out how they intended to react to the Brexit vote, both in speeches and in white papers. Their intended direction and, consequently, their ideology was clear. They were firmly committed to globalization and political correctness.

For May, Brexit was not a rejection by the people of globalization, but instead, the Brexit vote was an opportunity to extend it, to replace subservience to the EU with subservience to a host of other international institutions, for example, the UN and the WTO. Importantly, May craftily substituted a pro-EU policy in the place of the Leave EU vote. 'Brexit means Brexit' was a useful slogan, but to May, Brexit meant a 'deep and special partnership with the EU'. In other words, the Leave vote should be ignored, and only a token sovereignty restored. Membership of the Single Market would be replaced with a comprehensive free-trade arrangement that, we were told, would require give and take (Britain gives, and the EU takes) and interim deals that span many years and include the continuation of payments to the EU, free movement, and subservience to the EU courts.

An understanding of Mayism can be achieved by examining six speeches and two white papers: May's speech to the UN in September 2016; Liam Fox's speech at the Manchester Town Hall in September 2016; May's speech to the Tory Party conference in October 2016; Hammond's speech to the Tory Party conference in October 2016; May's speech to the US Republicans in January 2017; May's EU policy speech in January 2017, setting out her approach to the Article 50 negotiations; and the two white papers in February and March 2017 relating to Article 50 and the repeal of the 1972 European Communities Act. In these speeches and white papers, a political stance was adopted and adhered to. That stance was one of globalization and political correctness.

The first key speech, shortly after assuming the leadership of the Tory Party and hence the premiership of the country, was in the USA to the United Nations in September 2016. In this speech, May naturally dealt with issues from an international perspective, but the importance of the speech was the extent to which she redefined national issues as being under the UN's remit – in particular immigration.

May began her speech to the UN by emphasizing the threats posed and that these were global. She listed the familiar threats as 'war, political instability, abuses of human rights and poverty' and the new threats as being 'global terrorism, climate change, and unprecedented mass movements of people', and she said: 'such challenges do not respect the borders of our individual nations and that only by working together shall we overcome them'.

May referred to the 'universal values that we share together' and that Britain would 'honour our commitment to spend 0.7% of our Gross National Income on development' and would 'drive forward the implementation of the Sustainable Development Goals' as well as 'continue to champion the rights of women and girls, making sure that all girls get the education they deserve, and tackling horrific abuses such as female genital mutilation and the use of sexual violence in conflict.' May pointed out Britain's role on the Security Council, its NATO membership, and its peacekeeping efforts. Revealingly, May said: 'We will continue to stand up for the rules based international system and for international law.' For May, national sovereignty was a secondary consideration and subordinate to 'the rules based international system and ... international law'.

May gave a sop that 'we must recognise that for too many of these men and women the increasing pace of globalization has left them feeling left behind', but she did not allow this concern to affect her commitment to globalization and quickly urged that 'we need this – our United Nations – to forge a bold new multilateralism'. She claimed that this was necessary as 'no country is untouched by the threat of global terrorism ... when extremists anywhere in the world can transmit their poisonous ideologies directly into the bedrooms of people vulnerable to radicalisation'. May referred to 'the mass displacement of people, at a scale unprecedented in recent history' and that 'when criminal gangs do not respect our national borders, trafficking our fellow citizens into lives of slavery and servitude, we cannot let those borders act as a barrier to bringing such criminals to justice'; she believed that the United Nations was best placed to respond: 'as an international community, we must work together to adopt and implement the most comprehensive national action plans to tackle both the causes and the symptoms of all extremism'. She wanted to 'focus' on both violent and non-violent extremism, 'Islamist and neo-Nazi – hate and fear in all their forms'.

Having delved towards the cultural and racial friction, May then focused on immigration and said:

> 'Just as we need the United Nations to modernise to meet the challenges of terrorism in the 21st Century, so we also need to adapt if we are to fashion a truly global response to the mass movements of people across the world and the implications this brings for security and human rights.'

May openly sought to transfer control of immigration away from the nation state to international bureaucracies such as the UN. May described the 1951 UN Convention on Refugees and its 1967 protocol as a 'bedrock' and that there were 65million displaced people across the world, a figure which she readily admitted 'has almost doubled in a decade' – a fact that proved the failure of the UN and of which May did not grasp the implication. However, May argued that 'UN appeals are underfunded; host countries are not getting enough support; and refugees are not getting the aid, education and economic opportunities they need. We must do more. And as the second largest bi-lateral provider of assistance, the UK remains fully committed to playing a leading role.' May promised that she would 'be championing' the 'financing [of] both humanitarian support and economic development' with 'a further UK financial contribution at President Obama's Refugee Summit' later that day. This is the 'We' argument: that the Ponzi class spend taxpayer's money on their pet projects. By 'we', May means somebody else; she has no intention of spending her own money – just taxpayers' money.

May pointed out that there was an 'unprecedented' number of economic migrants using 'the same unmanaged channels' as refugees and that this 'affects all of us'. May's response was to say that 'I believe we have to use the opportunity afforded by this General Assembly for an honest global debate to address this global challenge.' She believed that 'controlled, legal, safe, economic migration brings benefits to our economies' but that countries needed to control their borders or else a 'failure to do so erodes public confidence, fuels international crime, damages economies and reduces the resources for those who genuinely need protection and whose rights under the Refugee Convention should always be fulfilled'. Once again, for May, the interests of the nation are secondary and subordinate to international rules and treaties. The 1951 UN Convention on Refugees is out of date and has been subject to politically correct abuse.

(The 1951 UN Convention on Refugees, which is implemented alongside the European Convention on Human Rights and the UN Contention on Torture, commits a signatory to offer refuge to someone who has a 'well-founded fear of being persecuted for reasons of race, religion, nationality, membership of a particular social group or political opinion'.[2] The UN convention had been introduced as a consequence of WWII and Nazism, as the 1930s restriction meant that German Jews had been unable to escape to safety. At the end of WWII, Europe had many refugees and holocaust survivors still living in refugee camps. The second paragraph of Article 1 states that the convention only applies to those who were refugees: 'as a result of events occurring before 1st January 1951'.[3] This meant that the convention would only have a temporary effect to deal with a specific problem. However, in the 1960s, wars in Africa caused large numbers of refugees. This led to the resurrection of the 1951 convention and the introduction of the 1967 protocol, which simply removed half the sentence with the date limitation. The UN convention was never intended to be used indefinitely in the way that it has been, nor was it intended to be used to facilitate mass and illegal immigration.)

May set out 'three fundamental principles' for dealing with immigration. First, she wanted refugees to claim asylum in 'the first safe country they reach' and said that allowing them to 'press on with their journey, can only benefit criminal gangs and expose refugees to grave danger'. She advocated greater support for those countries receiving these refugees. She made no mention of the need to end the pull factor of Western countries allowing illegal immigrants to stay regardless of the merits of their migration. Second, she wanted 'to improve the ways we distinguish between refugees fleeing persecution and economic migrants'. She wanted to 'reduce the incentives for economic migrants to use illegal routes'. Third, she wanted better management of economic migration 'which recognises that all countries have the right to control their borders' and that 'we must all commit to accepting the return of our own nationals when they have no right to remain elsewhere'. This was wishful thinking; if countries were prepared to accept their own citizens, they would already be doing so. May merely nattered that states do what they have already shown they will not do. Britain, or Western countries, do not need to ask permission from the UN to secure their borders.

President Trump, during his election campaign, advocated the creation of 'Safe Havens' to accommodate refugees. These could be set up near failed states to accept displaced people and so end any justification for immigrants to invade the West. Despite her supposed concern for refugees, May makes no statement of support for this idea.

May thus believed that 'a managed and controlled international migration response' combined with 'investing to tackle the underlying drivers of displacement and migration at source' would allow the rejection of 'isolationism and xenophobia' as well as 'achieving better outcomes for all of our citizens'. This was political correctness. May dismissed as 'isolationism and xenophobia' the idea that government should also tackle the pull factors, such as the lack of border controls and so-called human rights nonsense that prevents illegal immigrants from being deported. For May, either someone believed in a 'controlled *international* migration response' or they believed in 'isolationism and xenophobia'.

May then turned to a pet subject, 'modern slavery', where:

> 'Organized crime groups, who are largely behind this modern slavery, lure, dupe and force innocent men, women and children into extreme forms of exploitation. Trafficked and sold across borders; victims are forced into living the kind of inhumane existence that is almost too much for our imagination. These criminals have global networks to help them make money out of some of the world's most vulnerable people. Victims are held captive in squalid conditions under the constant shadow of violence and forced into sex and labour exploitation.'

May said that as these organized crime groups operated internationally, and 'We must use our international law enforcement networks to track these criminals down, wherever they are in the world, and put them behind bars where they belong'. May advocated:

> 'We need our law enforcement agencies to work together, with joint investigation teams working across multiple countries. Victims will only find freedom if we cultivate a radically new, global and co-ordinated approach to defeat this vile crime. Together we must work tirelessly to preserve the freedoms and values that have defined our United Nations from its inception.'

Once again, May displayed her globalism. She saw immigration control as a matter for international bureaucracies and not the nation state. She did not state that Britain would be taking back control of its borders, despite the referendum vote.

In conclusion, May said:

> 'The United Kingdom has always been an outward-facing, global partner at the heart of international efforts to secure peace and prosperity for all our people. And that is how we will remain. For when the British people voted to leave the EU, they did not vote to turn inwards or walk away from any of our partners in the world.'

Importantly, she said (italics my own emphasis):

> 'Faced with challenges like migration, a desire for greater control of their country, and a mounting sense that globalization is leaving working people behind, they demanded a politics that is more in touch with their concerns; and bold action to address them. *But that action must be more global, not less.* Because the biggest threats to our prosperity and security do not recognise or respect international borders. And if we

only focus on what we do at home, the job is barely half done. So this is not the time to turn away from our United Nations. It is the time to turn towards it.'

In this way, in her speech, May concentrated not only on assuring the UN that nothing was going to change in Britain, despite the EU referendum vote to Leave, but deftly sought to transfer responsibility for many problems, in particular immigration, to being global problems requiring global solutions and not national ones ('action must be more global'). May's entire argument rendered national immigration control redundant. This was lunacy. The solution to mass immigration, and all the attendant criminal networks that have sprung up to make vast profits from it, is to stop mass immigration. It is the fact immigrants know that once they get inside the West, Britain in particular, that they are unlikely to be deported that encourages them to migrate. Being prepared to allow in anyone who claims to be a refugee is not a response to a migration crisis, but the cause of it. What is needed, and what the British people voted for, is a government policy to end mass immigration by whatever means are necessary, including the repeal of the various so-called human rights legislation and also a withdrawal from the 1951 UN Convention on Refugees. Britain is full.

Also in September, a speech about free trade at the Manchester Town Hall was given by Liam Fox, who, as the international trade secretary, naturally concentrated on trade issues. As May demonstrated her commitment to globalization at the UN regarding immigration, likewise, Fox demonstrated his commitment to globalization regarding trade. In his speech about the virtues of free trade, one cannot deny that Liam Fox was bold and ambitious:

> 'Although the principles of free trade are the same today as set out by Smith in the 18th century, the trading environment has changed beyond recognition. Today, we stand on the verge of an unprecedented

> ability to liberate global trade for the benefit of our whole planet with technological advances dissolving away the barriers of time and distance. It is potentially the beginning of what I might call "post geography trading world" where we are much less restricted in having to find partners who are physically close to us.
>
> It is an exhilarating, empowering and liberating time yet this bright future is being darkened by the shadows of protectionism and retrenchment. History teaches us that such trends do not bode well for the future. Those of us who passionately believe in the case for open and free trade therefore have a clear mission. To succeed in this great task we need to get back to first principles.
>
> I want to remake the intellectual and philosophical case for free trade for I believe the arguments are overwhelming.'

Thus, at the very start, Fox proceeded down a road of disinformation and a corruption of what Adam Smith advocated (see *The Ponzi Class*, in particular the chapters 'List and the Classical School' and 'Joseph Chamberlain and the Tariff Reform Campaign'). He further misrepresented the lessons of history, which demonstrate that free trade is not an unqualified success and that all countries, apart from Britain, regard a degree of protection as both necessary and normal. The issue is to get the right balance. However, Fox adopted a confrontational stance against any criticism of what he defined as free trade:

> 'Its modern-day critics would do well to evaluate the devastating failures of alternative economic models throughout history and to compare them with the recent success gained by countries such as China, India, or Vietnam. My message today is a simple one – free trade has, and will continue to, transform the world for the better, and the UK has a golden

opportunity to forge a new role for ourselves in the world, one which puts the British people first.'

Fox asserted that 'free and fair trade' is 'fundamental' to Britain's prosperity and that of 'the world economy'. The inclusion of 'fair' is at least a recognition that unilateral free trade might not be unquestioningly desirable, yet the whole thrust of his speech demonstrated that he saw nothing wrong with, or did not recognise, the unfair trading activities of countries such as China or the EU. Fox pointed out that overseas trade was 'equivalent' to more than half Britain's 'national income'; this claim is achieved by adding both imports and exports together, and on this basis, an increase in imports is a success. A trade deficit is likewise a success, and if the deficit grows, then that is an even bigger success! To Fox, free trade is a 'significant job creator' leading to higher living standards and increased tax revenues.

Fox described the repeal of the Corn Laws in 1846 as being 'a watershed in our country's relationship with free trade'. It is true that the repeal of the Corn Laws was a positive reform. It allowed the population to increase, as it could be fed with the help of imported foodstuffs. People could be better fed. But what Fox missed is that Britain was able to pay for those imported foodstuffs with exports of manufactured goods. The reform was therefore beneficial to Britain, as it allowed a larger, better-fed population, it allowed foreign countries to sell their foodstuffs in Britain, and it allowed an increase in the exports of British manufactured goods to countries who, in turn, were wealthier, as they were selling more foodstuffs to Britain; therefore, everyone became wealthier and had a better standard of living with a genuine increase in growth of all involved countries.

Where Fox lost the plot is that he tried to apply a 'lesson' from this reform as being a blanket dogma in favour of free trade. He made no mention of how or why Britain became so dominant economically by the time of the Corn Laws and so misrepresented the lessons to be learnt (see *The Ponzi*

Class, pages 15 and 37). When he spoke of 'putting the consumer first', he ignored that consumers are also producers and therefore have an interest in ensuring a viable, successful industry and an interest in securing the tax revenues generated by a viable, successful industry.

Fox asserted that 'free trade forces businesses to innovate to compete'. As a point of fact, this is simplistic. The car producer British Leyland did not compete; it failed and was closed down, with the more attractive parts of the business ultimately falling into foreign ownership. Fox asserted: 'Free trade also allows markets to specialise in the production of goods where they have the greatest efficiency ... This process of specialisation means that global output increases and ultimately, we pay less at the checkouts for the products we actually want.' This is a theory, and in justifying the theory, Fox focused on 'global output increases' – not national increases in output nor increases in national standards of living. He is supposed to be representing British interests.

Fox was bold about his commitment to globalization. He said that Indian investment in the British car industry was beneficial for the Indian car sector and that British investment in India's chemical industry benefited British pharmaceutical firms: 'That is the glorious joy of free trade – it is not a zero-sum game, it really can be win-win.' Fox said that those living below the poverty line in India had fallen from 45% in 1993 to 22% in 2011. He said that it was 'no coincidence' that this was accompanied by India having 'embraced globalization and started to liberalise its economy'. This play on words does not assert, let alone prove, that India's improved standard of living is because of free trade or globalization. He ignored India's protectionist measures.

In an attempt to bolster his argument, Fox gave North and South Korea as an example. He described North Korea as a closed economy that had 'turned inwards'. He described South Korea as having 'embraced open trade and free markets'. In fact, North Korea is a communist state, and its backwardness is therefore inevitable. South Korea was determinedly protectionist until relatively recently. It was South Korea's protectionist economic policies that propelled that country to rapid industrialization and strong growth (see *The Ponzi Class*, page 261). Fox grossly misrepresented reality. This is the British trade secretary.

Fox drew a distinction between a 'general increase in prosperity' and those sectors that could not 'cope with competition', and he cautioned against 'pander[ing] to short-term protectionist instincts'. While it is true that consumers, with free trade, might have a choice of 'a greater range of goods and services at lower prices', that choice has to be paid for. A trade deficit has to be funded – either by borrowing from abroad or from selling national assets – and consumers are also producers and can find their wages lowered or find that they have lost their jobs as a result of globalization. Overseas producers may not have the regulatory costs or may be able to pay far lower wages; they may also be protectionist themselves and therefore be manipulating their currencies to give their producers an artificial advantage. For example, India unashamedly relies on coal regardless of climate change issues, China is manipulating its currency, and the one-size-fits-all euro artificially makes northern EU countries' goods cheaper and British goods more expensive than would otherwise be the case. The post-referendum boom in manufactured exports, for which the fall in the value of sterling has been credited, demonstrated the damage done to the British economy by this currency manipulation. Fox completely ignored this beyond saying: 'It is an insecurity that fuses together and is fed by a number of factors: new technologies that threaten long established industries; the social and economic impact of high levels of immigration and the fear that international trade means the export of jobs and an inability to compete.' Instead, he said that 'arguments against globalization and free trade will give rise to protectionist retrenchment with damaging economic consequences that future generations will have to endure'. The costs of mass immigration, for example, were ignored, as were the economic consequences of a trade deficit. While heaping praise on the North American Free Trade Agreement (NAFTA), Fox ignored the scale of the USA's trade deficit or the disquiet that NAFTA has caused in the USA. The newly elected President Trump could scarcely wait to renegotiate NAFTA, which he has described as a bad deal.

Fox continued to assert that 'barriers to trade raise prices' (as do all taxes on business and business regulations) and that protectionism might be a 'short-term vote winner or temporarily prop up failing industries' but that consumers 'lose out'. However, he made some concession to practicalities by saying: 'This is not however, to argue that temporary measures are never needed or that we should not take action against anti-market measures such as dumping where our own industry is threatened by uncompetitive behaviour.'

This anti-dumping sentence was quickly sidelined in Fox's speech when he claimed that WTO reports showed that G20 countries had become more protectionist since the 2008 recession. Fox said that although some of this was due to countries responding to 'unfair competition, such as dumping', nevertheless, 'the biggest economies need to lead by example' if there is to be a world of 'more open trade'. This is an important admission. Rather than ensuring that present trade deals are rolled over post-Brexit, with those countries neither in the EU or with whom Britain might wish to alter the trading relationship, or moving to agree free-trade deals with those countries that have already indicated that they would wish to do such deals (Australia, New Zealand, Canada, and the USA now that Trump has been elected), or signalling a determination to bring an end to the very large trade deficits with both China and the EU, Fox sees his role as to 'lead by example' for global free trade.

Fox said that the WTO had been a 'bedrock of the international trading system' and that Britain should work with the WTO to further reduce tariffs and 'axe red tape across borders'. Fox said that only 11% of British companies export, which was lower than other European countries. Fox pointed out that 'We also cannot leave our current account deficit, which currently stands at a record level of 5.4% of GDP, to be dealt with at some point in the future.' He therefore urged that Britain needed to improve productivity and said that 'We must also rebalance our economy through trade in a holistic way with exports, inward investment and overseas investment all playing a part.' This was no more than waffling.

For reasons set out in *The Ponzi Class*, the 'inward investment' – ie selling off assets to fund the trade deficit – merely perpetuates the trade deficit (*The Ponzi Class*, pages 254–258). This policy is a cause of the trade deficit, as it increases the value of sterling and so reduces the competitiveness of manufacturing, both in the home and export markets. The lessons of history show that tariffs will rebalance the economy and that rebalancing will lead to a boom as, finally, British industry will increase output to meet demand created by the tariffs increasing demand for British goods in the home market. The post-referendum surge in the exports of British manufactures due to the fall in the value of sterling shows the positive effects that tariffs would have.

The next major speech was May's speech to the Tory Party conference in October 2016. Much attention was heaped onto the speech, with even senior UKIP people breathless about it.

It would be churlish to deny that Theresa May did not make an effort to stamp a new ethos and approach onto the Tory Party following the EU referendum. She did not flinch from rooting out from the government some who deserved to go.

What is important with the speech is not what it said but what it did not say. The May Government's foot dragging regarding getting out of the EU had already infuriated many Leave voters and had already allowed the EU fanatics the time to regroup and begin their wrecking tactics. Progress was so slow that it was already doubtful even then whether anything resembling Brexit would actually be achieved.

The conference speech attracted so much attention because it seemingly told people what they wanted to hear. May wanted people to believe that she understood their angst. She dealt with this early on and said:

> 'In June people voted for change. And a change is going to come. Change has got to come because as we leave the European Union and take control of our own destiny, the task of tackling some of Britain's long-standing challenges – like how to train enough people to do the jobs of the future – becomes ever more urgent.
>
> But change has got to come too because of the quiet revolution that took place in our country just three months ago – a revolution in which millions of our fellow citizens stood up and said they were not prepared to be ignored anymore.'

To explain this 'revolution', May continued:

> 'The referendum was not just a vote to withdraw from the EU. It was about something broader – something that the European Union had come to represent. It was about a sense – deep, profound and let's face it often justified – that many people have today that the world works well for a privileged few, but not for them. It was a vote not just to change Britain's relationship with the European Union, but to call for a change in the way our country works – and the people for whom it works – forever. Knock on almost any door in almost any part of the country, and you will find the roots of the revolution laid bare.'

May said that 'Our society should work for everyone,' but this was not perceived to be so by those struggling to buy their own home, those who found their children in a bad school, or those who were struggling with a stagnant income. She further identified a perceived failure of democracy when people's complaints 'fall on deaf ears'. She continued:

> 'The roots of the revolution run deep. Because it wasn't the wealthy who made the biggest sacrifices after the financial crash, but ordinary, working class families. And if you're one of those people who lost their job, who stayed in work but on reduced hours, took a pay cut as household bills rocketed, or - and I know a lot of people don't like to admit this – someone who finds themselves out of work or on lower wages because of low-skilled immigration, life simply doesn't seem fair. It feels like your dreams have been sacrificed in the service of others. So change has got to come.'

May then said that there was 'unfairness all around', between an older generation and a younger one (an ominous comment), between London and other parts of the country, and between the rich and 'their fellow citizens'. For May, there needed to be a 'spirit of citizenship':

> 'That spirit that means you respect the bonds and obligations that make our society work. That means a commitment to the men and women who live around you, who work for you, who buy the goods and services you sell. That spirit that means recognising the social contract that says you train up local young people before you take on cheap labour from overseas. That spirit that means you do as others do, and pay your fair share of tax.
>   But today, too many people in positions of power behave as though they have more in common with international elites than with the people down the road, the people they employ, the people they pass in the street. But if you believe you're a citizen of the

world, you're a citizen of nowhere. You don't understand what the very word "citizenship" means.
So if you're a boss who earns a fortune but doesn't look after your staff...

An international company that treats tax laws as an optional extra...

A household name that refuses to work with the authorities even to fight terrorism...

A director who takes out massive dividends while knowing that the company pension is about to go bust...

I'm putting you on warning. This can't go on anymore.'

The point about those who consider themselves to be 'a citizen of the world' is valid. However, May's list of offenders completely excluded the entire state sector – for which May is directly responsible. She made no mention at all of, for example, civil servants, quangocrats, judges or politicians, who have a decisive influence on the problem she identified. May deftly redirected focus away from the most important members of the Ponzi class.

May averred that she intends to act: 'A plan that will mean government stepping up. Righting wrongs. Challenging vested interests. Taking big decisions. Doing what we believe to be right. Getting the job done.' This was nice-sounding, meaningless waffling. May continued:

'And to put the power of government squarely at the service of ordinary working-class people. Because too often that isn't how it works today. Just listen to the way a lot of politicians and commentators talk about the public. They find your patriotism distasteful, your concerns about immigration parochial, your views about crime illiberal, your attachment to your job security inconvenient. They find the fact that more than seventeen million voters decided to leave the European Union simply bewildering.'

May here identified a threat to the rule of political elites across the West. Liz Kendall, a Labour MP, had recently voiced an appreciation of this when she had said that there was a problem with the view of many ordinary people that the elites regarded them with contempt, that the problem had been there for a while and had now bubbled up with the Brexit vote and with Donald Trump.

May then declared that it was 'time to reject the ideological templates' of both 'the socialist left' and 'libertarian right' and 'embrace a new centre ground' with more government intervention 'to act on behalf of us all'. This would include a support of free markets but being prepared to intervene when they were not 'working as they should', as well as 'encouraging business and supporting free trade, but not accepting one set of rules for some and another for everyone else.' While May asserted that she wanted 'a confident global Britain that doesn't turn its back on globalization but ensures the benefits are shared by all,' she failed to see the nature of globalization or the flaws of unilateral free trade. Once again, the problems were swept under a carpet of platitudes.

Boldly, May committed 'to stop quibbling, respect what the people told us on the 23rd of June – and take Britain out of the European Union. Because it took that typically British quiet resolve for people to go out and vote as they did: to defy the establishment, to ignore the threats, to make their voice heard.' She then declared that it was time for 'that same resolve now' and that Article 50 would therefore be 'triggered no later than the end of March' and that there would be 'a Great Repeal Bill to get rid of the European Communities Act' introduced in the next session of Parliament, and hence, 'the authority of EU law in this country [would be] ended forever'. She did not make clear that the effect of the 'Great Repeal Bill' would be deferred until the negotiations triggered by Article 50 were successfully concluded. So the outcome of the Article 50 process, which requires *all* EU states and the EU parliament to agree, was a block on leaving the EU.

May said that the negotiations with the EU would be 'tough' and would 'require some give and take'. The agreement she sought would include:

> '... free trade, in goods and services. I want it to give British companies the maximum freedom to trade with and operate within the Single Market – and let European businesses do the same here. But let's state one thing loud and clear: we are not leaving the European Union only to give up control of immigration all over again. And we are not leaving only to return to the jurisdiction of the European Court of Justice. That's not going to happen.'

The problem with this is that it was too centred on free trade, and the commitment to have control over immigration is not the same as a commitment to end mass immigration. Nor was there any commitment to stop making payments to the EU – something that has remained on the agenda.

May betrayed her wet liberal leanings with her talk of 'a Global Britain' and that there will be no 'retreat from the world' – whatever that is supposed to mean. (This is a recurring theme of May's since becoming prime minister. Repeatedly, and especially when abroad, she has been forever on about Britain being open for business and of not retreating from the world. Her guilt complex has dominated her thinking.) In her speech she stated that Britain would 'forge a bold, new confident role ... on the world stage', would be 'keeping [its] promises to the poorest people in the world' and 'providing humanitarian support for refugees in need', would be 'cracking down on modern slavery' and be the 'strongest and most passionate advocate for free trade right across the globe'. This was important, as May defined Britain's ex-EU position in terms of giving money away in foreign aid, letting refugees into Britain (this was what she meant) and pursuing free trade as if it were a global system (which was delusional); this unilateral free-trade stance closes off any attempt to use Brexit to bring Britain's trade back into balance.

May identified 'structural problems' such as 'the shortage of affordable homes' and infrastructure, as well as a 'need to rebalance the economy across sectors and areas in order to spread wealth and prosperity around the country'. She spoke of 'a new industrial strategy' to support strategic industries, including finance, and to revive 'our great regional cities'. She spoke of correcting dysfunctional markets, giving the access to broadband as an example, and highlighted again the problem of housing:

> 'High housing costs – and the growing gap between those on the property ladder and those who are not – lie at the heart of falling social mobility, falling savings and low productivity.
>
> We will do everything we can to help people financially so they can buy their own home. That's why Help to Buy and Right to Buy are the right things to do. But as Sajid said in his bold speech on Monday, there is an honest truth we need to address. We simply need to build more homes.'

That was untrue. It is not simply a lack of house building that has led to the housing shortage, but the sheer scale of mass immigration that has created that shortage. It is noteworthy that May did not mention this at all. Also, were it not for the need to house all the immigrants, instead of packing people into affordable housing like sardines, we could have concentrated on better housing so that people had more space, privacy and nicer homes. May further stated:

> 'And I want us to be a country where it doesn't matter where you were born, who your parents are, where you went to school, what your accent sounds

like, what god you worship, whether you're a man or a woman, gay or straight, or black or white.'

This is all politically correct pap. May proceeded to highlight that she had introduced the 'first ever Modern Slavery Act' and restricted police stop and search by two thirds due to the 'disproportionate targeting of young, black men', and she gave several alleged examples of how discriminated against she considered ethnic minorities to be, notably: 'People in ethnic minority households are almost twice as likely to live in relative poverty as white people.' Consequently, she said:

> 'That's why I have launched an unprecedented audit of public services to shine a light on these racial disparities and let us do something about them. Because they are all burning injustices, and I want this government – this Conservative Government – to fight every single one of them.'

May continued, saying that she wanted a Britain based 'on merit not privilege' and 'when we overcome unfairness and injustice, we can build that new united Britain that we need', and this required government action 'identifying injustices, finding solutions, driving change. Taking, not shirking, the big decisions. Having the courage to see things through.'

This is political correctness – race war politics in particular. A very major reason why so many ethnic minorities in Britain are less wealthy than the indigenous British is because those ethnic minorities are also immigrant communities who have migrated to Britain from poorer parts of the world. It is therefore inevitable that they are less wealthy. This is not a 'burning injustice' of society for which the nasty white British nationals are to blame, but a direct and inevitable consequence of government immigration policy. It should also be noted that she was focused on 'relative poverty', not absolute poverty. May's proposed 'audit of public services' was simply a prelude to quotas and yet more anti-English ethnic cleansing.

Instead of wallowing in political correctness and race war politics, May would have been best advised to stop stirring up a sense of grievance and victimhood among her targeted minorities. She should not stir up anti-English hatred.

Of importance was also the Hammond speech at the conference, in which some points need highlighting. Hammond rehashed the failed Remain arguments of the referendum campaign:

> 'No ifs, no buts, no second referendums. We are leaving the European Union. But it is equally clear to me that the British people did not vote on June 23rd to become poorer, or less secure. So our task is clear: repatriate our sovereignty; control our borders; and seize the opportunities that the wider world has to offer……but do all of this while protecting our economy, our jobs and our living standards. The message may be simple, but the process will be complex. Successful negotiation with the EU27 will demand patience, experience, meticulous planning and steely resolution.'

And:

> 'But let me repeat the Prime Minister's pledge yesterday: As we negotiate our exit from the EU…… and our future relationship with it, this Government will fight for the best possible deal for British business and British workers. The best possible access to European markets for our manufacturing and services industries. And the best possible freedoms for our entrepreneurs and global exporters……ensuring Britain after Brexit will remain one of the best places in the world for a business to invest, to innovate and to grow.'

Hammond concluded his speech by asserting that 'we are not going to turn our backs on the nations of Europe' and that 'we will remain the best of neighbours' and 'the closest of trade associates' and 'the strongest of security partners'. He said that a future Britain would be 'attracting the brightest and the best', 'not a country turning inward' but 'reaching out'.

What should be noted here is that Hammond still saw the concept of leaving the EU in terms of problems and a threat to the economy. He further reiterated that he saw the issue as a long process (as he had stated to MPs in July), and that Britain would be seeking EU permission to leave. He saw Britain's future in terms of globalization.

Hammond hit the nail on the head by stressing Britain's low productivity: 'long-term sustainable growth requires us to raise our national productivity', which was not only lower than that of Germany and the USA, but also lower than that of France and Italy. This meant 'that millions of British workers are working longer hours for lower pay than their counterparts in Europe and the US', a situation Hammond said:

> 'That has to change if we are going to build an economy that works for everyone in Britain. If we raised our productivity by just 1% every year, within a decade we would add £250 billion to the size of our economy; £9,000 for every household in Britain.'

As an example of the changes ahead, in March 2017, a report from PwC predicted that robots will replace more than 10million workers over the next 15 years. Yet the impact of this new technology was ignored, as was the impact of immigration and its effect on productivity.

Having identified a key problem and the necessity of fixing it, Hammond failed to stress the need to end mass immigration, which reduces productivity (as firms prefer to hire cheap labour rather than modernize). He even went so far as to say that 'Quite simply, we're not building enough new homes. This is a long-term challenge.' After lobbing a few £billion at the problem, Hammond said: 'Making housing more affordable will be a vital part of building a country that works for everyone. And this Government is determined that the dream of home ownership should be for the many, not the few.' Of course, this is laudable, but Hammond missed the point that by flooding Britain with immigration, he then has to switch scarce resources away from investment elsewhere, such as manufacturing (which creates wealth), towards housing (which does not), and he advocated this despite also pointing out: 'The deficit remains unsustainable. And the decision to leave the EU has introduced new fiscal uncertainty. Last year, the government borrowed £1 in every £10 we spent.'

The May doctrine was repeated in her speech to the US Republicans in her visit to the USA in January 2017. In her speech, May quoted Churchill, someone President Trump greatly admires:

> 'We must never cease to proclaim in fearless tones the great principles of freedom and the rights of man which are the joint inheritance of the English-speaking world and which through Magna Carta, the Bill of Rights, the Habeas Corpus, trial by jury, and the English common law, find their most famous expression in the American Declaration of Independence.'

May said that this 'is something Britain has always understood'. She cited this understanding as to why Britain was the only G20 country apart from the USA that was spending 2% of GDP on defence and 0.7% of GDP on 'overseas development', why Britain was working to the defeat of ISIS, why Britain had sent troops to Estonia and Poland as a part of NATO, why Britain had troops deployed in various 'peacekeeping operations', and 'why Britain is leading the way in pioneering international efforts to crack down on modern slavery – one of the great scourges of our world – wherever it is found. I hope you will join us in that cause' – so-called modern slavery being a particular favourite topic of May's.

May asserted that the vote to leave the EU created 'the opportunity to reassert our belief in a confident, sovereign and global Britain, ready to build relationships with old friends and new allies alike'. May said that 'We will build a new partnership with our friends in Europe. We are not turning our back on them, or on the interests and the values that we share. It remains overwhelmingly in our interests – and in those of the wider world – that the EU should succeed.'

May believed that Britain's future would see 'us restore our parliamentary sovereignty and national self-determination, and to become even more global and internationalist in action and in spirit'. Britain would have control of its immigration policy and be free to make its own laws. But she emphasized that Britain would

> 'step up with confidence to a new, even more internationalist role, where we meet our responsibilities to our friends and allies, champion the international cooperation and partnerships that project our values around the world, and continue to act as one of the strongest and most forceful advocates for business, free markets and free trade anywhere around the globe.'

She regarded this as necessary due to the world being 'increasingly marked by instability and threats that risk undermining our way of life and the very things that we hold dear'.

Boldly, May said that 'One of the lessons of fighting terrorism in the last 15 years or so is yes, killing terrorists can save innocent lives. But until we kill the idea that drives them, the ideology, we will always have to live with this threat.' Given that the growth of terrorism is linked to the growth of Islam in the West, then this idea raised all sorts of implications. May pointed out that as the terrorists 'are defeated on the ground', they are 'exploiting the internet and social media to spread this ideology that is preying on vulnerable citizens in our own countries, inspiring them to commit acts of terror in our own cities'. This line portrays the terrorists as 'vulnerable citizens' who are preyed upon. More wisely, May did identify the ideology as 'the ideology of Islamist Extremism'. She said that she hoped to work with President Trump to defeat this 'evil'. However, May's determination was fleeting, as she continued:

> 'But of course, we should always be careful to distinguish between this extreme and hateful ideology, and the peaceful religion of Islam and the hundreds of millions of its adherents – including millions of our own citizens and those further afield who are so often the first victims of this ideology's terror. And nor is it enough merely to focus on violent extremism. We need to address the whole spectrum of extremism, starting with the bigotry and hatred that can so often turn to violence.'

This exonerated Islam itself for the terrorism, defining the religion as 'peaceful', which it is not, and by focusing on a sweeping 'whole spectrum of extremism, starting with the bigotry and hatred', May redirected the problem away from 'Islamist extremism' onto anyone who is deemed politically incorrect. She ignored culture totally. May wanted more international action to 'secure a political solution in Syria'.

May then promoted her commitment to globalization by saying:

> 'To deal with the threats of the modern world, we need to rebuild confidence in the institutions upon which we all rely. In part that means multinational institutions. Because we know that so many of the threats we face today – global terrorism, climate change, organized crime, unprecedented mass

movements of people – do not respect national borders. So we must turn towards those multinational institutions like the UN and NATO that encourage international cooperation and partnership.'

May did advocate that 'those multinational institutions' needed to work with the countries 'that formed them', as they had 'no democratic mandate of their own'. She said she shared the US's 'reform agenda' and hoped to work with the USA to make those institutions 'more relevant and purposeful than they are today'. She rightly said:

> 'Yet the most important institution is – and should always be – the nation state. Strong nations form strong institutions. And they form the basis of the international partnerships and cooperation that bring stability to our world. Nations, accountable to their populations – "deriving" as the Declaration of Independence puts it "their just powers from the consent of the governed" – can choose to join international organizations, or not. They can choose to cooperate with others, or not. Choose to trade with others, or not.'

Therefore, May was happy for the other EU countries to 'integrate further', as this is what they had chosen to do. Britain, she said, had 'chosen to take a different path', as Britain's 'history and culture is profoundly internationalist'. Britain had 'always looked beyond Europe to the wider world. We have ties of family, kinship and history to countries like India, Pakistan, Bangladesh, Australia, Canada, New Zealand, and countries across Africa, the Pacific and Caribbean.' Once again, this is a politically correct reworking of British history and a reworking of why Britain voted to leave the EU.

May ended on a globalist note, saying that globalization had left some people behind and that, in Britain, there would be reforms 'to ensure wealth and opportunity is spread across our land' so that those 'left behind' could see that 'free markets, free economies and free trade can deliver the brighter future they need. And it can maintain – indeed it can build – support for the rules-based international system on which the stability of our world continues to rely.' In saying this, May was contradicting President Trump's belief that bilateral deals are to be preferred, and she was pretending that there was a genuine global market with international institutions making decisions rather than national ones. This extreme globalization was neither necessary for free trade, nor was it what the British electorate voted for in the referendum. It further abdicated the May Government from responsibility for bringing Britain's trade with the EU into balance. May continued and said that the 'Global Britain that emerges after Brexit is even better equipped to take its place confidently in the world.' This commitment to globalization is a key part of Mayism, and May was strenuously reinterpreting the Leave vote to promote her vision of globalization.

Also in January 2017, May made a much-heralded speech about the government's policy on leaving the EU. This speech was very warmly received. In this long-awaited speech, May finally gave more detail of the government's policy. The speech was met with great approval from the media and those who wish to leave the EU – including UKIP.

Matthew Elliott, the chief executive of Vote Leave, tweeted: 'Superb speech from PM – everything we campaigned for @vote_leave. Inspiring vision for #GlobalBritain. Loved "Take Back Control" reference.' Nigel Farage, the former UKIP leader, tweeted: 'I can hardly believe that the PM is now using the phrases and words that I've been mocked for using for years. Real progress.' Suzanne Evans, a former UKIP leadership candidate and someone not in the Faragist wing of UKIP, said:

> 'I was chuckling at some of it, to be honest, it seemed as if she was channelling UKIP. There were various phrases there that I've used myself again and again,

and I think her 12 priorities were all extremely sound, good priorities for a proper 'clean' or what some people called 'hard' Brexit – I overwhelmingly welcome the speech.'

Some in Labour described May's proposals as 'Soft Brexit'.

In fact, the speech revealed that May's political correctness steadily guides her approach – as does her obsession with free trade. Furthermore, she advanced a rationale very similar to Osborne's when he was trying to frighten voters to vote Remain in the referendum (for example, in the second Treasury report, Osborne aligned a Remain vote with 'a country that faces out to the world' rather than 'retreating from the world' and that 'Openness to trade and investment will be a key driver of the UK's future economic security'). At the UN, May deployed a similar argument and continued to do so and did so again in this speech – *that is because she is a Remainer and sees things from a Remain point of view*. She does not understand the case for Brexit.

Throughout her speech, May ladled on her belief in globalism. She started in the third sentence: 'They voted to leave the European Union and embrace the world,' in reference to the referendum vote. In another example, she said that 'It was the moment we chose to build a truly Global Britain.' May explained the Leave victory in the referendum as 'not simply because our history and culture is profoundly internationalist, important though that is,' but also because 'Many in Britain have always felt that the United Kingdom's place in the European Union came at the expense of our global ties, and of a bolder embrace of free trade with the wider world,' and she said that the vote was 'a vote to restore, as we see it, our parliamentary democracy, national self-determination, and to become even more global and internationalist in action and in spirit.' This rewriting of history is telling. People did not vote Leave because they wanted more globalization. They were motivated by a rejection of it and were concerned about more down-to-earth issues. As the Lord Ashcroft research disclosed (see above), even the Remain voters were evenly split regarding globalization, and the Leave voters regarded it as a something bad. The Leave voters further rejected multiculturalism and political correctness.

Correctly, May pointed out that Britain should take: 'the opportunity of this great moment of national change to step back and ask ourselves what kind of country we want to be'. Leaving the EU gives Britain the opportunity to tackle its problems. But May ignored this:

> 'I want this United Kingdom to emerge from this period of change stronger, fairer, more united and more outward-looking than ever before. I want us to be a secure, prosperous, tolerant country – a magnet for international talent and a home to the pioneers and innovators who will shape the world ahead. I want us to be a truly Global Britain – the best friend and neighbour to our European partners, but a country that reaches beyond the borders of Europe too. A country that goes out into the world to build relationships with old friends and new allies alike. I want Britain to be what we have the potential, talent and ambition to be. A great, global trading nation that is respected around the world and strong, confident and united at home.'

This might all sound nice, with lots of talk of being global, but it is meaningless. There was no mention of the size of the trade deficit (a problem totally ignored in the speech, not even being mentioned once, despite the EU's responsibility for a great part of it), of ending mass immigration, or of the need to free Britain from other damaging entities such as the human rights courts and legislation. Leaving the EU gives Britain the opportunity to negotiate a trade deal that would end the trade deficit with the EU, but May did not even see that as an aim. She did mention that the government would get its spending deficit down and spend more on infrastructure as it did so. In fact, the deficit was likely to stay high, and the government was actually increasing it above the level planned by the previous chancellor, George Osborne.

May claimed that Britain's historical global aspirations are 'why we are one of the most racially diverse countries in Europe, one of the most multicultural members of the European Union'. In fact, Britain is 'racially diverse' etc due to the unwillingness of successive British governments to stop the ever-increasing scale of immigration despite the firm opposition to mass immigration from ordinary people. Multiculturalism has been imposed on the British public and is not something they have ever voted for.

May set out twelve objectives:

- Certainty
- Control of our own laws
- Strengthen the Union
- Maintain the Common Travel Area with Ireland
- Control immigration
- Rights for EU nationals in Britain and British nationals in the EU
- Protect workers' rights
- Free trade with European markets
- New trade arrangements with other countries
- The best place for science and innovation
- Cooperation in the fight against crime and terrorism
- A smooth, orderly Brexit

May rightly promised to 'convert the "acquis" – the body of existing EU law – into British law' (after which it can be reviewed and amended/repealed at leisure) and that the outcome of the deal negotiated would be put to a vote in parliament.

May said that in the future, laws would be made in 'Westminster, Edinburgh, Cardiff and Belfast', that there was 'a Joint Ministerial Committee on EU Negotiations, so ministers from each of the UK's devolved administrations can contribute to the process of planning for our departure from the European Union', that there had already been a paper from the Scottish Government', and that the government expected 'a paper from the Welsh Government shortly'. She also said that the government looked 'forward to working with the administrations in Scotland, Wales and Northern Ireland to deliver a Brexit that works for the whole of the United Kingdom'. She promised that the government would work 'very carefully to ensure that – as powers are repatriated from Brussels back to Britain – the right powers are returned to Westminster, and the right powers are passed to the devolved administrations of Scotland, Wales and Northern Ireland'.

There was no mention of the English or English interests. There was no commitment to seeing power devolved to an English parliament, despite the fact that the English are funding the whole of Britain. May saw nothing wrong with anti-English discrimination and did not even mention the issue, simply taking it for granted as a normality.

The speech did nothing to reassure voters that mass immigration would end. May boldly asserted that 'We will continue to attract the brightest and the best to work or study in Britain – indeed openness to international talent must remain one of this country's most distinctive assets' and that 'we will always want immigration'. Instead, there was a sop:

> 'In the last decade or so, we have seen record levels of net migration in Britain, and that sheer volume has put pressure on public services, like schools, stretched our infrastructure, especially housing, and put a downward pressure on wages for working class people. As Home Secretary for six years, I know that you cannot control immigration overall when there is free movement to Britain from Europe.'

As home secretary, May did virtually nothing to curtail either legal or illegal immigration. Immigration was at record levels, with roughly 650,000 pouring in each year. The government had even been using the Royal Navy to ferry illegal immigrants across the Mediterranean and had recently been searching Europe for, and bringing into Britain, mature, if not middle-aged, men who claimed to be child minors. May made no commitment that anything would change.

May did rule out continuing membership of the EU Single Market. Although this was seen as radical, in fact, it was simply what people had voted for in June 2016 (both sides of the referendum campaign admitted that a vote to leave would mean leaving the Single Market). Instead, May promised to 'pursue a bold and ambitious Free Trade Agreement with the European Union' that would give Britain tariff-free access to the Single Market 'on a fully reciprocal basis'. Since the Remain case was that we needed to stay in the Single Market in order to benefit from the completion of the Single Market regarding services, which was supposedly where Britain had a competitive advantage, then we did not have free trade 'on a fully reciprocal basis' now, but only in goods, where the EU has a competitive advantage (this is the Remain's own logic, and it is logic that the May Government has eagerly adopted).

There was no commitment to dealing with the unfair advantage that the Northern European countries have, in particular Germany, due to, for them, the undervalued euro. There was no commitment to bring trade with the EU back into balance, nor any evidence that the May Government even grasped the importance of this issue. This was a serious defect in the government strategy. It would also affect the trade in services. Furthermore, although May said that Britain would no longer 'contribute huge sums to the EU budget' and that 'the days of Britain making vast contributions to the European Union every year will end'. They key term was 'will end'. This was something that might happen some date in the future – if the May Government did not cave in. It should be noted that May did commit to 'make an appropriate contribution' for specific programmes with which Britain might wish to stay involved.

May enthused about free trade, saying that a 'Global Britain' must enter into 'trade agreements' with countries across the world. She cited China, Brazil, the Gulf States and India, as well as Britain's daughter nations of Australia, New Zealand and Canada and the USA (our American cousins), which was now keen to strike a trade deal as soon as possible. May bemoaned that since joining the EU, trade as a percentage of GDP for Britain has 'broadly stagnated' and stated the need for Britain to 'rediscover its role as a great, global trading nation'. To enter into free trade deals with Third World countries would be ruinous, given their much lower wages, living standards and scant levels of regulation, and any such deals would need to be approached cautiously. A free-trade deal with the communist, protectionist China would not be worth the paper it was written on. There was already a whopping trade deficit between Britain and China. The statistic about trade as a percentage of GDP was irrelevant. What mattered was the growth rate of the British economy, which would be determined by the competitiveness of British manufacturing and its ability to successfully thrive, primarily in the home market. Britain was the superpower of the 19th century because it was a great manufacturing nation. It was the competitiveness of British industry that was the source of British economic power and the engine for the increase in living standards.

In order to avoid a 'cliff-edge' when leaving the EU (the term 'freedom' would be more accurate), May proposed that:

> 'We believe a phased process of implementation, in which both Britain and the EU institutions and member states prepare for the new arrangements that will exist between us will be in our mutual self-interest ... This might be about our immigration controls, customs systems or the way in which we cooperate on criminal justice matters. Or it might be about the future legal and regulatory framework for financial services. For each issue, the time we need to

phase-in the new arrangements may differ. Some might be introduced very quickly, some might take longer. And the interim arrangements we rely upon are likely to be a matter of negotiation. But the purpose is clear: we will seek to avoid a disruptive cliff-edge, and we will do everything we can to phase in the new arrangements we require as Britain and the EU move towards our new partnership.'

It should be noted that these were Remain arguments. The whole approach was that leaving the EU would be detrimental. That leaving would be a change for the better was absent from the rationale. Furthermore, the opening proposal was that Britain, having spent from June 2016 to March 2017 doing nothing other than consider what it might want to do, would then spend two years in negotiations, which may or may not even result in an agreement, before putting anything agreed on to not only the British parliament but also all the other EU parliaments, including the European parliament, who can veto the deal; then, after all that, it was proposed that there should be an interim period before the vote of June 2016 is finally honoured. This interim period could be many years. In the meantime, there would not only be elections in Britain, but also across the EU and its 27 member states; and importantly, the 'vast contributions to the European Union every year' would continue, the flood of immigrants would continue to pour in, EU laws would continue to be enforced upon Britain, Britain's fishing grounds would continue to be plundered by foreign fishing vessels, and the balance of trade deficit would continue to balloon. And this was May's ideal! From this ideal position, as is the nature in negotiations, there would be compromises, fudges and sell-outs. May's opening stance was a losing position – especially so given her desperation to reach a free-trade deal with the EU. That desperation put the EU in a strong position. Revealingly, May said:

'Trade is not a zero sum game: more of it makes us all more prosperous. Free trade between Britain and the European Union means more trade, and more trade means more jobs and more wealth creation. The erection of new barriers to trade, meanwhile, means the reverse: less trade, fewer jobs, lower growth.'

This was a simplistic presentation of 19th century free-trade *theories*. It is not automatic that free trade increases more growth, jobs or wealth creation. In practice, there is a balance to be struck between free trade and a degree of protectionism. The question is: does Britain have the right balance? The scale of, and reasons for, the continuing balance of trade deficits with both the EU and China proves that it does not. Britain cannot continue selling off assets and borrowing to fund its trade deficit, and it needs a strategy to pay for imported goods by selling exported goods. Selling more British goods in the British home market would be the key part of this long-overdue correction. Interestingly, May pointed out that a failure to reach a deal with the EU 'would risk exports from the EU to Britain worth around £290 billion every year'.

May concluded her speech by saying 'when future generations look back at this time, they will judge us not only by the decision that we made, but by what we made of that decision'.

This speech was followed up by a white paper in February 2017 which formally restated the issues set out in May's speech. In the forward, May stated that 'We do not approach these negotiations expecting failure, but anticipating success. Because we are a great, global nation with so much to offer Europe and so much to offer the world' and that her aim was 'Not merely forming a new partnership with Europe, but building a stronger, fairer, more Global Britain too.' (To avoid repetition, a full analysis of the white paper 'The United Kingdom's exit from and new partnership with the European Union' is at Appendix A.)

The white paper for the Great Repeal Bill was submitted to Parliament in March 2017. In the forward, written by May, the white paper stated that the government sought certainty 'as we negotiate a new deep and special partnership with the European Union'. This was not what the people voted for. We voted to leave.

The white paper was dishonest regarding leaving the EU when it stated: 'Article 50 is the only legal route by which we can leave the EU. It sets out that the UK has two years to negotiate a withdrawal agreement with the EU, after which our membership of the EU will end unless an extension is agreed with the European Council.' By this logic, prior to the invention of Article 50, it was impossible to leave the EU. In fact, there are agreed international rules (the Vienna Convention on the Law of Treaties) for the termination of a treaty (which can be achieved by giving as little as three months' notice), and the British Parliament always has the right to repeal legislation. It is only the repeal of the 1972 European Communities Act that will get Britain out of the EU. Article 50 is a process intended to keep the EU in charge and to require the country that wishes to leave to ask permission to do so. The white paper was clear that the government 'will continue to negotiate, implement and apply EU law' until Britain has exited.

As a former world power with an empire, Britain should be experienced in how a nation state can establish sovereignty and how to grant independence. Britain granted independence to its colonies far more quickly than apparently we are given to understand it is possible to leave the EU, and the issues of decolonization were immeasurably more complex. Another useful comparison is the dissolution of the Soviet Union, which had its own version of Article 50 – Article 72 – including a law 'On the procedure for resolution of issues in connection with a withdrawal of a Union republic from the USSR.'[4] The process was for there to be a referendum in the 'member state', after which it would notify the Supreme Soviet of the Union, which would then refer the matter to the Congress of People's Deputies, who would then set up a transitional period of up to five years 'to resolve the issues arising in connection with the withdrawal of the Republic from the USSR'. USSR law would continue to be enforced during the transitional period.[5]

Within two years of this law being passed, all 15 Soviet Republics had withdrawn from the USSR, and *not one of them* followed the procedure. All 15 republics made a Unilateral Declaration of Independence by passing a motion in their own parliaments and withdrew unconditionally. The USSR made threats, objected and demanded that if necessary, there should be an 'amicable divorce' by following the procedure. The USSR's objections and threats were ignored.[6]

The white paper itself acknowledged that it is only by repealing the 1972 Act that Britain can leave the EU:

> 'The Great Repeal Bill will do three main things:
> a. First, it will repeal the ECA and return power to UK institutions.
> b. Second, subject to the detail of the proposals set out in this White Paper, the Bill will convert EU law as it stands at the moment of exit into UK law before we leave the EU. This allows businesses to continue operating knowing the rules have not changed significantly overnight, and provides fairness to individuals, whose rights and obligations will not be subject to sudden change. It also ensures that it will be up to the UK Parliament (and, where appropriate, the devolved legislatures) to amend, repeal or improve any piece of EU law (once it has been brought into UK law) at the appropriate time once we have left the EU.
> c. Finally, the Bill will create powers to make secondary legislation. This will enable corrections to be made to the laws that would otherwise no longer operate appropriately once we have left the EU, so that our legal system continues to function correctly outside the EU, and will also enable domestic law

once we have left the EU to reflect the content of any withdrawal agreement under Article 50.'

The white paper continued:

> 'The ECA gives effect in UK law to the EU treaties. It incorporates EU law into the UK domestic legal order and provides for the supremacy of EU law. It also requires UK courts to follow the rulings of the Court of Justice of the European Union (CJEU) ... As a first step, it is important to repeal the ECA to ensure there is maximum clarity as to the law that applies in the UK, and to reflect the fact that following the UK's exit from the EU it will be UK law, not EU law, that is supreme. The Bill will repeal the ECA on the day we leave the EU.'

Of course, the day Britain leaves the EU has been delayed by the May Government. Were the repeal of the 1972 Act to be done immediately rather than delayed, then Britain would leave immediately. It is only by repealing the 1972 Act that Britain ends 'the supremacy of EU law' and leaves the EU.

The Great Repeal Bill was intended to remove the EU's Charter of Fundamental Rights from British law, and tellingly, it promised: 'The ECHR is an instrument of the Council of Europe, not of the EU. The UK's withdrawal from the EU will not change the UK's participation in the ECHR and there are no plans to withdraw from the ECHR.' The May Government remained committed to the ECHR.

SUMMARY

The Ponzi Class examined the evolution and impact of the policy of globalization and political correctness upon society, primarily from Britain's perspective. The turmoil of the EU referendum out of which the May Government emerged was an opportunity for change. There was a chance that the ideological obsessions causing Britain's decline – as well as the decline of the West – might be confronted. They have not been.

Despite what May herself might choose to dismiss, there is something describable as Mayism. Mayism is distinct. An examination of May's speeches to the United Nations, her conference speech, her speech to American Republicans, her speech setting out her approach to Brexit as well as the two attendant white papers demonstrated that May is a politically-correct globalist. She is not a patriot. She has been consistent. Accompanying speeches from Fox and Hammond endorsed the May stance and proved that the Tory Party as a whole has remained firmly committed to the policies of globalization and political correctness. This commitment was the opposite of what people voted for in the referendum and the opposite of what was needed to resolve the underlying problems bedevilling Britain. A responsible prime minister would have accepted the referendum vote and united the country behind a new policy of patriotism and a rejection of globalization. The Ashcroft poll revealed that even half of the Remain voters opposed globalization, in addition to the overwhelming majority of Leave voters.

May's career has been unremarkable. She has made a few abrasive comments and has been steadily politically correct. As home secretary, she talked occasionally and did little. On immigration, there was the odd speech of the need to control it, followed by inaction. As prime minister, she has proceeded in the same manner. She announced that 'Brexit means Brexit' and then did nothing for 12 months. It was not until June 2017 that the May Government embarked upon the Article 50 negotiations, the first act of which was to capitulate and agree that there should be no negotiations on the future trading arrangements until Britain had got the EU's permission to leave; this permission depended upon paying up to £80billion or so.

The May Government's handling of the referendum vote was the product of both May's and her minister's globalism and political correctness. To them, the restoration of British national sovereignty was something bad and to be avoided. May herself was deft in her method of steering the Brexit process in a globalist direction. She pronounced that the British felt constrained by the EU and wanted more globalization. May was resolute in her determination to continue giving away taxpayer's monies in foreign aid despite knowing how unpopular that was. She continued to advocate international rights ('universal values that we share together').

Regarding immigration, May told the UN that she wanted some changes in 'a managed and controlled international response' to the present difficulties with mass migration and that she rejected 'isolationism and xenophobia'. She did not intend to deal with mass immigration to Britain by adopting policies to end it. She transferred the issue to international bodies and the need for international agreements, and she advocated more globalization as a solution to problems caused by globalization ('action must be more global, not less. Because the biggest threats to our prosperity and security do not recognise or respect international borders ... So this is not a time to turn away from our United Nations. It is a time to turn to it'). She repeated this line in her speech to the US Republicans.

May was not alone in her globalism. The Tories revelled in it. As trade secretary, Liam Fox positively advocated free trade, irrespective of the honesty and reliability of the states he was keen to do deals with. He lauded China as an example of a country succeeding due to free trade. This is a travesty of the truth – as is his comparison between North and South Korea. Fox did not see his role as to ensure that present arrangements with countries across the world would continue and that they would continue to trade with Britain on the same terms – irrespective of whether Britain is in the EU or in the WTO. He saw his role as to 'lead by example' for global free trade.

Free trade is only a theory, and only a particularly flimsy theory would be based on historical misrepresentations and be unable to be modified to take account of the reality of both the EU's and China's protectionist endeavours. Britain needs more than Fox's globalist planetary pretensions and a flimsy theory to tackle its problems.

Fox noticed that Britain had a major trade deficit, but he failed to offer a solution beyond saying that Britain needed to improve productivity and that we needed to 'rebalance our economy through trade in a holistic way with exports, inward investment and overseas investment all playing a part'. Such waffling was as much a cop-out as it was nonsense. It was meaningless. Britain has a massive trade deficit with both the EU and China, both of which are manipulating their currencies to the disadvantage of others. The USA was alert to this (although President Trump has yet to act), but Britain was in denial. An imposition of tariffs would solve the problem. In a triumph of dogma over practical common sense, Fox and the May Government refused to contemplate this.

May made a memorable speech to the Tory conference in which she condemned those she said considered themselves to be 'citizens of the world' ('if you believe you're a citizen of the world, you're a citizen of nowhere. You don't understand what the very word "citizenship" means'). While this met with widespread adulation, what those gushing over it missed was that to May, those who were guilty of regarding themselves as 'citizens of the world' excluded the state sector. Deftly, she redirected public anger that she had noticed expressed in the Brexit vote away from the prime culprits. This was a major success for the Ponzi class, as they escaped criticism for what they had done and intended to continue to do – as would soon be seen.

Fatally, May decided not only to embrace Article 50, rather than simply leave, but also set the goal as being to try and forge some sort of new partnership with the EU. This put the government in a losing position, as it was then dependent upon a deal with the EU – to which the EU was unlikely to agree. It further guaranteed a long, drawn-out process. May compounded this with a multitude of promises of interim deals, transition periods, exemptions etc. With a stated aim of a 'Global Britain', May manoeuvred Brexit opinion behind her losing position. Amazingly, May had full UKIP endorsement for her manoeuvrings and redefinition of Brexit. UKIP confined itself to making the odd comment about holding May's feet to the fire over Brexit if she did not deliver. If fact, if they meant business, then May's feet would already have been so deep into the fire that they would be able to hear her howling in Vladivostok; in fact, the residents should have been complaining about the noise.

May has been politically correct throughout her political career. It was she who coined the phrase 'the nasty party' to summarize what she said people thought of the Tories. It was she who embraced the so-called Equality Act introduced by Labour. Now, as prime minister, May pursued a politically correct agenda openly and even at the Tory conference. She alleged that ethnic minority households were more likely to be 'in relative poverty' than white ones and announced that there would be 'an unprecedented audit of public services to shine a light on racial disparities' that she described as 'burning injustices'. This was pure race war politics.

Of great significance, in both her speech on government EU policy and in the white paper on Brexit, May set obtaining a free trade deal with the EU as an aim, while bringing trade with the EU back into balance was not. This was as incredible as it was ruinous.

For all her talk about fairness, May saw nothing unfair in being openly willing to involve the devolved administrations in Scotland, Wales and Northern Ireland in the Brexit process – but not the English. May saw nothing wrong with the English being second-class citizens in their own country. Like her predecessor, May saw no need for an English parliament. This would soon prove vital.

PART FOUR

THE JUNE 2017 GENERAL ELECTION

Despite repeatedly ruling out an early general election, on April 18, 2017, May called an early general election. May said in a speech to the press outside No 10: 'At this moment of enormous national significance there should be unity here in Westminster, but instead there is division. The country is coming to together, but Westminster is not.' She continued: 'Our opponents believe the government's majority is so small that our resolve will weaken and that they can force us to change course. They are wrong.' May said that Labour had threatened to vote against the final Brexit deal, that the Liberal Democrats had threatened to 'grind the business of government to a standstill', and that 'unelected members' of the House of Lords had 'vowed to fight us every step of the way'.

A snap poll gave the Tories a 21-point lead over Labour. Such a lead would increase the May Government's working majority in the House of Commons from 17 to more than 140.

The campaign focused on May and denigrated Corbyn. Tory candidates were instructed by Central Office that every poster must include the slogan 'Standing with Theresa May'. A Tory source said that voters needed to be reminded as to the choice of who would be prime minister. By comparison, many Labour candidates were refusing to say whether Corbyn would be mentioned on their campaign literature at all.

Brexit, at the start, was a major issue. The campaign was described as the Brexit general election. The Tories emphasized the need for stability with a slogan 'Strong and Stable', as opposed to the alternative 'Coalition of Chaos' prospects under a Labour government. May was presented as someone fit to negotiate a Brexit deal, whereas Corbyn was presented by the Tories as someone unfit for high office.

The EU continued to cause trouble. Before the election was called, the EU was steadily ramping up the pressure and the demands it was making. On April 5, the Spanish warship Infanta Christina, which had sailed well into Gibraltar's territorial waters, had to be challenged by the British patrol boat HMS Scimitar before leaving. The EU had recently agreed to give Spain a veto on any Brexit deal. The next day, a photograph emerged showing a Spanish policeman at the crossing into Gibraltar waving a handgun. The Royal Gibraltar Police were reportedly investigating the incident, which occurred when the Spanish started carrying out extensive passport checks. Those at the normally free-flowing border experienced up to five-hour delays as a result. The German MEP Manfred Weber, a close ally of Frau Merkel, said: 'Let me say to people of Spain and Ireland, you will not have to deal with London alone. Irish and Spanish interests are European interests.'

It was leaked to a German newspaper that Juncker and May had had a bad-tempered dinner at No 10. Allegedly, Juncker had told May that 'Brexit cannot be a success' and subsequently had told Frau Merkel that May was 'living in a different galaxy'. Of the disputed dinner, May said: 'During the Conservative Party leadership campaign, I was described by one of my colleagues as a bloody difficult woman. And I said at the time the next person to find that out will be Jean-Claude Juncker.' Guy Verhofstadt said: 'Any Brexit deal requires a strong and stable understanding of the complex issues involved. The clock is ticking – it's time to get real.'

On May 4, May decided to speak out. She said:

> 'Threats against Britain have been issued by European politicians and officials. All of these acts have been deliberately timed to affect the result of the general election ... Whatever our wishes, and however reasonable the positions of Europe's other leaders – there are some in Brussels who do not want these

talks to succeed. Who do not want Britain to prosper. So now more than ever we need to be led by a prime minister and a government that is strong and stable.'

The EU's attacks stopped.

The local election results went well for the Tories and reinforced the sense of Tory supremacy. The Tories gained an extra 563 councillors and 11 councils. UKIP, whose voters the Tories coveted, bombed. UKIP lost 145 councillors and only got one elected. Arron Banks said that UKIP needed 'a strategic bullet to the back of the head'. He added:

> 'If we use the analogy of UKIP as a racing car, Nigel [Farage] was a skilled driver who drove the car around the track faster and faster, knowing when to take risks, delighting the audience. The current leadership has crashed the car at the first bend ... UKIP under the current leadership, without positive radical policies, is finished as an electoral force.'

Arron Banks had for some time been trying to muscle into becoming chairman of UKIP as an alternative to starting his own political party with Nigel Farage.

Cameron said that May needed a large majority to take on the Brexiteers: 'This is one of the most defining elections I can remember where it's so important the Conservatives win and win well so Theresa can negotiate that deal and stand up to people who want an extreme Brexit.' Ruth Davidson had made a similar comment, that the purpose of the election was to give May a big enough majority that she could ignore the so-called hard Brexiteers.

The opinion polls remained favourable to the Tories. A YouGov survey for *The Financial Times* revealed that around 60% of those who backed Brexit planned to vote Tory. Furthermore, only 22% of voters wanted to stay in the EU while 68% wanted the government to complete Brexit. Support for Remain had collapsed from its 48% referendum high.

Then the Tories launched their manifesto. Unlike the Labour manifesto, which contained a number of populist pledges, in particular to abolish tuition fees for students, the Tory one offered more austerity, political correctness, and hid behind the 'Strong and Stable' slogan. The Tories announced the abolition of free school meals for those aged four to seven, but also announced that every primary school pupil would have access to a breakfast club at school. They ignored that mothers preferred to have free school lunches and get their own children's breakfast. Cost saving was cited as justification for the change. (A full response to the manifesto is in Appendix B).

Worse, the Tories launched a three-pronged assault on pensioners: the end of the triple lock on pensions, a means-testing of winter fuel payments, and a death tax to fund social care that become known as a dementia tax.

Of the proposed move away from a triple lock for pensioners to a double lock, the IFS said: 'Getting rid of the 2.5 per cent element of the triple lock does little to change the projected long-run generosity of the state pension.'

The means-testing of the winter fuel allowance did not extend to Scotland on the basis that Scotland was colder. Scottish pensioners would not face cuts in the winter fuel allowance.

Regarding the dementia tax, Damian Green said on the Andrew Marr Show: 'We have set out this policy which we're not going to look at again.' Jeremy Hunt stated that the idea of any cap on costs was being dropped: 'Not only are we dropping it ahead of a general election and we're being completely explicit in our manifesto that we're dropping it. We're dropping it because we've looked again at this proposal and we don't think it's fair.'

The new policy increased the threshold fourfold, to £100,000, beyond which people needed to pay. But this now also applied to those needing care in their own homes and not just residential care home costs. Furthermore, there was no cap on the costs. Some Tories argued that it was not only right that the government 'allowed' people to keep £100,000 of their wealth, but also that it was right that they should lose everything else.

Of the proposed dementia tax, Sir Andrew Dilnot said:

> 'People will be left helpless knowing that what will happen is, if they're unlucky enough to suffer the need for care costs, they'll be entirely on their own until they're down to the last £100,000, all of their wealth including their house. If the Tories get into power, we're going to end up with a world where we have a sort of inheritance tax that is social care specific, so if you're unlucky enough to get dementia, all of your accumulated wealth will be taken away.'

The Dilnot Commission into the care home charges (those getting care in their own homes would continue to get that care for free) recommended a cap of £35,000, along with a £100,000 threshold below which people would pay nothing. The aim was to lessen the practice of councils seizing pensioners' homes should they need to be admitted into a care home. The estimated cost was only an extra £1.7billion (see *The Ponzi Class*, page 295, to see how the Tories ratted on a previous manifesto commitment on this issue).

According to the Alzheimer's Society, the costs of dementia would require the saving of £800 per year for 125 years. On average, dementia patients live for five years. The Alzheimer's Society based their analysis on a cost of three years of care at home of about £39,000 and another two years in a care home of about £62,000.

While the costs to ordinary people were substantial, the monies needed to resolve the problem were comparatively puny compared to the May Government's extravagance elsewhere (such as foreign aid). With the Local Government Association estimating that another £2.6billion was needed by 2020, and the IPPR estimating that another £13billion would be needed by 2030, dealing with these shortfalls – even if they are underestimates – was well within the government's means. But the Tories were obsessed with their new 'intergenerational fairness' discovery.

As the polls slipped and with adverse feedback on the doorstep, with advice from the campaign strategist Sir Lynton Crosby (who was carrying out his own research as to voter reaction), and with three Cabinet ministers privately threatening to go public with their concerns about the dementia tax, May announced that the planned reforms would include a cap of some description, about which there would be consultations. May denied that this was a change. 'Strong and Stable' had become 'Weak and Wobbly'. Hunt now said:

> 'We want to make sure that people who have worked hard and saved up all their lifetimes do not have to worry about losing all their assets through a disease as random as dementia. That's why we want to introduce an absolute limit on the amount of money anyone has to pay for their care.'

At a press conference, May declared: 'Nothing has changed. Nothing has changed. We are offering a long-term solution for the sustainability of social care for the future.' Days later, in a live debate with voters on Sky News, May said: 'I want to take that risk away, ensuring no one will have to sell their house to pay for care in their lifetime and ensure they can have protected at least £100,000.' She further explained: 'I saw a lot of scaremongering and recognised there would be a lot of worry, and clarified that there would be a cap.'

On Monday, May 29, it was reported in the *Daily Mail*:

> 'May will today attempt to relaunch the Tory election campaign amid fears Labour could be about to take the lead in the polls. The Prime Minister will return to the campaign trail with a promise to protect the child victims of domestic violence ... May will unveil proposals to appoint a domestic violence

commissioner to stand up for victims and hold the police and criminal justice system to account.'

With a promise of longer sentences for offenders, May was quoted as promising: 'We will launch a relentless drive to help survivors find justice and increase the number of successful prosecutions.'

The Tories had overlooked the fact that Corbyn, as he had demonstrated with his initial election to be leader of the Labour Party and with the subsequent contest against a challenger that he had won easily, was an accomplished campaigner. He was at his best when out campaigning. Now he was in his element again, with a popular manifesto to promote. But all was not plain sailing, as Labour figures, in particular Dianne Abbott, repeatedly did not know the costs of their array of promises.

Corbyn himself came unstuck in a radio interview with Emma Bennett in which he was unable to explain the costs of Labour's childcare policy. Bennett was subjected to internet abuse from Corbyn supporters. She was branded a 'Zionist shill' and a 'Zionist Torygraph writer' writing 'Zionist drivel' and likened to Miss Piggy.

The Tories accused the BBC of anti-Tory bias after a live debate took place in front of noisy left-wing audience. The BBC denied the charge and insisted that the audience had been balanced between the parties. Rumours circulated that Corbyn supporters had got into the audience by calling themselves Tories, and so the audience had been swamped with ardent leftists.

When pressed on the issue of immigration, May's response was to stick to making a promise to reduce it to the tens of thousands at some unspecified date in the future. When asked if what Brandon Lewis, the policing minister, had said was correct, when he had stated that net immigration would be reduced to the tens of thousands by 2022, May responded: 'That's what we are working for. We're working to bring immigration down to the tens of thousands. But having been Home Secretary for six years this isn't something that you can just produce the magic bullet that suddenly does everything. What you have to do is keep working at it.'

The campaign was shockingly disrupted by Islamist terrorism in Manchester and then in London. These two attacks came after an earlier one on March 22, when Khalid Masood drove a hired car onto the pavement and into pedestrians on Westminster Bridge, killing five people and injuring another 50, before running towards Parliament, where he stabbed and killed a police officer. He was shot dead by the police. In Manchester, on May 22, Salman Ramadan Abedi, a suicide bomber, killed 22 people and injured another 59 at the Manchester Arena at a concert of the American singer Ariana Grande. Then there was an attack by three Islamists on London Bridge, who drove a white van into pedestrians before jumping out armed with knives and attacking people. Seven people were killed, and 48 injured. The terrorists were shot dead.

Corbyn made much of how the Tories had reduced police numbers. The Labour Party manifesto had already promised to increase police spending and the numbers of police. As Home Secretary, May had been responsible for the cuts. The law and order issue was no longer a Tory strong point.

On June 7, 2017, the day before the vote, May said:

> 'We need to make sure that police and security and intelligence agencies have the powers they need. We should have longer prison sentences for people convicted of terrorist offences. We should make it easier for the authorities to deport foreign terror suspects. And we should do even more to restrict the freedom and the movements of terrorist suspects when we have enough evidence to know they present a threat, but not enough evidence to prosecute them in full in court. If our human rights laws stop us from doing it, we will change the laws so we can do it. If I am elected as Prime Minister on Thursday, I can tell you that this vital work begins on Friday.'

This was heralded by some in the press as a pledge to amend, if not repeal, human rights legislation. It was no such thing.

Nearly all the opinion polls still gave the Tories a lead, and some polls predicted a large lead and a landslide. However, two polls did not. The pollster Survation, who had predicted a Tory win on an eve-of-vote poll in 2015 (but had discounted their opinion poll, as it was out of step with all the others), predicted a narrow Tory lead of around 1%. They differed with the other pollsters particularly in that they forecast a high turnout of young voters who would vote Labour. The Tories were confident of a decisive victory of around 90 seats. The Survation poll was confirmed by the exit poll, which predicted a hung parliament, and that was the outcome.

Overall results for the main parties:

Tories won 318 seats (down 12) with 42.4%
Labour won 262 seats (up 30) with 40%
SNP won 35 seats (down 21) with 3%
Liberal Democrats won 12 seats (up 4) with 7.4%
UKIP won no seats (down 1) with 1.8%

The Tory vote of 42.4% was higher than the Thatcher landslide of 1983, and the 13,650,900 votes were more than the Blair landslide of 1997. The breakdown for the various parts of the United Kingdom of Great Britain and Northern Ireland were:

England:

Tories won 297 seats (down 21)
Labour won 227 seats (up 21)
Liberal Democrats won 8 seats (up 2)
Greens won 1 seat (no change)
UKIP won no seats (down 1)

Wales:

Tories won 8 seats (down 3)
Labour won 28 seats (up 3)
Liberal Democrats won no seats (down 1)
Plaid Cymru won 4 seats (up 1)

Scotland:

Tories won 13 seats (up 12)
Labour won 7 seats (up 6)
Liberal Democrats won 4 seats (up 3)
SNP won 35 seats (down 21)

Northern Ireland

DUP won 10 seats (up 2)
Sinn Fein won 7 seats (up 3)

The election turnout of the under 24-year-old voters was estimated to be as high as 72%, compared to 43% in the 2015 general election. Labour's £11billion pledge to abolish tuition fees was credited as being a major factor in this. Even the Tory bastion of Kensington was lost to Labour, after three recounts.

The UKIP leader, Paul Nuttall, resigned. UKIP had lost 3million votes and had been unable to contest as many seats as previously (when almost all had been). UKIP was short of money and candidates. UKIP had adopted an immigration policy akin to that of the Tory one (focusing on net immigration), with a slogan of 'one in one out': for every emigrant there could be an immigrant. This was a slogan masquerading as a policy; that a pensioner has decided to retire in Spain is not a reason to allow an immigrant in from Pakistan, nor could any government know who was leaving sufficiently to balance them with a corresponding number of immigrants (although UKIP did say it would seek parity over a number of years). In short, the slogan/policy was an unworkable cop-out on a key issue.

More controversially, UKIP adopted a new policy billed as an 'integration agenda to bring communities together'. This included proposals: a law 'against wearing of face coverings in public places'; the abolition of postal voting on demand due to 'electoral fraud and vote-stealing, especially among minority communities'; a ban on Sharia and 'a legal commission to draw up proposals to disband Sharia courts'; medical checks in schools on girls at 'high risk of suffering FGM', with a failure to report FGM 'a criminal offence itself'; the CPS to cite that where the victims of grooming gangs were of a different race or religion than the paedophiles, then that should be considered 'an aggravating feature'; 'immediate closure' of schools proven to be teaching Islamist ideology and a 'moratorium on new Islamic faith schools until substantial progress has been demonstrated in integrating Muslims into mainstream British society'; and for the CPS 'to treat a so-called "honour" dimension of any act of violence as an aggravating factor' and the incident to be given higher priority.

Were it to be enacted, the UKIP Integration Agenda might confront some issues stemming from the mass immigration of Muslims into Britain, but UKIP did not reconcile the policy with their policy of continued mass immigration, nor explain why those who adhere to a supremacist creed should even try to assimilate given that they expect to become the majority. Nor did UKIP justify why the English (it is England where most Muslims settle) should take responsibility for the Muslim unwillingness to assimilate. Nor did UKIP explain the conflict both within Islamic countries and between Muslims and non-Muslims across the world.

The UKIP Integration Agenda caused open opposition from within the party both during and after the campaign. Some senior figures in UKIP blamed it for their poor result. Those figures did not regard UKIP aping the failed Tory immigration policy to be a problem.

May was reportedly talked out of resigning immediately after the result. David Davis had to dash to No 10 to 'shore up' May. A planned reshuffle was abandoned in favour of only minor changes. Many Tory MPs spoke out that May's position was untenable: 'There is no way she makes it past conference,' one said. MP Anna Soubry said: 'She needs to consider her position. It was a dreadful campaign, and that's me being generous.'

Chancellor Philip Hammond, whom May's advisers had been briefing would be removed, challenged May directly about the rumours and adverse briefings. May 'mumbled that it wasn't her'. Hammond demanded that May's two advisers, Nick Timothy and Fiona Hill, be sacked.

Rob Wilson, a former minister who lost his seat, said that the manifesto 'put an Exocet through the heart of our main supporters – older people.' MP Nigel Evans said:

> 'We didn't shoot ourselves in the foot, we shot ourselves in the head. The campaign was going swimmingly well until we launched our own manifesto, when we did the triple assault on our core vote, the elderly. And quite frankly, from then on in people were not interested in the Labour party's manifesto. All they wanted to know was were they going to lose their winter weather payments and what the impact of the so-called dementia tax was going to be. We hijacked our own campaign and from then on it was an absolute disaster.'

Philip Davies MP said: 'people are tired of austerity' and that 'I think it's fair to say we made a bit of a pig's ear of the national campaign really, to be honest. The manifesto wasn't very good, particularly in terms of social care. Dropping a policy on people a few weeks before an election that seemed to come out of thin air was clearly a bad mistake.' MP Sarah Wollaston, chairman of the Commons Health Committee, said: 'I cannot see how the inner circle of special advisers can continue in post. It needs to be far more inclusive in future.' Lord Lamont said that 'there have been a lot of complaints about Mrs May's inner circle.' One minister said that Timothy and Hill should be 'taken out and shot'. Another minister said: 'Fiona and Nick will have to go – the Prime Minister might try to protect them but the Party will not wear it.'

Timothy, nicknamed Rasputin, was blamed for placing the dementia tax into the manifesto without consulting the Cabinet. Both Timothy and Hill had angered many ministers with their abusive and bullying attitude, including the use of swearing and insults. Hammond had described Timothy as 'economically illiterate'. One senior minister said: 'There is huge resentment at the collapse of Cabinet government. Politicians have been relegated to the sidelines by unelected unaccountable advisers.'

On the Saturday after the election it was reported that May had been given an ultimatum to sack Timothy and Hill or else she would face an immediate leadership challenge on Monday, with the necessary signatures already being available. Timothy and Hill resigned within the hour. These resignations turned the tide, although Osborne called May a 'dead woman walking'. This comment, if anything, was seen as disloyal to the Tory Party and rallied support to May. Boris Johnson sent a message to Tory MPs saying: 'Folks we need to calm down and get behind the Prime Minister.' In the limited reshuffle, May brought Gove back into the Cabinet. Boris Johnson posted on Twitter: 'It's a GOVErnment of all the talents. Welcome back to Michael.' Leadsom was moved to become the leader of the House of Commons, where she would be responsible for getting the Brexit legislation through Parliament. May appointed Steve Baker, a hard-line Brexiteer to the Brexit department.

The Remainers took the poor election result as an opportunity to try and challenge the Brexit strategy. Ruth Davidson said: 'What's really clear is that the Conservative Party, having failed to win a majority, now needs to work with others. And that means that we can look again at what it is we want to achieve as we leave the European Union, and I want to be involved in those discussions.' She proceeded to call for 'open Brexit', prioritising free trade rather than cutting immigration and saying, 'That's about making sure we tear down barriers rather than put them up.'

According to the *Evening Standard*, edited by Osborne, those Cabinet ministers who wanted a softer line taking on Brexit had been nicknamed the 'sensibles', and some were reportedly in talks with Labour. One unnamed Tory minister claimed that the EU policy was now a 'question for parliament' and not the government. May's new chief of staff, Gavin Barwell, blamed Brexit for the Tories' poor election result.

Of a meeting with May, Ruth Davidson, the Scottish Tory leader, told the BBC:

> 'I wanted to speak to her about what this election taught us as a party. It taught us that the country want us to be in government, but they do not want us to have a majority and that means we have to work with others on the big issues of the day, and that for me includes Brexit. We do have to make sure that we invite other people in now. This is not just going to be a Tory Brexit, this is going to have to involve the whole country.'

Nicola Sturgeon claimed that plans for a so-called hard Brexit were 'dead in the water', adding:

> 'The approach to Brexit ... has to change in light of this election. The Prime Minister has got to include more people in this process, different parties, all of the nations of the UK. And I think it must be an approach that starts with a determination to retain our place in the Single Market, because that's right for jobs and investment.'

David Davis pointed out 'Something like 80% of the British people voted for the parties that have accepted that we have to leave the EU ... The reason for leaving the Single Market is because we want to take back control of our borders.'

Lord Hague, a former Tory leader, called for May to reach out to Labour. Hague suggested that there could be a cross-party commission. Cameron told a conference in Poland: 'It's going to be difficult, there's no doubt about that, but perhaps an opportunity to consult more widely with the other parties on how best we can achieve it. I think there will be pressure for a softer Brexit,' and he added that 'parliament deserves a say'. Cameron also said: 'Scotland voted against Brexit. I think most of the Scottish Conservatives will want to see perhaps some changes with the policy going forward.' Hammond had reportedly told his German counterpart that there could be a change in the Brexit policy.

Sir John Major spoke out against doing a deal with the DUP (to give May a Commons majority), saying that it might threaten the Northern Ireland peace process. Major said that May should try and run a minority government. Lord Trimble said: 'There's no connection between the agreement and the European Union and Brexit, and all the rest of it. People are just trying to grab this and argue as a stick to beat the Government with and I think it's really quite silly.'

May abandoned any idea of making changes to the Human Rights Act, with government sources saying this was due to the lack of a Commons majority. Also binned was the three-pronged attack on pensioners – the dementia tax was scarcely mentioned again. However, the political correctness remained, with the Queen's Speech saying: 'My government will make further progress to tackle the gender pay gap and discrimination against people on the basis of their race, faith, gender, disability or sexual orientation. Legislation will be brought forward to protect the victims of domestic violence and abuse.'

Of great importance was the abuse and intimidation of political opponents dished out by the hard left during and after the general election campaign. Having won control of the Labour Party, the hard left had set about getting control of the country. In June 2017, the Tory MP Sheryll Murray, during Prime Minister's Questions in the House of Commons, said:

> 'Over the past month I've had swastikas carved into posters., social media posts like "Burn the witch" and "Stab the cunt", people putting Labour Party posters over my home, photographing them and pushing them through my letterbox, and someone even urinated on my office door.
> Hardly kinder, gentler politics. Can you suggest what can be done to stop this intimidation, which may well be putting off good people from serving in this place?'

May replied:

> 'You are absolutely right to raise this issue and you were not the only person who experienced this sort of intimidation during the election campaign, particularly – I'm sorry to say – this sort of intimidation was experienced by female candidates during the election campaign. I believe this sort of behaviour has no place in our democracy.'

Murray had been forced to stop holding hustings after a man threatened her.

In July, a cross-party report revealed that Tory candidates at the general election had experienced anti-Semitic abuse, racist graffiti daubed in a polling booth, paedophile smears, as well as a multitude of insults and abuse. Three serious death threats were reported to the police. Maria Caulfield, whose car tyres were slashed while it was parked outside her home, said that the abuse had got much worse and that she had had her posters daubed with 'Kill the Tories'.

It emerged that even the BBC's political editor, Laura Kuenssberg, had been given 'personal protection' during the general election in response to online threats from Corbyn supporters. She had been accused of anti-Corbyn bias.

The intimidation within the Labour Party also continued. In July, the moderate Labour MP Luciana Berger, whose local branch had been taken over by Corbyn supporters, was threatened with deselection unless she apologised for past criticism of Corbyn and got 'on board quite quickly now'. Miss Berger had previously received a deluge of anti-Semitic abuse (up to 2,500 messages in three days at one point) on the internet, including threats to rape or murder her. Some messages contained the yellow star used by the Nazis.

Jess Phillips, the Labour MP for Birmingham Yardley, in reference to a recent photo and threats against fellow Labour MP Yvette Cooper, wrote on Twitter: 'This can no longer be seen as individual incidents, this is targeted to control, isolate and manipulate. It has to stop. If I caught someone taking stalker pics of me, I'd throw their phone on the train tracks.' The attack against Miss Cooper on an anonymous site (the site's users were unmasked as leftist extremists) called her 'a cunt' and boasted that 'we're in charge forever'. Miss Cooper had recently been threatened with deselection.

A planned debate about the intimidation of MPs in the House of Commons was cancelled as a result of a Labour filibuster. Leadsom, the Commons leader, said: 'Members on both sides of this House have been victims of vile abuse from anarchists and hard-left activists, but obviously Labour are not interested.'

The general election had also been corrupted by voter fraud. The Electoral Commission announced that it would be investigating the matter of double voting by students in the general election. Many students had registered to vote at both their home and their university addresses. Many had boasted on the internet that they had voted twice. The Commission had received more than 1,000 email complaints from the pubic and 38 complaints from MPs. The Tory MP Peter Bone said: 'There were a number of students on social media boasting that they had voted in more than one place.

Did it affect the outcome of the election? I think it might have done. There were lots of seats where 40 or 50 votes made all the difference.'

Figures showed that there were 2.28million students at universities in 2015/16. Those areas with high student populations experienced a 10% increase in voter registration. A spokesman for the Electoral Commission said: 'It is troubling that some voters appear to have admitted voting more than once at the general election, which is an offence. Urgent action is needed to reduce both the scale and the administrative impact of duplicate registration applications.' The Labour Party refused to support a ban on duplicate registration.

Meanwhile, the EU announced that it wanted a greater say in regulating the City of London's euro clearing market. The market had a turnover of £750billion per day. Miles Celic, of TheCityUK lobby group said:

> 'While these proposals appear to fall short of the worst case scenario, the European Commission is holding back any real detail on when or how it might pull the trigger on a location policy. Despite the Commission recognising the costs that a clearing location policy would pass on to European savers and businesses, it appears politically committed to exploring this further.'

EU officials refused to say whether the new rules might require London clearing houses to move.

This move by the EU was not lost on the May Government. Hammond picked up on it in his Mansion House speech hours later. This speech was important, as Hammond was positioning himself as the soft-Brexit leadership hopeful in the event of May resigning (or being forced out), and he also displayed a firm commitment to the stance adopted by May while staying true to the Remain arguments that he had previously advocated.

In his Mansion House speech, Hammond rightly acknowledged that 'Stronger growth is the only sustainable way to deliver better public services, higher real wages and increased living standards,' but he remarked that 'I thought we had won that argument. But I learned in the General Election campaign that we have not.' He correctly pointed out that it is investment that leads to increases in productivity.

Hammond said that Britain should have continued mass immigration ('we do not seek to shut it down') and quoted from the Tory manifesto: 'Britain is an open economy and a welcoming society and we will always ensure that our British businesses can recruit the brightest and best from around the world.' He said that Britain had 'benefited from globalization'. However, in his judgement, too much of the thrust of globalization thus far ('"Globalization 1.0" if you like') had been focused on goods rather than services, of which he believed Britain was more competitive. Therefore, he said, 'So for the UK to be able to share fairly in the benefits of globalization, we need to lead a global crusade for liberalisation of services,' and that 'we must employ that logic in our Brexit negotiations, to agree a bold and ambitious free-trade agreement with our EU counterparts that covers both goods and services.' He therefore supported the May Government's policy of seeking 'a comprehensive trade agreement in the context of a deep and special partnership that goes much wider than trade.'

Hammond accepted that Britain had voted to leave the EU and said that 'we will leave the EU, but it must be done in a way that works for Britain.' He gave three objectives to achieving this:

> 'Firstly, by securing a comprehensive agreement for trade in goods and services. Secondly, by negotiating mutually beneficial transitional arrangements to avoid unnecessary disruption and dangerous cliff edges. Thirdly, by agreeing frictionless customs arrangements to facilitate trade across our borders –

and crucially – to keep the land border on the island of Ireland open and free-flowing.'

Hammond further emphasized that there should be 'a pragmatic approach to one of our most important EU export sector – financial services'. He warned of protectionist measures that were being advanced under the guise of 'regulatory competence, financial stability, and supervisory oversight'. This was a reference to the EU signal that it wanted more supervisory powers to regulate the City of London hours before. Hammond argued that it was in the EU's interests not to harm the City due to its dominance, upon which the other EU countries depended. He therefore wanted joint British/EU regulations for 'cross-border business'.

Hammond's prioritisation of financial services stemmed from the Remain campaign. In the Treasury's second report, 'HM Treasury analysis: the long-term economic impact of EU membership and the alternatives' (see above), it had been stated that future economic reform of the EU would 'include the next stage of development of the Single Market, with a focus on bringing down the remaining barriers to trade in services, energy and digital, alongside completing major ongoing trade deals' and that 'The financial services industry is crucial to the success of the UK economy. EU financial integration have helped UK financial firms grow both in size and in the breadth of services they offer. Financial services exports have increased from 1.6% of GDP in 1991 to 3.5% of GDP in 2015.'

As with the British government's promotion of the interests of the City to the exclusion of the wider economy after WWI, especially with the return to the Gold Standard at pre-war parity, once again, the City had priority – this time, even more stupidly so, as 3.5% of GDP is a small fraction of the total and the export of financial services to the EU is only a part of that 3.5% and is smaller still.

In her speech setting out the government's policy regarding Brexit in January 2017 (see above), May said that a failure to reach a deal with the EU 'would risk exports from the EU to Britain worth around £290billion every year' (this would only apply if Britain were prepared to impose tariffs, which May has ruled out and is desperate to avoid). In a television interview in June 2017, David Davis also referred to this £290billion figure, which he compared to a figure of around £230billion for Britain's exports to the EU. The figure is for goods and services for 2015. However, by mid-2017, the figures for 2016 were available, giving a more up-to-date picture.

To start with the total picture, Britain's payments deficit has continued and even reached an unprecedented 5.5% of GDP in the final quarter of 2015.[7] On an annual basis, the deficit for 2013 was 4.4% of GDP; for 2014, it was 4.7% of GDP; for 2015, it was 4.3% of GDP; and for 2016, it was 4.4% of GDP. These figures reveal a deep-seated problem that shows no signs of correcting itself – despite free trade *theories* and floating exchange rates.

To focus on the EU, as even Hammond urged as a prelude to his commitment to a 'global crusade for liberalisation of services', which is fully consistent with Fox, the Trade Secretary, and his commitment to global free trade. The transactions with the EU are split into four broad sectors: goods, services, primary income (mainly investment income), and secondary income (mainly government transactions). Britain once used to have a healthy surplus in investment income (money earned on investment abroad exceeded money paid to foreigners on their investments within Britain). Britain once used to rely upon investment income to mask its deteriorating trade in goods. For example, in 1924, the trade deficit of £214million was more than covered by 'invisible earnings' on investments of £272million, giving a surplus of £58million. Another example: the surplus on investment income was £30,150million in 2005 and had fallen to a surplus of £18,671million in 2011, the last year it was in surplus.

Dealing with the EU, in 2016, the deficit in primary income was £10,346million (down from a deficit of £18,544million in

2015), and the deficit in secondary income was £11,304million (almost the same as 2015). The surplus in services was £24,195million in 2016 (down from £28,365million in 2015).[8] In other words, in 2016, the surplus in all services, of which financial services are only a part, was enough to cover the deficit in primary and secondary income. That leaves the trade in goods. This has been in deficit for a very long time.

To take the most recent years, the trade (in goods) deficit with the EU was £58,354million in 2012, £69,408million in 2013, £79,262million in 2014, £88,955million in 2015, and £95,629million in 2016.[9] In 2016, the export of goods to the EU totalled £144,175million, and the imports totalled £239,804million.[10]

The 2016 figures for combined goods and services exported to the EU was £240,560million, while the total imported was £311,994million. That Davis preferred to stick with the 2015 figures is understandable.

The trade deficit in goods of £95,629million with the EU was vast, and the clear trend shows that it will continue to worsen. This is a disaster and is ruining the British economy. Selling off assets and borrowing to fund the trade deficit will simply entail more payments in dividends and interest to foreigners and so will make the primary income deficit worse. The prospect of an expansion of financial services exports sufficient to cancel out the trade deficit is delusional. Worse, those in the May Government, with the Hammond master plan devolved from the Remain campaign, have convinced themselves that if they can only enter into some sort of partnership with the EU post-Brexit, then they might be able to liberalize trade in services (as Osborne was prattling about in his Treasury report) and so create more financial services exports − ignoring the corresponding likelihood of more services imports, ignoring the EU's protectionist moves, and ignoring that Britain is supposed to have left and so should not be meddling with the EU's affairs. One can recall that Junker said that May was 'living in a different galaxy'. Brexit means exit. Britain voted to leave.

The EU is exploiting what is for the northern countries, Germany in particular, an artificial and undervalued currency, the euro, to price their exports more cheaply than would otherwise be the case and to push up the price of imports. Britain is suffering from this, and its economy is being harmed. The trade deficit with Germany in 2016 was £31,717million (it was £31,079million in 2015). China has also been manipulating its currency as well as adopting other protectionist measures (for example, see *The Ponzi Class*, pages 248–250, 269 and 270). The trade deficit with China in 2016 was £27,101million (it was £23,864million in 2015). Britain has a £58,818million trade deficit with Germany and China alone. This deficit is worsening. Germany and China are taking Britain to the cleaners.

A responsible trade policy would be one in which existing arrangements with other countries, apart from those with the EU and China, are rolled over irrespective of the WTO. Britain could then concentrate on bringing its trade with the EU and China back into balance, if necessary by using tariffs. A 20% tariff on the imported goods from the EU would raise £47,961million (£62,399million for both goods and services), while a 20% tariff on imported goods from China would raise £8,118million (20% of £40,588million).[11] This is enough to eliminate the government spending deficit. In practice, demand would be redirected towards British goods, and so there would be fewer imports but correspondingly extra economic activity, thus also generating tax revenues.

Were the £95,629million deficit in goods with the EU eliminated, then the extra demand would, as people spent the extra money thus earned, in turn generate further demand (this is described as the multiplier effect) and tax revenues. Britain would boom, just as it did when it resorted to tariff reform after crashing out of the Gold Standard (see *The Ponzi Class*, pages 131 and 135–140).

The May Government did not even have eliminating the trade deficit as an aim, and this deficiency was backed by UKIP. It was a triumph of dogma over intelligence.

SUMMARY

In calling the surprise election, May had taken a bold step based on what looked to be an impregnable lead in the opinion polls. Yet, like a tragic character in a Shakespearean play, May's political correctness and globalism would bring her down.

The campaign started as almost a presidential contest with the 'Strong and Stable' slogan being rammed down the electorate's throat with grating repetition. It was assumed that May was fit to conduct the Brexit negotiations but that Corbyn was not. However, the Tories had overlooked that Corbyn was in his element campaigning. He was supported by a populist manifesto. As for the Tory manifesto ...

Confident of their commanding lead, the Tories wallowed in political correctness and globalism. Their manifesto verged upon an insult to their core voters, whom they openly intended to fleece. Labour attracted a high turnout of young voters and a portion of former UKIP voters. UKIP saw its election effort collapse, and its vote did likewise. May had rightly anticipated this but not that Labour would pick up many of the former UKIP voters.

Opinion polls showed that 68% of voters wanted to see Brexit completed and only 22% still wanted to stay in the EU.

May's political correctness sank the Tory campaign. As a civic nationalist (see *The Genesis of Political Correctness*, the chapter 'Citizenship and National Identity'), she believed that people owed allegiance to the state and to her, not that the government was there to represent the people. She genuinely expected people to accept and vote in favour of the dementia tax and to give the state their life savings.

Meanwhile, foreign aid flowed out to a variety of spendthrift entities, and the payments to the EU continued despite the referendum vote. May's eyes might have twinkled at the thought of the extra tax revenues arising out of the proposed dementia tax, but the voters were appalled. Even when the extent of public hostility was clear, May could not cope with reality. She became robotic in her response to the fallout. Cocooned in a globalist/politically correct bubble, she could not understand the views of ordinary people, whose objections she found 'simply bewildering' – to quote her own Tory conference speech in reference to the ruling class's reaction to the Leave vote; in that speech, May scoffed at those who considered themselves to be 'a citizen of the world' without appreciating that she considered herself to be one. The flaw in Mayism was apparent from the outset. It manifested itself in the unenthusiastic approach to Brexit and proved devastating to the prospects of success in the general election.

Regarding immigration, May's idea of dealing with public concern was to make yet another manifesto commitment to reduce *net* immigration to the tens of thousands. The number and savagery of the terrorist attacks did not alter her view. She genuinely believed that making manifesto promises constituted governing.

After years of indecision, UKIP finally embraced the policy of an English parliament. Cameron had spoken of English Voters for English Laws (EVEL) after the Scottish referendum on independence. That referendum had been won after a scare regarding the surge in the independence vote, with a multitude of promises of extra powers for the Scots. Consequently, Cameron unexpectedly made his pledge. However, EVEL fell well short of an English parliament. Nevertheless, the policy ultimately adopted by the Tories was to fiddle about with the standing orders regarding voting procedures in the House of Commons: the English MPs had a veto in the committee stage of legislation, but all MPs from all parts of the United Kingdom still had the vote on English affairs.

The result of the 2017 general election was that the Tories won handsomely in England (with 297 seats to 227 seats for Labour and a 61-seat overall majority). But the phalanx of MPs from Scotland, Wales and Northern Ireland (each of which, unlike England, had their own parliaments) meant that the Tories were narrowly short of a majority. The governance of England was determined by non-English MPs. This is in addition to the large number of non-English voters allowed to vote and the abuses of the postal ballots. Then there was the out-of-date constituency boundaries. The vote was rigged against the Tories by the Tories. Instead of fudging and waffling, they needed to govern. They were too useless to introduce an English parliament, and they paid the price. They preferred to appease a coalition of anti-English vested interests who were out to plunder the English for all they could get – Plaid Cymru, the SNP, Sinn Fein, a multitude of supposedly oppressed groups (militant homosexuals, feminists, ethnic minorities, Muslims, etc) and the EU. No one stood up for the English.

Given that the number of Tory MPs in Scotland (the wealthiest part of Britain outside London and South East England) increased by an extra twelve to a total of thirteen, the Scottish Tory leader, Ruth Davidson, was heralded as an election genius. Without those extra twelve Tory MPs, the May Government might well have lost office to a Corbyn-led coalition. This achievement by Davidson needs to be kept in perspective. In fact, the Scottish Tories won 13 out of 59 seats; ie the Tories lost the election in Scotland by a huge margin. In England, by comparison, the Tories won 297 out of a total of 533 seats; ie the Tories handsomely won an overall majority in England despite all the vote rigging and despite the appalling campaign. And yet Davidson subsequently exploited her newfound status to push for more immigration (the immigrants are settling in England) and a watered-down Brexit (the costs of the payments to the EU are met by England). There was no justification for this whatsoever.

Following the unexpected loss of an overall majority, the pro-EU Tories saw their opportunity to thwart the referendum vote and undermine Brexit (made easier by May's own intention to do the same). The EU resumed its belligerence. A prime example was when the May Government made an offer to the EU regarding the rights of EU citizens living in Britain. The EU rejected the British offer and further demanded that the European Court of Justice retain authority over those citizens and their 'rights'. The fact that a British government was asking permission of the EU about the internal affairs of Britain signified the weakness of the May Government. Those EU immigrants should be expected to abide by British laws. That is what sovereignty means. It is subversive to try and create a new class of EU immigrants who would have privileged status in Britain.

Lord Tebbit, when he reminded the House of Lords that these EU immigrants were foreigners and that Britain's responsibility is to its own citizens, was greeted with gasps of horrified shock by the other lords. This confirmed the lack of patriotism amongst the ruling Ponzi class, and of their snobby disdain for anything so vulgar as acting in Britain's interests.

While allowing EU immigrants to remain in Britain generally, might be less problematic than trying to expel them, this largesse on the part of Britain should not be ignored. For example, these EU immigrants occupy housing. The government has estimated that there are around 2.8million EU immigrants. Migration Watch UK put the figure as totalling more than 3.5million by the time that Britain is supposed to leave in 2019.[12] With around 92% of these being of working age and with an average household occupancy rate of 1.92, then around 1,708,708 new houses would be required to increase the housing stock to meet the increased demand.[13]

Average house prices in England in March 2017 were £232,530. This average figure hides wide variations. Average house prices in London and the South East, where a disproportionate number of immigrants settle, were £471,742 and £311,514 respectively.[14] There are believed to be one million EU immigrants in London, and immigrants tend to settle in cities where the costs of housing are more expensive. To use ballpark figures, the cost of housing the EU immigrants is at least £500billion and could well be far, far higher. There is in addition the discrepancy between the official figures for number of EU immigrants and the number of national insurance numbers issued (indicating that the true number of immigrants is considerably greater). Furthermore, the strain on the housing stock is worsened by the numbers of non-EU immigrants. The children of immigrants, in turn, eventually need houses.

Britain has a desperate housing shortage, with something in excess of £1trillion of housing stock taken by immigrants. Britain does not have the resources to make good that cost, which, ultimately, is born by ordinary people in the form of higher costs for mortgages and rents, and lower standards of living by being denied home ownership etc. Furthermore, there are the other costs of immigration as well. Yet the EU has poured scorn on Britain's offer to confer residency rights on EU immigrants post-Brexit and has even had the gall to demand up to £90billion in a divorce payment! In reality, Britain should be billing them.

The situation got worse. Although the May Government had been offering a number of fudges and sell-outs to the EU, the EU was not inclined to compromise. The EU refused to even begin to negotiate a future trade deal until Britain had agreed to terms for the Irish border and the rights of EU nationals in Britain, and agreed to pay the EU a divorce bill. Despite promising 'the row of the summer', David Davis immediately capitulated and accepted the EU's agenda. In July 2017, it was reported that the EU planned to remove the freedom of British citizens living in the EU to move from one country to another in the EU. The one million British ex-patriots would be confined to the country they presently lived in. This was despite the EU continually stating that they would negotiate as one bloc. Britain had indicated that it was willing to give voting rights to EU nationals in Britain, but it was unwilling to agree that the European Court of Justice should implement any deal.

Meanwhile, it emerged that the Tory MP Nicky Morgan was circulating a letter that she proposed to send to May demanding that Britain remain in both the EU Customs Union and the Single Market during any transition period. The letter alleged: 'The economic dislocation that would result from a sudden and incomplete negotiation poses a serious risk to investment, profitability, operations and the livelihoods of the people they employ. They are particularly concerned about an immediate exit from the Single Market and the customs union.' This letter was leaked against a background of Hammond, with increasing boldness, announcing that there would be a transitional deal following March 2019, during which Britain would stay in the Single Market. This would, of course, have implications regarding free movement.

One cabinet minister reportedly said: 'Most of the Brexiters now realise that the timetable for exit is very short and that a substantial transitional period is needed.' Allegedly, No 10 had even agreed to leave open the option of Britain staying under ECJ control and that payments to the EU might continue during a transitional period, which would allow the EU to continue spending regardless of Brexit.

The ardent Remainer Matthew Parris, a former Tory MP, wrote to the Brexiteers in *The Spectator* magazine: 'Suspect a plot by my lot to procrastinate until you lot slip out of vogue. Deadlines for any "transition" can be put back until kingdom come. Allow us to lure you into these thickets and you lose.'

Stories that the Cabinet had agreed that free movement would continue were confirmed when Gove spoke out publicly and said: 'As we leave the EU we will have an implementation period which will ensure we can continue to have not just access to labour but the economic stability and certainty which business requests.' Whether it was called free movement or not, it was clear that mass immigration from the EU was to continue. Increasingly, it was obvious that the voters were to be fobbed off with the six-year delay and 'a slightly beefed up version of Mr Cameron's attempted renegotiation' that, in July 2016, Redwood said was not what people had voted for (see above). In an article for *The Financial Times*, Amber Rudd wrote:

> 'I will today be asking the Migration Advisory Committee, the government's independent advisers, to carry out a detailed assessment of migration from the EU and the European Economic Area in relation to the economy in England, Scotland, Wales and Northern Ireland. We will be asking the committee to examine the British labour market, the overall role of migration in the wider economy and how the UK's immigration system should be aligned with a modern industrial strategy. This advice will build on the government's own work and allow us to take these vitally important decisions based on the best advice possible. The MAC will look at the overall picture, moving beyond individual bits of anecdotal evidence and allowing us to make policy on high-quality evidence. The committee will be beginning its work shortly. This will be a chance for businesses and employers to express their honest opinions, independently of the government. It is critically important the views of each industry are reflected accurately in this evidence, so I would encourage industry representatives to get involved in the process. I also want to reassure businesses and EU nationals that we will ensure there is no "cliff edge" once we leave the bloc. In addition to the MAC's work over the coming months, I will be joining colleagues from across the government in speaking to businesses, trade unions, educational institutions and many others. The comments and considerations we hear in the course of these discussions will combine

with the MAC's evidence to help shape our thinking and our future immigration policy. In the autumn, the government will set out some initial thinking on options for the future immigration system. We will take account of the MAC's evidence and the views of a range of stakeholders before any measures are finalised. Put simply, the UK must remain a hub for international talent. We must keep attracting the brightest and best migrants from around the world. And we must implement a new immigration system after we leave the EU that gives us control and works in all of our interests.'

This article demonstrated that Rudd was unchanged from her stance in the referendum debate when she attached so much importance to the opinions of experts (see above). Rudd, like Hammond, took the view that Remain might have been outvoted in the referendum, but that was not the same as being wrong. Rudd still regarded Brexit is something bad and to be mitigated, if not avoided (as she said in the first referendum debate: 'being in the EU makes us money – there is no saving from leaving the EU'). Nor did she take on board that only a small minority of firms export to the EU (Leadsom put the figure at 'only 6%' in the first debate) and that the interests of the other 94% of companies, and the interests of the wider public, might be more important.

The article did not attract criticism from the Brexiteers. No longer did Boris Johnson believe that the levels of mass immigration needed democratic consent. No longer did it matter that 'a city the size of Newcastle' was 'arriving every year' – for which the government could not afford any provision, either for housing, schools, hospitals, transport, etc.

In Rudd's article, she spoke only of the Ponzi class and ignored the interests and opinions of ordinary people. For her, only the views of experts and stakeholders mattered (ie vested interests) and not those of the smelly hoi polloi. For Rudd, and other Remainers, the referendum *decision* would be superseded by the opinions of experts and vested interests. Democracy was abandoned in Britain in July 2017.

Rudd was very keen to repeat the mantra about Britain attracting immigrants who are the 'brightest and the best ... from around the world'. That cliché might appeal to the politically correct, but what the British people want is a government that will strive to make the British the 'brightest and the best' in the world. Once it was considered normal to do the best for our own people.

What was completely absent was any mention of where the money was coming from to pay for this proposed transition period. With immigration from the EU running at 268,000 a year, a transitional period from March 2019 until the next election due in June 2022 would mean around another 871,000 immigrants from the EU. Then there are those getting National Insurance numbers but not included in the immigration figures (see above). If only a million immigrants moved to Britain (and there could be very many more, especially once those illegal immigrants claiming to be refugees get EU citizenship), then that will be another £110billion or so drain on the housing stock. The intention is that this cost, along with all the other costs (including the costs of immigration from the referendum in June 2016 until March 2019), will be simply dumped on ordinary English people whether they like it or not. Then there is all the non-EU immigration.

There was also the problem of the trade deficit with the EU, which was running at around £100billion per year. If the present rate of deterioration continues, then it will be nudging a deficit of £150billion per year by 2022. Neither Hammond nor any of the other Remainers have set out how this is to be funded. Taken together with the costs of immigration on the housing stock, then these are gargantuan sums of money. Unless the May Government is stopped, in practice, they will not pay these costs, pretend that the costs do not exist, and simply continue to offload them onto the general public. This is Ponzi economics.

One potential danger posed by the general election outcome, was that, as a prime minster no longer has the power to call a general election without the consent of parliament (due to the Fixed-term Parliaments Act, which the Tories never got around to repealing), should the May Government fall, then a Corbyn-led Labour Party has the option to try and form a government. Corbyn and his allies (eg Abbott and McDonnell) are Trotskyites (or else communists of some faction). The Labour Party has been taken over by communists, and that takeover continued to tighten its grip. As with Tsarist Russia, although Rasputin has gone, a weak and incompetent government is presiding over a deteriorating country, with a restless populace turning to the revolutionary left for solutions. The Brexit vote was the patriotic opportunity to tackle Britain's problems, and that has failed. The general election in June 2017 witnessed the electorate turning to communists. Britain is in danger of sliding into a Venezuelan-style communist revolution – if not worse. In the event of Corbyn taking power, then the intimidation experienced by Labour moderates, and by some Tories during the general election, would be a foretaste of coming attractions.

On July 7, 2017, it was reported that the latest YouGov poll put Labour on 46%, the Tories on 38%, the Liberal Democrats on 4%, and also UKIP on 4%. If a general election were called, then Labour would win.

CONCLUSION

Despite the ambitious hopes of the Brexit vote, the hegemony of the Ponzi class has remained. Little of substance has changed. There has been a lot of talk, a lot of media excitement and much political chatter, but nothing has actually been done. The payments to the EU continue, the immigrants still flow in, there remains a substantial trade deficit, foreign aid flows out with abandon, and political correctness remains the basis of morality. Austerity might have been formally discontinued following the election debacle, but it was simply a slogan anyway, and Ponzi economics reigned supreme and has continued to do so.

It is an oft-stated observation that in a democracy, the pendulum tends to swing back. That if things go too far in one direction, then there is a correction as public opinion asserts itself. The Brexit vote was a clear move by the public to make a correction, to get the pendulum to swing back towards the nation state and its proper governance in the nation's interests. Yet the Ponzi class has successfully jammed the pendulum and successfully demonized the public for daring to disagree with the ruling orthodoxy.

The failure of the Brexit revolution to produce a Tory leader who was a Brexiteer was a key moment that had profound consequences. But the seeds of the survival of the Ponzi class lie further back in the EU referendum campaign itself. The preposterous economic arguments churned out by the Remain campaign were not properly challenged, and the Leave side were reliant upon the Economists for Brexit, who were *unilateral* free traders. Understandably, the Vote Leave campaign did not wish to attack the Tory economic record, but UKIP should have. UKIP should have presented a critique of the trade deficit and of Ponzi economics, but they did not.

The Remain mantra that Britain had to remain a member of the Single Market and that economic catastrophe would be the outcome of leaving the EU (at the time, openly admitting that a Leave vote would mean leaving the Single Market) survived the Leave vote and became the mantra for a policy of seeking tariff-free access to the Single Market. Relying upon WTO rules, which the Economists for Brexit advocated, was deemed to be not an option. This locked Britain into having to negotiate with the EU. The May Government, May being a Remainer, refused to leave the EU at once, despite the EU saying they wanted a quick deal and despite Corbyn saying that he would support triggering Article 50 at once. Instead, May opted for an Article 50 withdrawal and opted to plump for tariff-free access to the Single Market. Tariff-free access was the government's overriding aim – not balanced trade. UKIP fully supported this, with Farage trying to get a seat at the negotiating table for himself. The May Government fully intended to continue to run a trade deficit and refused to take Brexit as an excellent opportunity to deal with the deficit problem.

Having opted for Article 50, the government prevaricated, procrastinated, vacillated, waffled and woffled, dawdled and dithered, and dithered and dawdled. The result being that one year after the referendum result, still nothing had happened – only talk of what might happen, and the bulk of that talk was of the sell-outs, opt-outs, interim periods, transition arrangements etc that the May Government was eager to offer the EU in the hope of securing a new partnership to include tariff-free access. This preoccupation totally obscured the trade deficit. This was a major victory for the Ponzi class.

A pivotal figure was Fox, the trade secretary, who saw his role not to secure Britain's trading relations post-Brexit, thus allowing the government to walk away from the EU regardless of any deal, but to champion global free trade. He treated Britain's trade deficit as something unimportant and not requiring attention from him as trade secretary. Globalization was presented by Fox as an inevitable process rather than a policy choice. To Fox, it was either globalization or a communist siege economy. This was a false dichotomy.

The morality of the Ponzi class is political correctness. The dominance of this creed has endured the Leave vote with scarcely any challenge. Leadsom, if the document spied upon was true, was steeling herself to counter the ideology. But May won the Tory leadership. May had a long history of political correctness. She was a keen devotee. Her premiership has been one of undiluted politically correct policies and gimmicks. Far from opposing it, which is what was needed, she extended it, not least with the Tory fixation with 'intergenerational fairness' (despite their desire to sow division, even the communists had not thought of this), which was simply a pretext to justify a very determined attempt to fleece pensioners. Militant feminism and race war politics flourished under the Tories. Race and sex quotas were enforced. Even elderly former soldiers have been persecuted in the British Inquisition, with dishonest lawyers pocketing large fees. Not even the terrorist atrocities dented the race war agenda. Freedom of speech has been under relenting attack.

Race war politics complemented the policy of mass immigration. A hatred of white people, the English in particular, was encouraged. Historical British figures were subject to attacks from immigrants. Allegations of racism were casually made with the flimsiest of excuses, while the tolerance of, in particular, Islamic hatred and intolerance was excused. Even the problem of paedophiles targeting English children continued. The prospect of the English becoming a minority in England persisted. The excuses to encourage mass immigration expanded. The impact on public services, especially housing, was ignored, as was the downward pressure on wages. Funds flowed to people smugglers. Human rights laws helped the criminals. Illegal immigrants were rarely expelled no matter how depraved their criminality. Not even the various acts of terrorism, nor the growing numbers of extremists, changed anything.

The result of the triumph of the Ponzi class was that the living standards of ordinary people continued to deteriorate. The prospect of future generations having a lower living standard, a process of de-civilization, was part of the reason for the young turning out to vote for Labour in the general election. It was not solely about tuition fees, but also about housing, home ownership, job opportunities and wage rates. Their lives have been ruined by the Ponzi class, and they saw hope in Corbyn's Labour manifesto.

Whether it be the targeting of pensioners (their pensions, their benefits or their homes), the underfunding of the NHS and social care (despite the Vote Leave pledge to allocate extra funding from the monies saved on ceasing payments to the EU), the pressure on schools, the desperate housing shortage, the squeeze on stay-at-home mothers, and the stagnant wages compared to the increasing inflation, living standards continued to fall.

Meanwhile, businesses were sold off to fund the trade deficit. British firms continued to receive no preference, and foreign ones continued to win lucrative government contracts. Crony capitalism flourished with ex-state sector entities bumping up prices as they paid out dividends to foreign owners. Taxes paid by multinationals in too many instances were so low as to be a sick joke. The government was alert to the issue of low productivity but refused to stop mass immigration (which is a major cause of it). No effort was made to eliminate the trade deficit.

Meanwhile, the living standards of the Ponzi class were as elevated as ever. Senior police officers, BBC presenters and big wigs, civil servants, charity workers, academics, NHS bureaucrats, peers, bankers, lawyers and even judges all have done very nicely. These are all people who parade their political correctness and their globalist credentials – all at somebody else's expense.

The Ponzi class has not only survived the referendum Leave vote, but its members have pursued their pet projects uninterrupted, and crucially, now they even threaten to thwart a genuine Brexit. Britain's exit from the EU is imperilled despite the referendum. As ever, the Ponzi class treats the views and interests of the general public with contempt.

In *The Ponzi Class,* I wrote: 'It is time to reverse Britain's economic decline or else we face not an economic Dunkirk, but an economic Fall of Singapore.' Despite the referendum vote, the scale of the adverse consequences of mass immigration, and the scale of the escalating balance of trade deficit, the Tories have been incapable of proper governance. They have proved themselves incapable of implementing the referendum decision. They have been unable to break free from their globalist, politically-correct mentality and have adopted a losing position regarding leaving the EU. Outrageous demands from the EU are met with immediate capitulation.

In *The Genesis of Political Correctness*, I explained that political correctness is a version of communism, and I wrote: 'Political correctness acts like a political version of Aids. It weakens a society's culture, identity, and its ability to defend itself, thereby allowing any opportunistic, hostile entity to attack.' The effects of political correctness have been evident in Britain, from the greed of those who wish to loot England for all they can get (it is the English who are the primary target), including the EU, to the jihadists who exploit the government's refusal to secure the borders in order to commit acts of terrorism. The ineffectual, blundering buffoonery of the Tory Party should be contrasted with the ruthless determination of the communist takeover of the Labour Party and the danger posed by that.

The British Ponzi class has survived the EU referendum. It remains to be seen for how much longer Britain can survive the British Ponzi class.

APPENDIX A

WHITE PAPER

The United Kingdom's exit from and new partnership with the European Union

Presented to Parliament by the Prime Minister by Command of Her Majesty
February 2017

A preface, written by David Davis, the secretary of state for exiting the European Union stated that 'The UK wants the EU to succeed. Indeed it is in our interests for it to prosper politically and economically and a strong new partnership with the UK will help to that end' and it reiterated the 12 principles that May had already set out regarding Brexit:

> '1. Providing certainty and clarity; 2. Taking control of our own laws; 3. Strengthening the Union; 4. Protecting our strong historic ties with Ireland and maintaining the Common Travel Area; 5. Controlling immigration; 6. Securing rights for EU nationals in the UK and UK nationals in the EU; 7. Protecting workers' rights; 8. Ensuring free trade with European markets; 9. Securing new trade agreements with other countries; 10. Ensuring the United Kingdom remains the best place for science and innovation; 11. Cooperating in the fight against crime and terrorism; and 12. Delivering a smooth, orderly exit from the EU.'

It also said that 'In this paper we set out the basis for these 12 priorities and the broad strategy that unites them in forging a new strategic partnership between the United Kingdom and the EU.'

1. Providing certainty and clarity

The white paper cited 'The Great Repeal Bill' as the means by which 'legal certainty' will be achieved. This bill will repeal the 1972 European Communities Act and 'convert the "acquis" – the body of existing EU law – into domestic law' (and it also amends 'secondary legislation to the laws that would otherwise not function sensibly once we have left the EU'). The white paper did not make clear that it is only by repealing the 1972 Act that Britain can actually leave the EU. All that Article 50 does is commence negotiations, and it puts the EU in charge. Incorporating the acquis into British law allows Britain to leave the EU without having to consider whether or not to repeal each and every little bit of EU legislation. A review of that acquis can then take place after Britain has left: 'It will be open to Parliament in the future to keep or change these laws.'

The white paper promised that the funding for present projects currently financed by the European Structural and Investment Funds, and the funding level for agriculture to 2020, would remain and that 'The Government will then put the final deal that is agreed between the UK and the EU to a vote in both Houses of Parliament.'

2. Taking control of our own laws

The white paper stated that The Court of Justice of the European Union, which rules on EU law, will lose jurisdiction over Britain, although Britain 'will of course continue to honour our international commitments and follow international law'. Britain would in the future rely upon other dispute resolution mechanisms for international agreements, of which there are already many, and these mechanisms, unlike the EU's, will 'not have direct effect in UK law'.

3. Strengthening the Union

The white paper highlighted that the government has already involved 'the administrations in Scotland, Wales and Northern Ireland to deliver an outcome that works for the whole of the UK'. There was no such representation for England. The paper stated 'The Prime Minister has already chaired two plenary meetings of the Joint Ministerial Committee, which brings together the leaders of the devolved administrations of Scotland, Wales and Northern Ireland.' Both Scotland and Wales had submitted papers, and Wales wanted 'a balanced approach to immigration linking migration to jobs and good, properly enforced employment practices'. The SNP had already argued that Scotland should also have a separate immigration policy.

The white paper stated that the government 'will work with the devolved administrations on an approach to returning powers from the EU that works for the whole of the UK and reflects the interests of Scotland, Wales and Northern Ireland'. Literally, England did not get a mention.

5. Controlling immigration

The white paper was open about the wonders of mass immigration. It extolled 'openness to international talent' and said that 'we will always want immigration, including from EU countries, and especially high-skilled immigration and why we will always welcome individual migrants arriving lawfully in the UK as friends'. The white paper promised that 'existing EU students and those starting courses in 2016–17 and 2017–18 will continue to be eligible for student loans and home fee status for the duration of their course. We have also confirmed that research councils will continue to fund postgraduate students from the EU whose courses start in 2017–18.'

The Paper said that the government was 'considering very carefully the options that are open to us to gain control of the numbers of people coming to the UK from the EU', that it was consulting 'businesses and communities', and that 'we will build a comprehensive picture of the needs and interests of all parts of the UK and look to develop a system that works for all'. The government was therefore leaning towards giving both the Welsh and Scottish nationalists what they wanted regarding immigration, despite the fact that England was where the vast majority of immigrants settled. However, England has no voice.

Ominously, the white paper stated that the new arrangements would be 'complex' and that 'Parliament will have an important role in considering these matters further'; also, the Paper stated that there 'may be a phased process of implementation to prepare for the new arrangements'.

6. Securing rights for EU nationals in the UK and UK nationals in the EU

The white paper put the number of EU citizens in Britain as numbering 2.8million, of which more than 900,000 are from Poland, and it put the number of British citizens living in the EU as numbering 1million, of which more than 300,000 lived in Spain and more than 150,000 live in France; many of these will be pensioners who have the capital to pay for a house.

8. Ensuring free trade with European markets and 9. Securing new trade agreements with other countries

The white paper stated:

> 'The Government will prioritise securing the freest and most frictionless trade possible in goods and services between the UK and the EU. We will not be seeking membership of the Single Market, but will pursue instead a new strategic partnership with the

EU, including an ambitious and comprehensive Free Trade Agreement and a new customs agreement.'

The white paper therefore stated that it is in both the interests of the EU and 'all parts' of Britain that 'the deeply integrated trade and economic relationship between the UK and EU be maintained' with 'the freest possible trade in goods and services', which would be 'as frictionless as possible'.

The white paper pointed out that with the trade negotiations, it would not be 'about bringing two divergent systems together', but about 'finding the best way' to continue existing arrangements with 'a new comprehensive, bold and ambitious free trade agreement'. The Paper asserted that the current trading relationship was mutually beneficial, and it pointed out that Britain has a large trade deficit with the EU: 'In 2015, while the UK exported £230 billion worth of goods and services to the EU, the UK imported £291 billion worth of goods and services from the EU. The UK's £61 billion trade deficit with the EU was made up of an £89 billion deficit in goods and a £28 billion surplus in services.' This figure is an understatement of the deficit, as it ignores both primary items and secondary items – only citing trade in goods and services.

Regarding agriculture and fishing, the white paper said: 'Whilst UK exports of agriculture, fisheries and food products to the EU were £11 billion in 2015, imports were £28 billion and over 70 per cent of our annual agri-food imports come from the EU. This underlines the UK and EU's mutual interest in ensuring continued high levels of market access in the future.' The Paper also notes:

> 'In 2015, EU vessels caught 683,000 tonnes (£484 million revenue) in UK waters and UK vessels caught 111,000 tonnes (£114 million revenue) in Member States' waters. Given the heavy reliance on UK waters of the EU fishing industry and the importance of EU waters to the UK, it is in both our interests to reach a

mutually beneficial deal that works for the UK and the EU's fishing communities.'

In fact, given that the EU fishes four times more fish from British waters than the British fishermen fish from EU waters, then the sooner Britain leaves the Common Fisheries Policy and regains full control of its own waters, like any other sovereign country, the better.

The white paper stated that 'Once we have left the EU, decisions on how taxpayers' money will be spent will be made in the UK. As we will no longer be members of the Single Market, we will not be required to make vast contributions to the EU budget.' However, Britain would be prepared to contribute to specific EU programmes if it is a participant. The Paper also stated that Britain would seek preferential trade deals with non-EU countries on leaving: 'We will be champions of free trade driving forward liberalisation bilaterally, as well as in wider groupings, and we will continue to support the international rules based system.' Ominously, the Paper stated (italics my own emphasis):

> 'Our approach to trade policy will include a variety of levers including: bilateral FTAs and dialogues with third countries, participation in multilateral and plurilateral negotiations, market access and dispute resolution through the WTO, trade remedies, import and export controls, *unilateral liberalisation*, trade preferences and trade for development.'

Unilateral free trade was openly back on the agenda. The white paper listed a number of countries with which Britain has already started negotiations, including China, Brazil and India. The Paper made clear that Britain will aim to rejoin the WTO in its own right.

12. Delivering a smooth, orderly exit from the EU

Although the white paper was optimistic about there being a deal, it stated: 'However, the Government is clear that no deal for the UK is better than a bad deal for the UK. In any eventuality we will ensure that our economic and other functions can continue, including by passing legislation as necessary to mitigate the effects of failing to reach a deal.'

Conclusion

In conclusion, the white paper confirmed that Britain will leave the EU and that the government sought 'an ambitious future relationship with the EU which works for all the people of the UK and which allows the UK to fulfil its aspirations for a truly global UK.' It also states:

> 'This strong partnership between a sovereign UK and a thriving EU will be at the heart of a new global UK: a UK which will emerge from this period of change stronger, fairer, more united and more outward-looking than ever before. A UK which is secure, prosperous and tolerant – a magnet for international talent and a home to the pioneers and innovators who will shape the world ahead. A truly global UK ...'

A second referendum was ruled out.

APPENDIX B

TORY PARTY JUNE 2017 GENERAL ELECTION MANIFESTO

May opened the Tory manifesto by asserting that 'The next five years are the most challenging that Britain has faced in my lifetime.' In the forward, she continued by saying that she wanted a Britain that was modern, prosperous, having 'world-class public services' with, ominously as it turned out, 'the first ever proper plan to pay for – and provide – social care', and 'a Britain in which burning injustices are tackled and overcome', including an end to 'the stigma of mental illness once and for all'. This morbid political correctness permeated the document.

The manifesto quickly revealed itself to be classical socialism as well as politically correct. It claimed that the May Government had 'delivered' 'strong and stable leadership' since the referendum and that there was a need for a 'strong economy'. It said that there was a need 'to deliver a smooth and orderly departure from the European Union and forge a deep and special partnership with our friends and allies across Europe'. Its globalism was displayed with the assertion that 'there is increasingly little distinction between domestic and international affairs in matters of migration, national security and the economy', which contradicted the notion of the importance of border controls. It alleged that there were 'enduring social divisions' and that the need to care for the elderly had to be balanced with being 'fair to younger generations'.

The manifesto boldly stated that 'The government's agenda will not be allowed to drift to the right' and that the government would seek to solve the 'long-lasting injustices, such as the lack of care for people with mental health problems, and the inequality of opportunity that endures on the basis of race, gender and class', as well as respecting 'the fact that society is a contract between the generations: a partnership between those who are living, those who have lived before us, and those who are yet to be born'. The May Government would therefore seek 'to restore the contract between the generations that provides security for older people while being fair to the young'.

This need for fairness towards the young did not extend to the government itself, which put off eliminating the spending deficit and only promised 'a balanced budget by the middle of the next decade'. These debts would have to be paid for by future generations.

That the Tories were loath to leave the EU was openly stated:

> 'As we leave the European Union, we want to negotiate a new deep and special partnership with the EU, which will allow free trade between the UK and the EU's member states. As part of the agreement we strike, we want to make sure that there are as few barriers to trade and investment as possible.'

This desperation for a 'deep and special partnership' was an attempt to circumvent the Leave vote. The manifesto made no mention of the trade deficit and committed to adhering to the present tariff regime when lodging 'new UK schedules with the World Trade Organization'. It further committed: 'We will continue to support the global multilateral rules-based trade system. We will introduce a Trade Bill in the next parliament.'

The manifesto said that a May Government would require employee representation on company boards, or the creation of 'a formal employee advisory council or assign specific responsibility for employee representation to a designated non-executive director', before then stressing the need to address Britain's 'slow productivity growth' for which there was 'a new £23 billion National Productivity Investment Fund', which would involve expenditure on infrastructure, skills, research and development, the railways, and housing (the manifesto stated that 'The North Sea has provided more than £300 billion in tax revenue to the UK economy' – this money has largely been wasted). Furthermore, the Migration Advisory Committee would 'make recommendations' as to the need 'to set aside significant numbers of visas for workers in strategically-important sectors, such as digital technology, without adding to net migration as a whole'. This would be combined with a promise to 'double the Immigration Skills Charge levied on companies employing migrant workers, to £2,000 a year by the end of the parliament, using the revenue generated to invest in higher level skills training for workers in the UK'. Interestingly, there was a specific pledge to 'take forward Sir John Parker's review of shipbuilding, helping our shipyards modernise and collaborate. We want to see shipbuilding growing on the Clyde and on the Forth, in Belfast and in Barrow, and in the north-east and south of England.'

While the manifesto spoke of how 'We will continue to work in partnership with the Scottish and Welsh governments and the Northern Ireland Executive, in a relationship underpinned by pooling and sharing resources through the Barnett Formula,' England had to be satisfied with devolution to local government, 'local enterprise partnerships', and 'newly elected mayors' – a sort of regionalization by the back door. The Tories were content to settle for a fiddling about with the standing orders in the House of Commons rather than a properly functioning English Parliament. Given the outcome of the election, this issue was central.

The manifesto pledged not only to 'bring the European Union's Charter of Fundamental Rights into UK law' but also that they would not 'repeal or replace the Human Rights Act while the process of Brexit is underway', and to only reassess this matter once Brexit is complete.

May's globalism was evident. The manifesto boasted that 'We will be the world's foremost champion of free trade. We will expand our global efforts to combat extremism, terror, and the perpetration of violence against people because of their faith, gender or sexuality.' It continued: 'We will continue to lead a global campaign for the education of women and girls, which is the key to progress in so many countries. We will lead the fight against modern slavery, just as we overcame the trade in slaves two hundred years ago.'

Of importance to the approach to Brexit, the manifesto said:

> 'The United Kingdom will be a global champion for an open economy, free trade, and the free flow of investment, ideas and information. Open and free trade is key to international prosperity, stability and security – it is an essential component of an economy that works for everyone. We believe the UK must seize the unique opportunities it has to forge a new set of trade and investment relationships around the world, building a global, outward- looking Britain.'

No mention was made of the trade deficit or of the need to end it.

That globalism was evidenced in the approach to the issue of immigration:

> 'We will ensure Britain remains a place of sanctuary for refugees and asylum seekers. The existing system, however, is geared towards people who are young enough, fit enough, and have the resources to get to Britain, rather than those who are most in need of our help.
>
> Wherever possible, the government will offer asylum and refuge to people in parts of the world affected by conflict and oppression, rather than to those who have made it to Britain. We will work to reduce asylum claims made in Britain and, as we do so, increase the number of people we help in the most troubled regions. We will continue to work with other countries in Europe, and the United Nations, to

review the international legal definitions of asylum and refugee status.

We will make sure our councils get the help they need to deal with people as they arrive, and establish schemes to help individuals, charities, faith groups, churches and businesses to provide housing and other support for refugees.'

The manifesto did not stop there:

'The UK is a global leader in fighting the evil trade in human beings – both around the world and in our own country – for sex and labour exploitation. As home secretary, Theresa May brought forward the Modern Slavery Act, the first of its kind in Europe, appointed the world's first anti-slavery commissioner and set up the Modern Slavery Taskforce to bring together the heads of MI5, MI6 and the National Crime Agency to co- ordinate our response to criminal gangs operating across the world.

We now need to go further. We need to focus on the exploitation of vulnerable men, women and children for their labour, people who are moved around our own country and between nations, as if they were not human at all. We will review the application of exploitation in the Modern Slavery Act to strengthen our ability to stop criminals putting men, women and children into criminal, dangerous and exploitative working conditions. And the UK will use its power to push the United Nations and other international bodies to make Modern Slavery a thing of the past.'

The immigration policy included a commitment that 'We will expect students to leave the country at the end of their course, unless they meet new, higher requirements that allow them to work in Britain after their studies have concluded.' In other words, students were likely to be allowed to stay.

This immigration policy was combined with the boast that the 'government [was] unafraid to confront the burning injustices of the gender pay gap, racial disparity, the stigma of mental health and disability discrimination.' It also asserted that 'If you are black, you are treated more harshly by the criminal justice system than if you are white.' The manifesto stated:

> 'Britain is one of the world's most successful multi-racial, multi-cultural, multi-religious societies. We are proud of our diversity, and the cultural and economic enrichment it brings.
>
> The enjoyment and pride we take in our diversity should not cause us to ignore the fact that in too many parts of our country, we have communities that are divided, often along racial or religious lines. To address this, we will bring forward a new integration strategy, which will seek to help people in more isolated communities to engage with the wider world, help women in particular into the workplace, and teach more people to speak English. We will work with schools to make sure that those with intakes from one predominant racial, cultural or religious background teach their students about pluralistic, British values and help them to get to know people with different ways of life.'

Having extolled the wonders of multiculturalism, the manifesto acknowledged that there was friction:

> 'Our enjoyment of Britain's diversity must not prevent us from confronting the menace of extremism. Extremism, especially Islamist extremism, strips some British people, especially women, of the freedoms they should enjoy, undermines the cohesion of our society and can fuel violence. To defeat extremism,

we need to learn from how civil society and the state took on racism in the twentieth century. We will consider what new criminal offences might need to be created, and what new aggravated offences might need to be established, to defeat the extremists. We will support the public sector and civil society in identifying extremists, countering their messages and promoting pluralistic, British values. And we will establish a Commission for Countering Extremism to identify examples of extremism and expose them, to support the public sector and civil society, and help the government to identify policies to defeat extremism and promote pluralistic values.'

The race war politics were combined with feminist ideology with the promise of 'measures to close the gender pay gap', including a target of 'parity in the number of public appointments going to women, and we shall push for an increase in the number of women sitting on boards of companies'. It further wanted in increase in the 'take-up of shared parental leave' with 'flexible work environments that help mothers and fathers to share parenting'.

Once again, the manifesto returned to race war politics with what it described as 'the race gap':

'Theresa May's first act as prime minister was to order an unprecedented audit of racial disparity across public services, to reveal the outcomes experienced by people of different ethnicities. That audit reports in July and a Conservative government will not hesitate to act on its findings, however uncomfortable they may be.

Alongside that assault on injustice, we will tackle those issues we already know about head on. We will strengthen the enforcement of equalities law – so that private landlords and businesses who deny people a service on the basis of ethnicity, religion or gender are properly investigated and prosecuted. We

> will legislate to mandate changes in police practices if "stop and search" does not become more targeted and "stop to arrest" ratios do not improve. We will reduce the disproportionate use of force against Black, Asian and ethnic minority people in prison, young offender institutions and secure mental health units and we will legislate here too if progress is not made. We will launch a national campaign to increase the number of Black, Asian and ethnic minority organ donors to cut the long waiting times for patients from those groups and save more lives. We will also ask large employers to publish information on the pay gap for people from different ethnic backgrounds.'

This was pure political correctness – race war politics in particular. It demonized ordinary people and businesses as being racist and fomented a sense of grievance in ethnic minorities. It advocated anti-English ethnic cleansing with the unashamed race quotas. It targeted the police for implied racism, ignoring the rising knife crime and Islamist terrorism. The Tories then blithely assumed that English people would be keen to go out and vote for all this.

The manifesto saved the best until last. First, it announced the end to the triple lock with 'Guaranteed annual increases in the state pension through a new Double Lock to be introduced in 2020', with the commitment to a minimum 2.5% increase being abolished. This would mean that 'pensions will rise in line with the earnings that pay for them, or in line with inflation – whichever is highest. We will also ensure that the state pension age reflects increases in life expectancy, while protecting each generation fairly.'

Next, the manifesto turned to social care:

> 'First, we will align the future basis for means-testing for domiciliary care with that for residential care, so that people are looked after in the place that is best for them. This will mean that the value of the family home will be taken into account along with other

assets and income, whether care is provided at home, or in a residential or nursing care home.

Second, to ensure this is fair, we will introduce a single capital floor, set at £100,000, more than four times the current means test threshold. This will ensure that, no matter how large the cost of care turns out to be, people will always retain at least £100,000 of their savings and assets, including value in the family home.

Third, we will extend the current freedom to defer payments for residential care to those receiving care at home, so no-one will have to sell their home in their lifetime to pay for care.'

Thus, pensioners stood to lose the entire worth of their assets above £100,000 if they needed either social care at home or in a care home. Presently, social care at home would not involve a claim against the house. Those with dementia would have been the most badly affected, as they need increasing levels of support for many years. Pensioners would lose their wealth, and their children would lose their inheritance. Those currently buying their own homes would be unable to pass those homes on to their children. Senior Tories repeatedly said that under the proposed scheme, people would be 'allowed' to keep £100,000 of their wealth, which their children might be 'allowed' to inherit. The Tories actually expected people to vote for this.

Regarding housing, which does affect young people, the manifesto resorted to the 'we' argument:

'We have not built enough homes in this country for generations, and buying or renting a home has become increasingly unaffordable. If we do not put this right, we will be unable to extend the promise of a decent home, let alone home ownership, to the millions who deserve it.

We will fix the dysfunctional housing market so that housing is more affordable and people have the security they need to plan for the future. The key to this is to build enough homes to meet demand.'

Consequently, the manifesto said 'We will meet our 2015 commitment to deliver a million homes by the end of 2020 and we will deliver half a million more by the end of 2022.'

1   *Hansard*, June 15, 2016, volume 611, 905437

2   Harriet Sergeant, *Welcome to the Asylum*, Centre for Policy Studies, London, 2001, page 7

3   Harriet Sergeant, *Welcome to the Asylum*, Centre for Policy Studies, London, 2001, page 7

4   Gerard Batten, *The Road to Freedom*, Bretwalda Books, Epsom, 2016, page 42

5   Gerard Batten, *The Road to Freedom*, Bretwalda Books, Epsom, 2016, page 42

6   Gerard Batten, *The Road to Freedom*, Bretwalda Books, Epsom, 2016, page 42

7   ONS AA6H

8   ONS, Balance of Payments, 2016 Q4

9   ONS, UK Trade: Jan 2017, 2

10   ONS, Balance of Payments, 2016 Q4

11   ONS, UK Trade: Jan 2017, 12

12   Migration Watch UK, 'The Rights of EU Nationals in the UK Post-Brexit', October 2014, updated 20th March 2017

13   Migration Watch UK, 'Household Projections and Immigration', March 2006

14   HM Land Registry, UK House Price Index (HPI) for March 2017, 16th May 2017

Printed in Great Britain
by Amazon